Integrative Counselling & Psychotherapy

Integrative Counselling & Psychotherapy

A Relational Approach

Ariana Faris and Els van Ooijen

Los Angeles | London | New Delhi
Singapore | Washington DC

SAGE Publications Ltd
1 Oliver's Yard
55 City Road
London EC1Y 1SP

SAGE Publications Inc.
2455 Teller Road
Thousand Oaks, California 91320

SAGE Publications India Pvt Ltd
B 1/I 1 Mohan Cooperative Industrial Area
Mathura Road
New Delhi 110 044

SAGE Publications Asia-Pacific Pte Ltd
33 Pekin Street #02-01
Far East Square
Singapore 048763

Library of Congress Control Number: 2011921405

British Library Cataloguing in Publication data

A catalogue record for this book is available from the British Library

ISBN 978-0-85702-126-7
ISBN 978-0-85702-127-4 (pbk)

Typeset by C&M Digitals (P) Ltd, Chennai, India
Printed by CPI Group (UK) Ltd, Croydon, CR0 4YY
Printed on paper from sustainable resources

Mixed Sources
Product group from well-managed
forests and other controlled sources
www.fsc.org Cert no. SA-COC-1565
© 1996 Forest Stewardship Council
FSC

Contents

About the Authors

Ariana Faris is a UKCP Registered Systemic and Family Psychotherapist and a Counsellor, having undertaken her initial training as a counsellor in the early 1990s. She currently works in private practice as a therapist, supervisor and trainer and runs groups in mindfulness-based cognitive therapy and mindfulness-based stress reduction. She was Programme Leader of the Postgraduate Diploma in Integrative and Cognitive Behavioural Counselling at the University of Wales, Newport for several years where she was responsible along with Els van Ooijen for developing the relational integrative model.

She has worked in a wide variety of contexts as a therapist and trainer including the addictions field, child and adult mental health settings, employee assistance programmes and higher education. In her professional role she is particularly interested in motivation and behaviour change as well as resource focused approaches to working with clients.

Dr Els van Ooijen offers psychotherapy, counselling and supervision through her private consultancy 'Nepenthe' in Bristol. She has been a visiting lecturer at the University of Wales, Newport since the early 1990s, contributing to their Postgraduate Diplomas and Masters programme in counselling and consultative supervision. Els has a background in the NHS and has written extensively for the nursing press on a variety of subjects.

Els holds an MA in Integrative Psychotherapy from the Bath Centre for Psychotherapy and Counselling as well as a Doctorate in Psychotherapy from the Metanoia Institute, both validated by Middlesex University. Her doctoral research focused on the development of the internal supervisor and involved an in depth reflection on her own psychotherapeutic practice.

Els writes regular book reviews for *Therapy Today* and has published two books on supervision: *Clinical Supervision, a Practical Guide* (2000) and *Clinical Supervision Made Easy* (2003), both published by Churchill Livingstone.

Foreword by Professor Neil Frude

In this book Ariana Faris and Els van Ooijen introduce the relational integrative model (RIM). This is an orienting framework that provides psychotherapists with a structured and coherent way of drawing upon theoretical ideas and therapeutic strategies from a wide range of psychotherapeutic approaches, including some which might initially appear to be highly incompatible.

All therapists are well aware of the rich and bewildering array of alternative therapeutic approaches. The 'big three' of psychodynamic, cognitive behavioural and humanistic psychotherapy all remain powerful forces in therapeutic practice and each of them has seen major developments in recent years. The field of psychotherapy continues to be as innovative as ever, and while such dynamism is exciting and uplifting, it also presents major challenges. Therapists, especially those still in training, are liable to become overwhelmed if they attempt to maintain a comprehensive understanding of this rich and increasingly complex field.

Many therapists are trained principally in a single approach and adhere to this in their thinking and their practice. Each approach has its loyal adherents who, in their bid to champion their favoured approach, sometimes become chauvinistic, ignoring, ridiculing or demonising other approaches. Too often, the result has been increasing polarisation as warring factions each condemn the infidels from the opposing camps. Conflict on fundamental questions has often led to extreme intolerance and fundamentalist rhetoric.

In recent decades, however, many therapists have become tired of the sloganising and the points-scoring and have come to recognise that much can be gained from adopting a more conciliatory position. In addition, as Ariana Faris and Els van Ooijen point out, the evidence that radically different therapeutic approaches have positive outcomes challenges the claims made by various camps that their own approach is uniquely 'valid' or 'effective'.

Therapists who recognise the potential value of drawing upon theoretical concepts and therapeutic techniques from a range of approaches may seek to widen their therapeutic repertoire by appending elements from other approaches. However, a more satisfactory alternative to such a 'bolting on' manoeuvre involves the therapist incorporating elements from several approaches within a coherent and integrated framework. The RIM is offered as an integrative framework for those who wish to follow such a developmental path.

The integrative enterprise has been greatly facilitated in recent years by a number of developments associated with each of the 'big three' approaches. Thus there has been a clear shift in psychodynamic thinking away from exclusively 'intra-psychic' accounts towards a more 'intersubjective' understanding of human experience and development. This move away from 'the doctrine of the isolated mind' also means that there is now a far greater acknowledgment of the influence of the wider social and cultural system. Another recent development, compassion therapy, although it originated within the cognitive behavioural therapy (CBT) field, is unquestionably humanistic in many respects. Cognitive therapy has also developed in such a way that it now considers deep (including unconscious) aspects of the individual's psyche (sometimes labelled 'schemas') and increasingly focuses on such aspects as meta-cognitions and mindfulness techniques.

It is as if the spaces in between the major approaches – once veritable chasms – are now being breached by sundry developments in theory and practice. At the same time, developments in other fields are providing insights that help to bridge gaps between different conceptual domains. Thus the new field of 'interpersonal neurobiology' has helped us to appreciate the prodigious plasticity of neural structures and has emphasised the fact that the relationship between brain structures and emotional experiences is by no means one-way or linear.

Although such developments are helpful to the enterprise of integration, the realisation of such a project still requires considerable vision. It is by no means an easy task to reconcile approaches that take radically different epistemological positions, that are based on conflicting theories and that advocate very different therapeutic styles. The RIM endeavours to square this circle by adopting a trans-theoretical approach and identifying concepts that are common across the different approaches.

Things that are different at one level may be recognised as similar if we ascend in the level of our analysis. Thus although a snake and a sheep appear extremely different in many ways, when we rise to a higher (less specific) level of description we immediately recognise and appreciate their similarity – they are both 'animals'. Similarly, by going up a level and using a broad trans-theoretical framework, the RIM is able to provide a higher-order framework that can assimilate the humanistic, psychodynamic and cognitive behavioural approaches to psychotherapy, despite their many differences.

This ambitious project could easily have resulted in a structure of overwhelming complexity, but the authors have taken great care to identify key dimensions of variation that together provide the basic architecture for the RIM. The multi-dimensional structure incorporates 'TIME' dimensions, comparing therapeutic approaches in terms of Temporal issues, Insight, Meaning making and Experience as well as using John Burnham's differentiation between 'approach, method and technique'. The authors then consider the different positions of the client, the therapist and the model within different therapeutic approaches and they incorporate Rowan and Jacobs's (2002) three styles of practitioner integration – 'instrumental', 'authentic' and 'transpersonal'. The framework is postmodernist and social constructionist in its epistemology and systemic ideas also permeate throughout the authors' thinking.

The authors prefer the term 'integrating' to 'integration' to emphasise the point that integrating is an ongoing and dynamic process. They do not regard the therapist as bringing a fully formed integrated approach to the therapy session. Rather, the therapist and client work together in an integrating collaboration. Between them they evolve the therapeutic relationship, the therapy style and the content of their sessions. Even the length of the therapy (that is, whether it is brief or otherwise) is determined in the course of the interaction. The idea that therapist and client together forge a narrative is common to several therapeutic approaches, but the RIM assigns a far more extensive set of tasks to the collaboration. Therapist and client do not simply work together as scriptwriters, but also as the rule-makers, the architects and the choreographers of what goes on in the room.

Although the therapeutic interaction is regarded as thoroughly collaborative, the roles of therapist and client are necessarily different. Transference dynamics will be different for the therapist and the client, and the interaction will be informed by the therapist's awareness and experience of ideas and practices from a wide range of different therapeutic approaches. The clinical agenda that evolves might well include the reduction of specific symptoms but it is also likely to include issues relating to existential security and personal growth.

Although the authors emphasise the importance of the therapist's use of reflective and empathic listening, they also recognise the usefulness of active Socratic dialogue and respectful challenge. In addition, they stress the significance of the therapist having access to a wide range of therapeutic strategies. Thus the RIM focuses on both the 'being' and the 'doing' aspects of therapy.

For me, one of the most fascinating aspects of the book is the consideration of the therapist's and the client's understanding of therapy and how they can work together to forge a common understanding of 'what this is all about'. The fact that many therapists have embraced postmodernist ideas and have adopted a social constructionist epistemology raises the possibility of a 'culture clash' between the therapist and the client. Most clients will have a 'naive realist' (or 'modernist') outlook and come to the therapist (whom they may regard as 'an expert', 'a pilot' or 'a guide') in order to 'get a problem fixed'. Those who refer clients, often medical practitioners, may have the same understanding and ambition.

Thus, very often clients come (or are sent) to therapy with broken hearts or worried brows, hoping that the therapist will 'cure' a specific symptom or 'solve' a specific problem. We need to be realistic about their images of us as therapists and we need to understand how they are likely to be thinking about therapy. Our duty not to bewilder our clients means that we may have to be especially careful when our words and actions in therapy are affected by the importance that we assign to, for example, 'curiosity' or 'outcome neutrality' since these are likely to be alien to the assumptions that the client brings to therapy, at least initially.

The authors provide a detailed and essential guide to the implications of working with the RIM for a range of professional issues including ethical therapeutic practice, training, supervision, therapist self-care, research and continuing professional development. The fact that the RIM takes a broad view of the potential impact of therapy and of how this might be evaluated leads the authors to make the interesting suggestion that evaluation might be viewed as an integral part of the therapy conversation. They also emphasise the possibility of using the framework to focus on clients' competence and personal resources rather than on their deficits. Thus the framework can foster a positive approach to therapy, identifying and opening up choices and new possibilities for the client.

The book is not a manual or a handbook containing a set of recipes to be followed. The framework does not provide a fixed protocol to be used in 'cases of OCD' or in 'cases of panic disorder'. The flexibility and bespoke nature of the RIM, and its dependence on the co-construction that takes place within therapy sessions, means that such a book could not be written. What we have instead is a carefully worked out framework for organising therapeutic thinking and therapeutic practice. The authors have taken on an ambitious challenge and the result is an impressive framework that goes far beyond mere eclecticism. The RIM provides a framework that affords therapists the opportunity to draw from a wide range of theories and to employ a wide range of therapeutic strategies while maintaining conceptual integrity. It therefore encourages and enables psychotherapists to craft their therapy in collaboration with the client while bringing to the therapeutic encounter the widest possible range of understanding, strategies and styles.

Acknowledgements

We are deeply indebted to the many clients, supervisees, colleagues and trainees that we have worked with throughout our years of practice, all of whom have contributed to the development of the ideas contained here. Without them this book would not have been possible. We wish to extend a very warm thank you to our critical readers for their helpful and insightful comments: Jeff Faris, Mary Morris, Annie Robinson and Christopher Wilson, and to Neil Frude for his foreword and generosity with both his time and commentary. Many thanks also to our editor Alice Oven for her continuing encouragement. Lastly we wish to thank our families and partners for their support and willingness to put up with us during the busy period of writing this book. And from Ariana a big thank you to Philippa Seligman for her wisdom and encouragement.

Introduction

IMPETUS FOR THE BOOK

Our current world may be characterised by a sense of alienation and separation on the one hand and a yearning for connectedness on the other. The phenomena of separation and connectedness are reflected in the fields of counselling and psychotherapy, where difference is sometimes emphasised more than similarity and common unifying principles are ignored or go unacknowledged. It is against this backdrop that we (the authors) wanted to develop a holistic and relational model that honours the perspectives from different theories.

As discussed in chapter 1 integration is a journey and a process rather than a final destination, not unlike the journey in the poem *Ithaka* (Cavafy, [1911] 1961). We are two psychotherapists from different orientations, who found ourselves charged with the task of developing a postgraduate counselling course that integrates humanistic, cognitive and psychodynamic approaches. We therefore decided to look at the cutting edges and frontiers of our own practice: one of us is a family therapist with a systems-based approach, the other trained in humanistic and integrative psychotherapy. The challenges and opportunities involved in the co-construction of a relational integrative model led us to ask these questions:

- How can we communicate when we speak different therapeutic languages?
- What gets lost in translation and what can be translated?
- How do we create a model that feels authentic?
- How do we create a model with relational heart?
- How do we create a holistic model that includes mind, body and spirit?
- How do we meet the demand to include evidence-based practice?
- How can we deepen our therapeutic connectedness in our work with clients and find ways of traversing boundaries, in order to create cross-cultural languages with our professional colleagues?

This book is based on our enquiry into the above questions. This enquiry took the form of a process reminiscent of action research, involving a recursive feedback cycle of reflection and action. We reflected deeply on our own practice, engaged in dialogue and reflection with each other, sought feedback from colleagues, students and clients and then integrated the results back into our developing model. This then led to another cycle of reflection, dialogue and so on. As discussed in chapter 1, our stance is one of continuing integration, a process that never stops. The relational integrative model discussed in this book should therefore be regarded as a staging post in a process of ongoing reflection and development, rather than as a final 'product'. Our ideas were (and are) continuously evolving; this book is therefore not quite the one we thought we were going to write. While we call the current synthesis of our thinking the 'relational integrative model', it represents a way of 'integrating' rather than an 'integration'. It should not therefore be categorised or manualised. Rather it requires each individual practitioner to work with the ideas contained within it; not unlike a new coat or a pair of shoes it may take a while for it to feel familiar and comfortable.

There were two areas where we saw eye-to-eye right from the beginning. The idea of a relational model spoke to both of us. For one of us systemic thinking has always been part and parcel of her theoretical and practical orientation, while the other has been strongly influenced by intersubjective systems theory within the psychodynamic field (Stolorow et al., 2002). Systemic therapy is an explicitly relational therapy; however, we were commissioned to teach psychodynamic, humanistic and cognitive behavioural approaches so we do not include it explicitly but rather incorporate systemic thinking and an intersubjective perspective in our presuppositions and conceptualisation.

Secondly as both of us have a longstanding interest in meditation, we were particularly keen to include mindfulness-based approaches.

CONTEMPORARY DEVELOPMENTS

A number of developments within the fields of counselling and psychotherapy are relevant to discuss at this point. Firstly (as discussed in chapter 1), since the middle of the twentieth century there has been a growing tendency to integrate aspects of different theoretical models (Flaskas and Perlesz, 1996). This may reflect a movement towards a postmodern way of thinking that entertains multiple perspectives. More recently, there also appears to be a more general movement towards each other by a number of therapeutic approaches and a willingness to integrate aspects of each other's philosophy and way of working.

Secondly, a 'relational turn' has been observed across theoretical approaches (Safran, 2003). As most of our wounds are sustained in and through relationship, it is increasingly recognised that healing happens through relationship too. The therapeutic relationship may therefore provide a microcosm within which intra- as well as interpersonal issues can be addressed.

The third development constitutes a 'contemplative turn', which is most obviously expressed in the growth of mindfulness-based practices that appear to be acceptable across modalities, irrespective of theoretical approach. These practices are also represented in transpersonal ways of working and therapies based on Buddhism. In developing the RIM we are strongly influenced by the relational and contemplative turns in contemporary psychotherapy.

THE WRITING PROCESS

We both have a strong wish to avoid the dangers of fixed, reified truths. Yet, at the same time, in our ongoing process of reflection and development, we have become aware of beliefs and ideas that we hold dear. To help us with this rather salutary realisation we have made use of Cecchin's invitation to be irreverent to one's own ideas (Cecchin, 1992). At times this has been (and inevitably continues to be) a struggle. At times we notice that we are cautious around each other and wonder whether that may be because we have not had enough 'fights' to thrash out some differences. Perhaps there are fights still to come as we continue to reflect, develop, work and write. We have tried to weave threads of connection into a whole; sometimes the threads may contain some knots, so that the final piece has character, but is also flawed. Yet, paradoxically, this is perhaps how it should be, and part of a stance and process of continuously integrating. As mentioned in chapter 5, the challenge is always to consider how it can be possible to have cross-cultural conversations and translate ideas between ourselves as authors, and also between theories, ideologies and preferred views. We leave it up to you, the readers, to decide whether the outcome of our process is an awkward synthesis of an uneasy alliance, or whether it constitutes an interesting dialogue that contains within it similarity and difference.

USE OF LANGUAGE

Within the therapy world there is a plethora of terms that are often used interchangeably, although the meaning (or intended meaning) of these terms may differ. Further complications may arise when two things are talked about as if they belong to the same frame of reference when they actually operate within entirely different frames. During discussions about psychotherapy or counselling practices, including matters of technical skills and decision making, methods of structuring practice and the philosophical and theoretical discourses underpinning these methods and techniques, there is much opportunity for confusion of levels of logical type. Burnham (1992) uses the broad term 'approach' to include approach, model, theory, assumptions and presuppositions. We define approach within our relational integrative way of thinking to entail our values and presuppositions, as these are instrumental in the choice of a particular theoretical orientation. We use Burnham's (1992) model to draw useful distinctions between 'approach, method and technique', in order to avoid confusion of frames of reference or of levels of logical type, in analysing different counselling and psychotherapy practices. These could include practices of teaching and learning.

Rather than the unwieldy phrase 'counsellor and/or psychotherapist', we use the words 'practitioner' or 'therapist'. This also avoids the need for the making of a distinction between counselling and psychotherapy, which in any case we regard as unhelpful.

As we are both women, we use the female voice for therapists and alternate between male and female voices for clients. The examples and case studies in the book are based on our own practice. However, in order to protect our clients' confidentiality we have created composite characters, which nevertheless stay true to our relational integrative way of working. An exception is the account and analysis of a dream in chapter 5, where permission has been sought and granted from the person concerned.

STRUCTURE OF THE BOOK

Chapter 1 contains a brief historical perspective on integration as well as a discussion of different methods of integration. In this chapter we also discuss Burnham's 'approach, method and technique' framework in more detail, define our own stance on integration and discuss current methods of training. Chapters 2–4 are organised according to Burnham's framework (approach – chapter 2; method – chapter 3; technique – chapter 4). Chapter 2 is in two parts. In the first part we outline the philosophical assumptions underlying the relational integrative model, followed in the second part by an account of those aspects of humanistic, psychodynamic and cognitive approaches that are in line with these assumptions. This section also contains a brief account of relevant developments in neuroscience as well as a discussion of seven core concepts that lie at the heart of the model. Method is discussed in chapter 3 in terms of a temporal framework of insight, meaning making and experience. Chapter 4 is also in two sections. In the first section we show how a relational integrative way of working is applicable to a variety of different problems and issues that clients bring, including trauma, abuse, loss, relationship and identity issues, eating disorders, alcohol addiction and anxiety and depression. The chapter's second part contains two examples of how the RIM may be applied to brief as well as openended therapy. In the last chapter we discuss a relational integrative view of a number of professional issues such as ethics, research, evaluation, supervision and personal development. Questions for reflection are included at the end of chapters as well as suggestions for further reading.

We hope that the book will be of use to student practitioners, their trainers and integrative practitioners in general.

1

Models of Integration

After a brief historical perspective, we first compare a number of different approaches to integration before discussing the 'approach, method and technique' framework. Next we define our own stance on integration and discuss current methods of training.

BRIEF HISTORICAL PERSPECTIVE ON INTEGRATION

When we have a problem or are feeling unhappy, some of us like to talk with a person who is not a friend or part of our family. In the past that was often someone respected in the community: a wise woman, a doctor or a spiritual leader such as a priest or shaman. These days that individual is often a counsellor or psychotherapist. It was not until the beginning of the last century, however, that therapy became a profession and developed its own body of knowledge and methodology.

Theories generally do not appear in a vacuum, but in relation to other developments. Freud, regarded as the founder of the 'talking cure', was influenced by the philosophy, literature and medical science of his time. This is not to deny Freud's brilliance; he was a truly original thinker. However, ideas about the unconscious, for example, were also being discussed by thinkers such as the Danish philosopher Harald Hoffding (Hoffding and Lowndes, [1881] 2004) and Carl Jung, whose conception of the unconscious differed significantly from Freud's view.

Freud's views were taken up, criticised, modified and developed further by others, a process that still continues; indeed, this is what happens with theories in all disciplines. Having just developed a groundbreaking theory of inner dynamics that may go on inside human beings, however, it was not easy for Freud to acknowledge that others might have ideas that contradicted some of his own. His falling out with, for example, Jung and Reich mark the beginning of the many 'turf wars' that have plagued the field from the beginning, such as 'Freudians' vs 'Jungians', followers of Melanie Klein vs those of Anna Freud or classical analysis vs attachment theory. Currently, we have disputes between those for and against cognitive behavioural therapy, and between the relational psychoanalytic movement and those favouring a classical psychoanalytic approach. While some of these divisions may be characterised as acrimonious, others have maintained a healthy dialogue of difference and innovation on a theme.

As early as the 1930s, French (1933) attempted to integrate aspects of psychoanalysis and Pavlovian conditioning. Reactions were mixed, with some rejecting the idea outright, while others thought it a potentially fruitful line of inquiry. A few years later Rosenzweig (1936) wrote an article with the now famous title, 'At last the Dodo said, "Everybody has won and all must have prizes"'. This quote from Lewis Carroll's *Alice's Adventures in Wonderland* ([1865] 1962, chapter 3) is referenced in current debates on psychotherapy's effectiveness, where the term 'Dodo Effect' is used as shorthand for a lack of evidence for any difference between approaches. Rosenzweig claimed that effectiveness was attributable to elements all therapies have in common, rather than with differences. He identified three factors:

- Effectiveness is related to therapists' personalities, rather than their theoretical approach.
- All therapies tend to help people see their problems differently.
- Although therapies differ in focus, all are likely to be helpful as change in one area will also affect other areas (Rosenzweig, 1936). (This claim seems to anticipate some principles within a systems approach, which we will discuss further in the next chapter.)

Many subsequent writers have been more interested in the similarities between therapeutic approaches than their differences. Until relatively recently, however, they were in the minority, perhaps because psychotherapy was still young and the zeitgeist was not yet ready to accept an integrative view. This began to change in the 1960s with Frank and Frank ([1961] 1993) discussing commonalities between psychotherapy and other forms of healing and Carl Rogers (1963) claiming that the traditional borders between the various therapeutic approaches were beginning to disintegrate. Interestingly the third edition of Frank and Frank's book *Persuasion and Healing* was reprinted in 1993, which seems to indicate that integrative ideas emerging in the 1950s and 1960s formed the roots of a general movement towards integration as a mainstream approach in therapy.

From the late 1980s onwards there has been increasing emphasis on the importance of the therapeutic relationship, irrespective of theoretical approach. Lazarus (1981) took a pragmatic view and saw no problem with therapists borrowing techniques from other modalities, without necessarily taking on board the theory upon which these techniques were based. Lazarus coined the term 'technical eclecticism' for this practice and later developed his ideas further into 'multimodal therapy' (Lazarus, 1981). The 1980s saw an explosion of publications and conference presentations and integration came to be regarded as a significant movement.[1]

In recent years we have observed two distinct phenomena. On the one hand, as mentioned earlier, there are ongoing disagreements between the proponents of a number of different theoretical approaches. On the other hand there appears to be a general growing together in the theory and practice of approaches hitherto regarded as distinct. We will discuss these phenomena in more detail in chapter 2.

---

[1]For a detailed history of psychotherapy see Goldfried, et al. (2005).

CURRENT APPROACHES TO INTEGRATION

Since the early founders of the 'talking cure', the body of therapeutic knowledge has increased dramatically, giving rise to many different models within three broad categories of approach: psychodynamic, humanistic and cognitive-based. Integrative approaches, which constitute a combination of two or more models within the above approaches, might be seen as a fourth category. We say 'might' as there is always the danger of setting any approach in concrete. Even within the three main categories, there are many new models that are influenced by several others. The fact that there are so many variations in theoretical approach indicates that the field is very 'alive' and developing in response to the complexity of human circumstances and the evolving nature of knowledge.

Re-invention of Wheels?

Our Western society appears to lend itself to pluralism and competition (O'Brien and Houston, 2007). Practitioners within one approach may be ignorant of other theories, resulting in duplication and 're-invention of wheels'. For example, there is a current movement within the psychoanalytic world towards a more relational (Mitchell and Aron, 1999; Mitchell, 2000) and intersubjective approach (Stolorow et al., 2002; Stern, 2009). At the same time this does appear to be a (re)discovering of many beliefs and practices that have always been a part of therapies based on a humanistic philosophy. It is not always clear whether these are true 'discoveries' or whether people are using work from other fields without acknowledging that they are doing so. For example, despite a great deal of overlap with the humanistic-existential field, Carl Rogers is never mentioned in psychoanalytic literature (O'Brien and Houston, 2007: 4).

Jungian psychology appears rather on the sidelines in the official psychoanalytic literature and is rarely included in training. At the same time, Jungian concepts such as 'complexes', or intro- and extraversion have filtered through into everyday language. The literary and artistic fields have been widely influenced by Jungian psychology. For example *Women Who Run with the Wolves*, by the Jungian analyst Clarissa Pinkola Estes (1997) became a bestseller, and the science fiction series *Dune* by Frank Herbert had the 'collective unconscious' as its main concept. Other artists influenced by Jungian ideas include Italian filmmaker Frederico Fellini, the painter Jackson Pollock and the singer-songwriter Peter Gabriel. The Myers–Briggs personality test (Briggs Myers, 1962), which is widely used within the business world, is based on Jungian typology and Jung's ideas also indirectly influenced the twelve-step programme of addiction recovery.[2]

---

[2]After meeting Rowland H, one of Jung's patients, Bob Wilson, one of the founders of Alcoholics Anonymous, became interested in Jungian psychology. Wilson later had a spiritual experience, which convinced him of the importance of change at a deep level. In a letter to Wilson Jung made a link between 'the craving for alcohol' and 'the spiritual thirst of our being for wholeness…' (C. G. Jung, letter to W. G. Wilson, Alcoholics Anonymous, Box 459 Grand Central Station, New York 17, 30 January 1961. In www.barefootsworld.net/jungletter.html (accessed 30 December 2010). See also Kurtz (1979).

Often, however, borrowing and sharing of ideas is acknowledged. Schema-based cognitive therapy, for example, acknowledges its use of Gestalt theory (Young et al, 2006). Overall it seems that the zeitgeist[3] is moving towards a more integrative stance, which (as we will discuss in chapter 2) is in line with postmodern philosophy. It may be that commentaries and critiques of therapeutic approaches recognise that the field is as subject to conceptual cross-fertilisation, analysis and synthesis as other fields of intellectual and scientific endeavour. The conditional nature of knowledge is well recognised in the so-called hard sciences (Kuhn, 1962; Popper, 2002). Therapy, which spans sciences, humanities and the arts is subject to similar social and theoretical evolution and integration. The challenge is to conceptualise such integration as a synthesis rather than a cacophony of jarring concepts thrown together randomly. At the same time – who is to judge?

This may also be a result of the field of counselling and psychotherapy beginning to mature (O'Brien and Houston, 2007).

KEY CONCEPTS OF INTEGRATION

The key concepts of psychotherapeutic integration are set out in the box below.

Key Concepts of Integration

Theoretical and practical limitations of single theory approaches.
Wide range of methods, tools and interventions.
Flexibility to meet individual clients' needs.
Lack of demonstrated effectiveness of any single theory for all clients.
Identification of common factors that facilitate efficiency and effectiveness.
Generic, rather than specific factors believed to facilitate change.

A Metaphor

This is an experience one of us had recently:

My partner and I had been invited to a dinner party out in the countryside. Although we had been there before, we could not remember the exact route. My partner decided to get directions from a travel site on the Internet and off we went. At first everything was fine. We followed the instructions and made good progress. But after a while things became unclear. 'Was that the second or the third turning? Did we miss one? Why is there a second roundabout when according to the directions

[3]'Spirit of the time' (German).

there should be only one?' We were lost, so retraced our steps to a point where things had still made sense and realised that we had taken a wrong turning. According to our directions we should be just outside the town of our destination, but we knew from previous experience that we still had a long way to go. Eventually, after another forty-five minutes of driving involving many turnings and roundabouts, our printout suddenly made sense again and we were indeed entering the town.

The above experience may be seen as a metaphor for different types of theory. Some may focus on one aspect of human experience, some on another, but none are likely to be able to encompass the entire richness of life. If we rely on just one theory, or only one set of instructions as in the above example, we might miss something important or lose our way. We believe that every theory offers useful reference points, which may be a reason why many practitioners are attracted to integration.

Typically integrative therapy involves combining different theoretical approaches and accompanying methods. As there are many models within the main theoretical approaches, it follows that there are also many different 'integrations', depending on which models or part models are being integrated. McLeod (2003b) fears that the proliferation of integrative models may add to the fragmentation of the field of counselling and psychotherapy. We do not share this fear and agree with O'Brien and Houston (2007: 4) who take the opposite view and regard integration as 'a corrective tendency in an over-fragmented field'.

The Happy Eclecticist

'As long as it works, I'm happy', said Sally. 'I really do not care whether a new technique such as EMDR or whatever fits with my original model. For me the main issue is – does it help this client at this moment?' Sally is a well-respected practitioner with a full practice and many satisfied clients. Clearly what she is doing works for her and her clients. We suspect that it is 'who she is' rather than the techniques she is using that makes Sally successful. She 'integrates' new techniques and experiences and makes them 'hers' and part of her professional repertoire.

The Eclectic–Integration Continuum

According to McLeod (2003b: 64) the world of counselling and psychotherapy is involved in an 'important debate over the relative merits of theoretical purity as against integrationism or eclecticism'. However, eclecticism, within which a practitioner may employ a wide range of techniques without a unifying theory, seems less popular than integrationism, which does attempt to unify different theories.

Mahrer (1989) identified six methods of integration comprising: the development of a new grand theory capable of encompassing all existing theories; using one theory

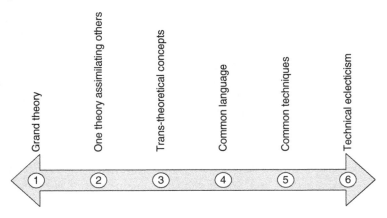

Figure 1 The Eclectic – Integration Continuum

to assimilate others; developing a common language, trans-theoretical concepts or techniques; and technical eclecticism – evidence-based approaches that marry specific problems with particular techniques (Dryden, 1984). The six approaches may be mapped onto a continuum with integration through a unifying theory at one end and the eclectic approach, focusing only on techniques, at the other.

According to Cooper and McLeod (2007) the 'grand theory' as well as some trans-theoretical attempts at integration may end up as unitary or purist rather than integrative models. We agree with Mahrer (1989) and Lapworth et al. (2001) that the trans-theoretical and technical eclecticist approaches seem the most viable options. What these approaches have in common is that, despite being placed in different positions on the continuum, each constitutes a partial rather than a complete integration. We see this as an advantage rather than a limitation (McLeod, 2003b: 69), as complete integration seems neither possible nor desirable. This is because each core theoretical approach is characterised by numerous sub-sections, which often do not see eye-to-eye. Also, we suspect that a grand theory that aims to contain all other approaches would be so general as to become meaningless.

Trans-theoretical Approaches Currently in Use

A trans-theoretical approach, which attempts to integrate theories through the identification of unifying concepts, seems to us the most fruitful. Well-established models such as Egan's ([1975] 1994) three-stage problem solving model, Andrews' (1991) self-confirmation model and Ryle's (1990) cognitive analytic (CAT) approach are said to fall into this category (McLeod, 2003b: 68–9).[4] Recent models include Cooper and McLeod's (2007) pluralistic framework, structured around the domains of 'goals, tasks and methods'. These domains operate as a meta-heuristic or meta-frame,

---

[4]Scott sees CAT as an integration of two models to make a third (Scott, 2004: 38), which would make it a unitary rather than a trans-theoretical model.

enabling therapists to select 'concepts, strategies and interventions from a range of therapeutic orientations' (Cooper and McLeod, 2007: 135). The authors see this framework as postmodern[5] in that it allows for the existence of conflicting but equally effective ways of working, and is respectful and inclusive towards 'otherness'.

Lapworth, Sills and Fish's multidimensional integrative framework has three dimensions: a core based on 'aspects of self experience' (2001: 43); context and relationship; and a larger frame of 'past, present and future' that surrounds the other two dimensions. This model helps therapists to assess clients' current needs, problems and deficits, thus serving as a useful guide to practice. Like Cooper and McLeod's pluralist model it allows the practitioner to choose strategies and ways of working from a wide range of theories.

Evans and Gilbert's relational-developmental model (2005: 3) uses the concept of the 'developing self' as a 'super-ordinate organising principle' that forms a bridge to others and the rest of the world. They take a 'two-person view of the therapeutic process' (2005: 2) in which what happens is co-constructed[6] between client and therapist and requires therapists' willingness to tolerate 'uncertainty, ambiguity and not knowing' (2005: 63).

O'Brien and Houston's (2007) model of integration is firmly focused on practice. Its nine components range from assessment and contracting to theoretical understanding and the use of codes of ethics, together forming a comprehensive framework.

APPROACH, METHOD AND TECHNIQUE – A FRAMEWORK FOR THINKING ABOUT INTEGRATION

What is it that attracts us to one type of therapy rather than another? Each of us brings a set of beliefs and theories, which form a system of thinking about human nature. These include ideas about the nature of mind, what constitutes mental health and wellbeing, how problems and difficulties arise and what mechanisms and processes bring about change. These personal maps or epistemologies determine which specific concepts we draw on from any psychological and therapeutic theory. This in turn will influence how we interpret information in the therapy session and how we choose to act. The actions we take include decisions about the therapeutic 'frame' (Gray, 1994): how and where we meet clients, the frequency and length of sessions, arrangements around breaks, our choices about how and what we communicate, and how we behave generally.

According to Burnham (1992), psychotherapeutic models comprise the three levels of approach, method and technique. 'Approach' is defined as the assumptions, values, theories and working ideas or epistemologies of a particular orientation; 'method' includes both the organisational patterns or frameworks and structures of practice and ways of working; 'technique' involves all the activities that take place

---

[5]We discuss postmodernism in more detail in chapter 2.

[6]Within the RIM we also take the view that whatever happens between client and therapist is co-constructed.

within actual practice. We use this framework to organise and conceptualise the different therapies that are included in our relational integrative model. In the next few chapters we will begin by exploring each theory at a level of approach and then go on to examine in detail the method and techniques that grow out of them.

Approach

Why Do We Do What We Do?

This is the theoretical store we draw upon to guide how we work with our clients, how we may understand and conceptualise our clients' experience and actions, and the processes that occur in the therapeutic encounter.

Method

How Do We Do What We Do?

This concerns whether the work is with individuals, couples, families, groups, etc; the length of sessions; whether the clients lie on a couch or sit facing us; whether there is a co-counsellor or a team behind a screen, as may be the case in family therapy; the length of the work, for example whether it is brief and time-limited or long-term and open-ended.

Technique

What Do We Do?

Technique constitutes the actions and behaviours we engage in when practising therapy. In other words, they are the skills, interventions and techniques underpinned by the approach, such as, for example, Socratic questioning, reflecting, active listening or setting homework tasks.

THE INTEGRATED PRACTITIONER

Most of the integrative models we discussed earlier share a focus on the 'client' and their needs. Rowan and Jacobs (2002), however, see integration differently and suggest that, rather than focusing on the practitioner's school or integration, it may be more fruitful to look at the therapist herself and the position she takes vis-à-vis her work. They outline three broad positions, constituting an 'actualisation hierarchy', a term taken from Eisler (1987) who sees it as analogous to the organisation of living organisms ranging from a single cell to a complex interlinked system of organs and processes.[7] The three positions

---

[7]See chapter 2 for a discussion of a systems approach.

('instrumental', 'authentic' and 'transpersonal') are created through an interaction of the 'confidence and development' of the therapist, the needs of the client and the 'place where the client currently is' (Rowan and Jacobs, 2002: 5). An advantage of focusing on the practitioner rather than the theory is that it allows for continuous growth and development of the individual. Perhaps inevitably there will be as many manifestations of a given integrative approach as there are practitioners using it.

The Instrumental Position

According to Rowan and Jacobs (2002) therapists occupying an 'instrumental position' are more likely to be in an 'I-it' (Buber [1923] 1958) relation to clients, and have curing the client of their problems or difficulties as their goal. Technical ability as well as evidence–based practice and manualisation are likely to be of great interest, although working with unconscious processes is also possible. Rowan and Jacobs (2002) claim that some cognitive behavioural approaches, neuro-linguistic programming and eclectic approaches without an integrating framework are examples of an instrumental position. It could be argued that they are jumping to unwarranted conclusions here, as it is not clear why wishing to cure, or evidence-based practice should preclude therapists from being in an I-thou or authentic (see below) relationship with their clients.

The Authentic Position

A therapist with an 'authentic' way of being is likely to be more occupied with the 'person-to-person' therapeutic relationship (Clarkson, 2003) than with specific techniques. Rowan and Jacobs (2002) see most humanistic therapists as coming under this umbrella, as well as Jungians, post-Jungians and many psychoanalytic therapists. The language used to denote what is valued in this position varies according to the theoretical approach, such as the more contemporary under-standing of countertransference, authenticity or 'healing through meeting' (Rowan and Jacobs, 2002: 6). This position may also be seen as a level of psycho-spiritual development (Wilber, 2000: 152). It is not entirely clear, however, on what basis Rowan and Jacobs (2002) include some approaches here and not others.

The Transpersonal Position

With a 'transpersonal' position or way of being, therapist and client may connect at a soul or heart level, in which the boundaries between them 'may fall away' and they let go of 'all aims and assumptions' (Rowan and Jacobs, 2002: 6). According to Rowan and Jacobs (2002) this level is the least well understood of the three and may involve much struggle and self-searching.

Therapist Rather than Therapy

The three positions identified by Rowan and Jacobs (2002) are helpful as they recognise that it is the therapist and who she is that is important, rather than the theoretical approach. However, their reasoning is inconsistent as they then group all therapists who practise within a certain approach as belonging to a particular position, although they might argue that it is the therapist's personal philosophy and position that leads her to choose a particular approach. Wilber's (2000) concept of 'transcend and include' that values rather than denigrates what has gone before may be helpful here. It provides a way to think about the three positions, in that each level is useful and therefore included, rather than negated or superseded by the next. This concept may also be applied to personal development generally. Whatever we have done, learnt or experienced becomes part of us; we do not discard, but continue building on and transcending, i.e. integrating, what we have learnt before. Although Wilber's concept of transcend and include does imply a hierarchy, it does not follow that we see the relational integrative model as better; it is just different. For example, Einstein's theory of relativity transcends Newton's theory and includes it when it is applicable (e.g. when bodies, such as satellites, move very slowly). It does not apply when bodies are moving extremely fast, or are very massive (e.g. black holes). Although Einstein's theory is 'better' in terms of its range of applicability, Newton's theory is 'better' as it is much easier to use and therefore better when it applies. Another example: the body includes organs, organs include tissues, tissues include cells – but we need them all. None are 'better' than the other.

THE RELATIONAL INTEGRATIVE MODEL'S DEFINITION OF INTEGRATION

> 'When I use a word,' Humpty Dumpty said, in rather a scornful tone, 'it means just what I choose it to mean – neither more nor less.'

> 'The question is,' said Alice, 'whether you can make words mean so many different things.' (Carroll, 1872: 72).

The word 'integration' is often used in a Humpty Dumpty kind of way with many practitioners professing to be 'integrative' without a shared understanding of what that means. What does 'integration' actually signify? According to the Collins English Dictionary (2000) 'to integrate' means 'to make or to be made into a whole, to incorporate or be incorporated, to amalgamate or mix, or to make up of parts'. Although subtly different, all four definitions involve a bringing together of different elements and creating something new. Scott (2004: 38) suggests four types of integration:

- Integration of a number of psychotherapeutic theories.
- Mental, physical, emotional and spiritual experience within the client.
- Integration of other disciplines such as philosophy or poetry.
- The use of humour or metaphor in the therapist's way of working.

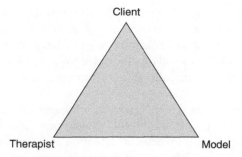

Client

Therapist   Model

Figure 2   The Three Aspects of Our Relational Integrative Approach

Our view of integration is influenced by Scott (2004) as well as Rowan and Jacobs's (2002) views as discussed above, in that we see integration as a continuous, holistic process involving the client, the therapist and the therapeutic model or theory. Different approaches to integration may vary, some emphasising theory and others being more concerned with the client's experience or the actual methods used by the therapist.

THE CLIENT

We see the purpose of therapy as helping clients come to terms with, digest or 'integrate' difficult experiences or aspects of their lives and relationships. Often someone comes to therapy because they feel that they are 'falling apart', are suffering and want to be healed and made 'whole'. This may involve an integration of different parts of herself, different experiences or sets of processes that may not sit easily together or the learning and integration of new strategies and ways of being. This is a dynamic process, and may involve the letting go of unhelpful habits (cognitive, behavioural, interpersonal), withdrawal of projections and re-integration of split-off parts, or the creation of new narratives.

> The word 'heal' is from the Old English word 'hal', meaning 'whole'. It is also related to the word 'hale' and the Old English toast 'Wassail' meaning 'Be Healthy'. The Middle English 'hool' meant healthy, unhurt or entire. So it seems that 'healing' implies the restoration of the whole. As such it offers a description not only of psychotherapy, but also of other traditions and ways of helping people with problems in living found in other cultures throughout the world.

THE PRACTITIONER

We aim to be and work with clients in a way that helps make their integrating process possible. As each person is unique, the relationship and the way we work with each individual is also unique.[8] The client–therapist relationship, or how we relate as two beings together, is not static but will also shift from moment to moment. This means that both of us (client and therapist) need to integrate what occurs between us. So the therapist's task involves allowing herself to notice what is happening, voice it and together with the client make sense of it, so that it can be digested, i.e. integrated psychically.

However, the client is not the only person who seeks internal integration. The practitioner also needs to be committed to a process of continuing integration, both personal and professional. This involves an intention or a continuous striving, rather than an actual achievement. This is not unlike Rogers's 'core conditions' (1957), which many of us aim to embody but rarely achieve fully. The minute we think we have 'achieved' full integration we are in trouble as it is a process and not a final state. Seeing integration as a finite state is likely to result in arrogance and a loss of openness. There is a danger of falling in love with our own approach and seeing it as superior to others.

Being committed to continuous integration can be challenging. In order to do this we need a secure base or framework that incorporates our values and beliefs. At the same time, however, it is important to hold theories lightly, and remember that they are metaphors, hypotheses or tools. We need to retain a stance of interest and curiosity and remain open to new knowledge and experience, even if these appear to invalidate some of our earlier beliefs, which is, after all, what we encourage our clients to do.

THE THEORY

We discuss our approach in more detail in the following chapters, but for now agree with Wahl according to whom therapeutic integration is:

> the discovery of an overarching concept or principle that reconciles apparently contradictory features of two or more therapeutic models. It is a way of saying: hey, if you look at things in this manner, what looked contradictory or irreconcilable no longer is. (2001: 7).

We prefer to talk of integrating rather than integration, as this expresses more clearly the continuing willingness of the therapist to learn and develop. Perhaps there is a difference between the therapist who, having been trained in a particular model, whether purist or integrative, is happy to stay within it, and the one who is curious to find out what else there might be. The latter is more likely to go on integrating continuously. McLeod (2003a: 72) suggests that the move away from pure theories, which are based on the ideas of their founders, towards a 'more sceptical stance' is characteristic of a postmodern way of thinking. A stance of continuously integrating therefore seems in line with this. We do not wish to imply a hierarchical relationship between a 'one model' therapy and a position of continuously integrating. If the position is right for

---

[8]This 'intersubjective' approach will be discussed further in chapter 2.

the therapist, who is thus able to practise congruently with her philosophical assumptions, it is likely that her clients will benefit. We therefore agree with O'Brien and Houston (2007: 16) who say that, 'the root to integration may lie in the therapist's careful monitoring of her subjective experience in the moment-to-moment interaction with the client followed by reflection on what she did and why'.

METHODS OF TRAINING INTEGRATIVE PRACTITIONERS

The Importance of Congruence between Training Method and Training Model

If there is no congruence between the values and philosophies of a therapeutic approach and how it is taught, the students will experience their trainers as 'do as I say, don't do as I do'. It is a fact of life that teachers are always in the 'gaze' of the students and often seen as embodying the particular approach they teach. As trainers we need to be aware that we are engaging with students' strongly held core beliefs, predispositions and assumptions, and will receive all kinds of projections from them, positive as well as negative.[9] For the teacher, being the recipient of a positive transference can be very seductive. However, most of us get our share of both types of projections, which helps keep us grounded, provided we acknowledge, name and work with them. Psychodynamic theory is helpful here as it provides a means of thinking and talking about these phenomena. If one's theoretical model does not include a means of working with transference and relational patterns then there may be a tendency to ignore what happens, which may result in unconscious acting out, both by trainers and trainees. Many trainers like to have supervision for their training work, either from their therapy supervisor or from someone who specialises in training supervision.

Ideally there would also be a consultation group within the training organisation, where people can support and challenge each other on their teaching practice. We see such a group as essential for trainers, to help them reflect on what happens in their groups and on themselves within the group and what actions might need to be taken. This would be an example of the organisation holding the trainers, so that the trainers can hold the students, which in turn will contribute towards the students being able to hold their clients. Trainers also need to be supported with administration, sufficient manpower so that the teaching groups do not get too large, a manageable workload and a say in how the organisation is run. If, however, there are problems within the larger organisation, this is likely to have a destabilising effect on the training team and will affect the students' experience negatively.[10] When, as is almost inevitable, problems do occur, it is essential that they are recognised, discussed and dealt with. This is not always easy; in some organisations, there

---

[9]The concepts of transference, countertransference, projection and projective identification originated in psychoanalysis.

[10]All parts of a system mutually influence each other.

can be a tendency to focus on the positive, but deny or ignore the negative. Reflexive processes, however, can help us to integrate the shadow[11] and pay attention to issues of power, thus avoiding the possibility of 'acting out', not just by the students, but also by the trainers or the organisation. Sometimes a training climate can be experienced as persecutory: as one therapist put it to us recently, 'some training organisations eat their young'.

Training: Single Model or Pluralist Approach

Despite the plethora of therapeutic approaches, training in a single approach is often advocated, as it is claimed to give trainees a good grounding in one model, upon which they can always build later. We feel that although this is certainly possible, it does very much depend on *how* that single model is taught. According to Summers and Barber (2010: 7), for example, 'traditional psychodynamic teaching methods can be more like catechism than intellectual exploration'. It seems likely that such methods, where what is taught is presented as 'the one and only true model', result in students being less open to looking at other models or ways of working. In other words, it could lead to Balkanisation, where the model's 'hypotheses' become reified and other approaches are treated with suspicion and hostility. Indeed the history of the therapy field is full of battles and conflicts. Training in a single approach may arguably make it more difficult to integrate new learning, so that something new may be at best 'bolted on' rather than integrated.

We see training integrative practitioners as helping trainees to engage critically with a number of ideas and open themselves up to the experiences offered. It may be wise to be suspicious of definite and simple answers, of people who claim to know the 'truth' or adhere to a reified truth as if it were doctrine. Truth is an elusive concept that often depends on 'whose' truth we are talking about. An integration of a number of approaches requires a clear understanding and knowledge of the premises behind each of them individually and a rigorous yet flexible stance, where the trainee is invited to entertain a number of ideas simultaneously holding all as *contextually* true.

Some training organisations prefer to teach a number of theories separately, and expect students to create their own integration. This can be challenging for students, particularly when on shorter (two or three year) counselling courses. This may result in confusion and the adoption of just one model, the one students like or find easiest, and a rejection of the others. Alternatively students may engage with each discrete model a little and say things such as, 'well first I worked psychodynamically by asking her about her childhood, then we did CBT because I asked what she was thinking, and then I worked in a person centred way and just listened'. This demonstrates not only a misunderstanding of what it means to work integratively, but also of the models mentioned, as what is said of each one of them sounds like a parody.

Students may be able to create their own integration, provided the training is long enough for this process to happen. In this case there needs to be clarity regarding the

---

[11]The shadow is a concept from Jungian psychology and denotes everything that we are not aware of, deny or reject. The shadow is often regarded as negative, but it can contain positive elements too.

organisation's underlying values and philosophies as well as a rationale for the teaching of particular theories and the exclusion of others. Lack of such clarity may leave students confused, particularly if there is also a lack of agreement between individual trainers regarding the usefulness of various therapeutic approaches.

INTEGRATION OF THEORY AND PRACTICE

We believe that successful training involves an integrative approach to three main areas: theory, practice and personal development. A typical training day might include sessions on theory, skills practice and personal development. During skills practice students take turns in functioning as client and therapist for each other. We find that theory is best introduced through inviting the students to actively participate in debate and discussion. Also, having been introduced to a particular aspect of theory, trainees are then asked to work with the new material in their skills practice, and reflect on what this means to them personally. This means that theory is not something dry and abstract, but comes alive through direct experience and practice.

TEACHING STYLES AND METHODS

Trainees are not the trainers' clients, but they are not their friends either. No matter how egalitarian therapy teachers try to be, the power differential cannot be denied. We are mindful of the fact that as trainers we are the people who mark trainees' work, observe their practice sessions, and will be influenced by our observations of them. As far as the course and their plans for the future are concerned, it may feel to trainees that their fate is in our hands, and to some extent it is. Training to be a therapist is not an easy experience. Not only do we ask people to learn a great deal of new material, they are also required to implement what they learn in their practice. We find that students are often very anxious, particularly when assessment looms near, and may need a great deal of support.

Although by definition everyone who trains as a therapist is an adult, the training itself can be curiously infantilising. So rather than a 'pedagogical' teaching style, which is based on the teaching of children, we advocate a stance of 'relational andragogy',[12] where students are treated as adults and therefore our equals. Within such an approach students are encouraged to take responsibility for their learning and are more likely to take an active part in the life of the training organisation. Feedback from students and ideas for improvement are actively sought and taken on board. How we like to be with clients – open, available, collaborative, invitational and creative – is how we like to be in our relationship with students.

---

[12]Andragogy is Greek meaning 'man-leading'. The term was first coined by the German teacher Alexander Kapp in 1833, and used by Knowles to develop a theory of adult learning. Andragogy emphasises 'process', not just content, and students' active involvement in their learning. Teachers act as facilitators rather than instructors. See Carlson (1989).

THE ROLE OF PERSONAL DEVELOPMENT

Personal and professional development is widely regarded as essential for all practitioners, whether qualified or in training, and an important aspect of our continuing integration of theory, practice and experience. As trainers we aim to help students become integrative practitioners through the integration of theory and practice, as well as the development of self-knowledge and self-awareness. There are at least three means by which trainees' self-knowledge and awareness may be facilitated: personal therapy, a personal development group and supervision.

Personal Therapy

Regarding the necessity of personal therapy, opinions appear divided, with many regarding it as absolutely essential throughout training, and others seeing it as an unnecessary expense, the value of which cannot be demonstrated. Interestingly, the writers of this book do not share the same opinion on the subject either. One author regards personal therapy as useful, though not essential, and one of several methods for gaining self-awareness. She questions how we can differentiate between models of training that pathologise their students, by defining their experience of the training process as one in which they are made aware of their deficits (which might then be 'cured' by their training therapists in mandated therapy), and those approaches that provide a resource to trainees, by recognising that an opportunity for reflection and personal development is a necessary component of the learning experience. However, the other author finds it hard to see how practitioners can help their clients go to places where they may not be prepared to go themselves and regards personal therapy as an essential part of training. This difference of opinion between us regarding mandatory therapy in therapy training is also reflected in debates in the field and different course requirements.

An argument in favour of therapy for trainees is that therapy training often shakes people's views and beliefs about themselves. This goes for every part of the course, even seemingly straightforward bits of theory. As discussed above, theory is best taught integratively, through asking students to check in with their own experience, observe their responses to theory, and ask themselves 'do I have strong reactions against anything?' A strong reaction is often a sign that there is something going on inside. It is therefore good to encourage students not to reject anything, but to be interested in their own wish to reject and reflect on what might lie underneath that wish. So therapy training involves helping students become interested in their own process and their own internal world and to develop a stance of curiosity.

Personal therapy can be hugely supportive and may provide excellent learning regarding 'how it is done'. A study by Rake and Paley (2009) reports how personal therapy helped people in three ways: it showed how to do therapy, developed their self-knowledge and helped to dissolve difficult personal issues. Congruence with the approach being learnt is therefore crucial. Practitioners who have had helpful therapy themselves are much more likely to have confidence in the therapeutic process than if they haven't, and their clients will sense that confidence.

Studies that attempt to link personal therapy to patient outcomes have so far been inconclusive (Beutler et al., 2004). This may be due to methodological problems, or the general difficulty of attributing single factors to client outcome, given the complexity and multidimensional nature of therapeutic work.

Personal therapy can also help trainees to learn the skills of being present with clients (such as developing attunement and advanced empathic responding) as well as learning to recognise and manage their own emotional responses. Some of the reasons for personal therapy during training may include: to provide the space to explore one's own inner world in order to help clients to do so, to gain support and help with processing of difficult experiences, to help with recognising blind spots and developing a stance of curiosity in self and others, and to learn to be with clients' as well as one's own emotional responses, and to learn to do therapy itself.

Reasons for Personal Therapy During Training

- Explore own inner world in order to help clients do so too.
- Support and help with processing of difficult experiences.
- Help with recognition and integration of blind spots.
- Help develop a stance of curiosity in self and others.
- Learn to be with clients' as well as own emotional responses.
- Learn how to do therapy.

The Personal Development Group

Many integrative courses include a personal development group where students can talk about and help each other to process their emotional responses to the course. For the successful functioning of a group, its members need to feel safe, so its first task is the development of a clear contract, which should include agreement on confidentiality. Personal development groups offer an excellent learning opportunity for students, provided certain parameters are adhered to: they should not be too large (no more than twelve people);[13] facilitators should not be involved in teaching or assessing the same group of students; and contracts should be clear.

Not all organisations are able to satisfy the first two criteria and run large personal development groups of around twenty people. A large group may leave some of its members too intimidated to speak, resulting in a few people actively participating while the others watch. If the group's facilitators also teach and assess, people may not feel safe and the group may function at a superficial level only. This would be unfortunate as in our experience personal development groups can be very supportive (as well as challenging) and offer fantastic personal learning opportunities for all concerned. The issue of personal development will be discussed further in chapter 5.

---

[13]See Johns (1996) on optimum group size.

Supervision of Practice with Clients

Supervision of practice is an important aspect of therapist development (Mehr et al., 2010). Supervisors can help trainees to talk about and integrate what they are learning and experiencing, and help them to 'be with' and engage with clients. Supervisors can also help trainees to notice their emotional responses to clients and reflect on what this might mean while, at the same time, listening to the client. Even though supervision is focused on practice, it has the potential to foster practitioners' personal awareness and development immensely.

Supervision of Skills Practice with Fellow Trainees

Trainees may also learn a great deal through observed work with each other – in vivo or recorded. We particularly like the use of audio/video recordings where trainees function as client or therapist for each other, which can then be shown and processed in small groups. This can be very revealing, so it is important for the facilitator or supervisor to hold the group and their anxiety, and ensure that the group reflection and discussions are respectful and supportive, so that all can learn.

The Value of Mindfulness

Both of us have integrated mindfulness practice into our daily life and in our work with clients.[14] It can also play an important part in the self-development of trainee practitioners (Chambers and Maris, 2010). In addition to teaching sessions on the use of mindfulness with clients, we therefore also like to include a brief period of mindfulness practice at the beginning of every training day.

SUMMARY

In this chapter we have discussed the history of psychotherapy integration as well as a number of different views of the subject. We concluded that a trans-theoretical approach seems the most fruitful and suggested the framework of 'approach, method and technique' as a useful way to think about integration. However, rather than seeing integration or an integrative model as static, we argued that it may be useful to think about integration as an activity. So instead of calling ourselves 'integrative' practitioners, we describe ourselves as engaged in a process of continuously integrating our relevant personal and professional experiences.

---

[14]The value of mindfulness in therapy and its practice has been adopted in humanistic approaches, contemplative and transpersonal therapies (Rowan 2005; Wellings and McCormick 2005) and integrated with a cognitive behavioural approach in the form of mindfulness-based cognitive therapy (Segal et al., 2002).

The remainder of the book will be devoted to all aspects of the relational integrative model and in the next chapter we introduce the theoretical ideas that form its basis.

QUESTIONS FOR FURTHER REFLECTION AND DISCUSSION

- How would you integrate concepts and methods from seemingly incompatible approaches?
- What do you think of the various types of integration? Are you attracted more to one type of integration than another? If so, what are your reasons for your preference?
- Is there a type of integration you would never contemplate using? If so, what are your reasons for its rejection?
- What do you think of Rowan and Jacobs's (2002) distinctions between therapists and therapies?
- What are your views on the various methods of personal development? What is your experience? What would you recommend to a new trainee practitioner?

FURTHER READING

Evans, K. R. and Gilbert, M. C. (2005) *An Introduction to Integrative Psychotherapy.* Basingstoke: Palgrave Macmillan.

Gold, J. R. (1996) *Concepts in Psychotherapeutic Integration.* New York: Plenum Press.

Lapworth, P., Sills, C. and Fish, S. (2001) *Integration in Counselling and Psychotherapy: Developing a Personal Approach.* London: Sage.

Norcross J. C. and Goldfried, M. R. (eds) (2005) *Handbook of Psychotherapy Integration* (2nd edn). Oxford: Oxford University Press.

O'Brien, M. and Houston, G. (2007) *Integrative Therapy: A Practitioner's Guide* (2nd edn). London: Sage.

Scott, T. (2004) *Integrative Psychotherapy in Healthcare: A Humanistic Approach.* Basingstoke: Palgrave Macmillan.

2

Approach

PART 1

THEORETICAL PRESUPPOSITIONS

In order to facilitate understanding and critical examination, it is important to clarify the broad perspectives and philosophical orientation that underpin a therapeutic theory. In the first part of this chapter we outline the core philosophical assumptions that underpin the synthesis that we call the relational integrative model. As described in the previous chapter the term 'approach' describes our theoretical orientation, which includes these broader assumptions. The RIM is based on a postmodern worldview and we begin by setting out what we mean by modernism before outlining our postmodern stance.

In the second part of the chapter we go on to discuss those aspects of the diverse ecology of ideas within the three main therapeutic schools that are included in the RIM. Each of the three main approaches (humanistic, psychodynamic and cognitive) has much to offer in the quest for useful ideas to alleviate pain and suffering. The challenge is how to successfully synthesise compatible aspects of these approaches into a coherent whole. We have called our synthesis the relational integrative model; however the preferences, prejudices and beliefs that a counsellor has will influence the balance of each theory within it.

KNOWLEDGE, EPISTEMOLOGY AND THE NATURE OF REALITY

Mahrer (1989) suggests that one strategy for integration is the determination of a wider trans-theoretical framework within which other theories can be assimilated. We therefore need to establish what this wider framework might be; what ideas we subscribe to and where they come from; what we understand by such concepts as 'the self', 'personality', 'identity' and 'change'. How we define these concepts and terms will influence our action as therapists. For example, if we believe that individual characteristics are inherited then, seeking to explain a person's behaviour, we would ask questions about the person's parents or grandparents. If we believe that depression is an illness caused by neuro-chemical imbalance, we might decide to treat the condition with drugs. If, on the other hand, we believe that someone displaying symptoms of this nature is possessed by evil spirits, the treatment would be of a very different order. It could be argued that all of these beliefs, as well as the activities and institutions that surround them, are socially constructed and, like all social constructions, culturally defined. We therefore asked ourselves the following:

How do we know what we know? What types of knowledge are there and how do we know that this knowledge is valid and reliable? Every theory is underpinned by an epistemological framework or lens that influences how we see and understand the world.[1] Frames of reference contain building blocks made up of propositions that are the starting point upon which theories are then constructed.

See for example the image below:

Figure 3   Rubin vase

The above figure allows two possible interpretations: a vase or two faces. The actual figure does not change, yet the mind's interpretation depends on perception. Once the image is seen in a certain way, it becomes difficult to see the other possible interpretation. It is impossible to 'see' both pictures – the vase and two silhouetted faces – at the same time. In other words the frame that is used influences how we make sense of something. Kuhn (1962) coined the term 'paradigm' to describe a collection of values, beliefs and assumptions about the nature of reality and knowledge that is shared by a society and culture at a given time. A paradigm is similar to

---

[1]The word epistemology is derived from the Greek 'episteme' meaning knowledge, and 'episte' meaning understanding, and can be defined as the study of the origins and nature of knowledge.

the frame we describe above. It forms the basis upon which we interpret or perceive reality. According to Kuhn sooner or later new discoveries will lead to the adoption of a new paradigm (a paradigm shift), which means that the old paradigm is rejected. So for example during the Age of Enlightenment in the seventeenth and eighteenth centuries, the prevailing paradigm involved the belief that valid knowledge of the world can only be obtained via observation, empirical testing and processes of reason. This was a reaction against the so-called Dark Ages, which were seen as dominated by superstition and irrational adherence to religious faith.

The humanist thinker Thomas Paine maintained that reality is always defined and mediated by human perception and experience while the eighteenth- and nineteenth-century Romantics argued that 'reason' cannot account for all phenomena such as the soul or God.

MODERNISM

Modernism is the dominant intellectual tradition of the scientific community and is underpinned by the idea that for knowledge to be valid there has to be an observer who measures, quantifies and tests that which is being observed. These views were introduced and developed by scientists and philosophers such as Isaac Newton and Descartes and gave rise to the scientific tradition and the view that science is the arbiter of truth.

Modernism suggests that in order for knowledge to be valid there has to be an observer who measures and quantifies that which is being observed and from these objective observations benchmarks for reality can be ascertained. The ultimate and eternal laws that govern the universe in this way can be discovered and known. The world is made up of matter and this matter and how it behaves and interacts can be understood on the basis of universal mathematical laws and thus can be predicted. Modernists, such as Newton, thought that with the right instruments, it is possible to observe and measure everything, including human behaviour and experience (McNamee, 1997). This resulted in a dualist position that separates the mind (consciousness) from the body (matter). The metaphor which best fits this view is that of 'world as machine' (Macy and Brown, 1998).

POSTMODERNISM

According to Kuhn (1977) it is not, however, possible to be a neutral observer as one always influences that which is being observed. The values, beliefs and prejudices of the observer will affect his or her interpretation of phenomena and their act of observation will influence what is being observed.

> When scientists must choose between competing theories, two men fully committed to the same list of criteria for choice may nevertheless reach different conclusions. (Kuhn, 1962: 324)

This means that each observer brings forth a reality that will change depending on who is doing the observing. This can be illustrated by the Pygmalion effect – according to which teachers' high expectations of pupils caused those pupils to do better (Rosenthal and Jacobson, 1992). A postmodernist worldview questions the notion of objectivity and suggests rather that the position or stance from which we construct a reality is just one way of starting. Postmodernism suggests that there are multiple perspectives on reality and it depends on the perspective we take as to which reality emerges. Contrary to a modernist paradigm, according to which reality can be pinned down and defined, categorised and known, postmodernism regards reality as subjective and 'truth' as provisional. So reality is created in the 'eye of the beholder' or brought forth by the observer as Cecchin (in Soderlund, 2009) says:

> You think that what you observe is there. But we find what we look for. The recent change in the past five or ten years is the realization that there is no reality to discover. You are not discovering reality, you are creating it.

Below is a table summarising the key difference between modernism and postmodernism:

Table 1 Modernist Science and Postmodernism compared

Modernist Science	Postmodernism
Reality exists independently of our perception of it. Humans can understand the world through objective analysis and reason.	Reality is always mediated by our interaction with it. Objectivity is approximated.
Pure reason, correct logical argument, and empirical observation are sufficient tools for determining rigorous scientific truth.	All arguments and systems of reasoning are contingent upon their point of departure, axioms, propositional rules and frames of reference. No argument can be proven by its own point of departure without falling prey to circular reasoning, tautology or paradox.
Universal laws can be obtained through objective measurement and reason. True knowledge about a phenomenon is eternal and universal.	Knowledge about a phenomenon is provisional and relative and holds as true until disproved. Other phenomena cannot be so reduced without losing understanding of their nature i.e. the whole is more than the sum of the parts.
We can know the true nature of a phenomenon providing that we obtain the right instrument of measurement or observation.	What we know about the nature of a phenomenon is always mediated by our perceptual, cognitive and socially constructed frame of reference.

Relevance to Therapy

Within the current therapy field the modernist and postmodernist worldviews are both represented albeit within different theoretical orientations, influencing the therapist's perceptions, beliefs and practice. Freud's development of psychoanalysis as a scientific method within the modernist paradigm for example should be seen against the backdrop of his studies on neuro-anatomy and physiology, which were well respected within the medical fraternity in the late nineteenth and early twentieth centuries. The tradition that he was trained in saw behaviour in purely bio-neurological terms (McLeod, 1998). From observation and analysis he inferred that the mind consists of psychic structures and mechanisms (instincts, drives), developed from past experiences and relationships that motivate behaviour and organise subjective experience.

This individual focus then led to the assumption that people's problems arise out of intra-psychic or internal mechanisms and processes. This perspective assumes that change occurs when something internal to the individual changes (Hayley, 1963). Insight is the mechanism by which such change is seen to occur: the person gains understanding and awareness of unconscious processes and this insight then brings about change and cure. The notion of insight as the primary vehicle for change has dominated Western psychologies for more than a century.

A logical conclusion of modernist psychological thinking is the attempt to determine benchmarks for human behaviours based on intra-psychic and structuralist[2] explanations. Normality is determined by ascertaining what the average behaviour might be, so that anything that falls outside the average range can be said to be abnormal (Haley, 1963: 6). From this perspective psychological difficulties are attributed to deficits or impairment of functioning or development. The therapist is a neutral observer who is able to diagnose whether a person's condition falls within or outside these norms. The American Psychiatric Association's development of the DSM,[3] which contains diagnostic criteria for specific conditions, falls within this tradition.

According to our postmodern perspective we understand that our realities are constructed or co-constructed. The therapist interprets what they observe in a particular way that is itself influenced by a particular context. This results in a particular description and will then determine the kind of therapeutic decisions that are made. For example a client may report feeling low, despondent and unable to get started on anything. If he were to see a GP they might wonder if the client is suffering from depression and ask whether he is sleeping well, has lost his appetite, and if so may come to the conclusion, based on diagnostic criteria, that he is indeed suffering from depression and prescribe anti-depressants to alleviate the symptoms. A psychoanalyst on the other hand may explore the client's history and early relationships in search for possible explanations and be interested in the way the client interacts with him for clues of early attachment patterns and will be interested in any defence mechanisms the client uses. In contrast a CBT therapist may look for negative automatic and distorted thinking and assumptions that are proving unhelpful to the client.

These examples illustrate that the treatment or approach used during this meeting will be determined by the therapist's or GP's interpretation of what it is she is

---

[2]Wilhelm Wundt was the pioneer of psychological studies of human cognition based on ideas that the mind functioned according to its underlying structures ([1874] 2002).

[3]Diagnostic and Statistical Manual of the Mental Disorders.

observing rather than something that is actually observable (Hayley, 1981). In other words, it is not possible to 'see' depression or anxiety in the same way that it is not possible to see cognitive distortions or a defence mechanism. These constructs are inferred by the observer and dependent on the observer's biases, prejudices and theories.

However, we also recognise that we need reference points to help us to read life. These constructs offer commonly agreed relative truths as well as a shorthand or language that can be shared with others so that we can have some understanding of what we mean by what we say. We can broadly agree, for example, that depression is a term that describes a certain set of symptoms when they are clustered together and occur in one individual.

INTERDEPENDENCE, SYSTEMS AND SOCIAL CONSTRUCTIONISM

> Shift from metaphor 'world as machine' to world as 'interconnected systems'. (Macy and Brown, 1998)

The early and middle part of the twentieth century saw an explosion of new ideas in the fields of physics and social science that included cybernetics, general systems theory and quantum physics. Key pioneers in this movement included philosophers, scientists and therapists such as Bateson, von Bertalanfy and Weiner. A crucial idea that emerged from the field of cybernetics (a term coined by Weiner in the late 1940s) is that life organises itself, so that parts of systems interact with each other by processes of feedback, thus creating patterns of interaction. This notion provides a cornerstone to the relational perspective in therapy. Bateson, an anthropologist, philosopher and social scientist, proposed a concept of mind based on the ideas of feedback and cybernetics (Capra, 1996). He made a crucial connection between the science of cybernetics and feedback that had originally been applied to machines and was the first to apply it to the processes of communication. Bateson's ideas formed the foundations of most of the presuppositions in the field of family therapy in the 1950s as well as influencing many psychiatrists such as R. D. Laing.

The group of therapists known as the Milan team and subsequently the post Milan team (including Boscolo and Cecchin) built on Bateson's theories in the 1970s and 1980s and applied them to the therapeutic context. Their groundbreaking contribution produced practical therapeutic methods based on the concepts of communication and systems theory, such as hypothesising, circular questioning and the notion of neutrality (Jones, 1993). Around the same time that Bateson was studying communication, neo-Freudians such as Harry Stack Sullivan, Karen Horney and Erich Fromm were moving away from a drive theory of human development, to propose an interpersonal or interactional theory of human behaviour and development. Fromm, for example, suggested that we have a fundamental need for relationship, as well as a sense of belonging and to be part of a social group. Stack Sullivan's ideas in particular had a huge, yet often unacknowledged, influence, precursing and shaping the development of object relations theory as well as relational psychoanalysis.

Collectively the ideas generated in this period brought about a shift from the metaphor of 'man as machine' to that of 'man as social being'. Human beings came to be seen as embedded in social networks or systems that operate according to processes of feedback (internal and external). Developments in neuroscience from the 1980s and 1990s onwards served to provide some neurobiological evidence for this interactional theory of human nature. These ideas inform the wider trans-theoretical framework (Mahrer, 1989) of the RIM, which include a postmodern, relational and social constructionist perspective as summarised below.

Presuppositions and Assumptions of the RIM:

- Reality is subjective and is co-constructed within a social context.
- Interdependence – all human beings survive and exist interdependently of one another.
- Human beings are embedded within systems – socio-cultural, political, historical, language systems.
- Objectivity is approximated – reality is mediated by our interpretation of it: a social constructionist perspective.
- Meaning and behaviour are products of interactional as well as intra-psychic processes.
- Intersubjectivity – interaction involves an exchange at a conscious and unconscious level; mutual influencing happens between participants. This means that the observer is not separate from the system that he or she is observing.
- Holistic perspective – whole is more than the sum of its parts.
- Ecological perspective – we are always part of a wider ecology and exist in networks of relationships and systems.

Contained within these presuppositions is the idea that people are primarily social beings and our 'selves' are constructed and created within relationships and via processes of communication and interaction. The very nature of what it is to be human is the process of being seen and acknowledged by another. Our sense of self is a construct that is built through internal and external responses to feedback from and with others. The shift from an individual to a two-person psychology therefore places a far greater emphasis on the relationship between therapist and client. It heralds a revolution in psychotherapeutic thinking, as the therapist can no longer be considered an objective observer of something 'out there'. A two-person psychology (and interactional/systemic thinking) acknowledges that therapist and client mutually influence each other. Communication in this sense is an evolving and emerging activity involving coordination and interpretation between people.

We are interconnected and interrelated. The relational paradigm and systems theory imply the mutually dependent nature of human existence. Systems thinking influences our definition and understanding of the term 'relational'. Systems are collections of parts organised and held together in a particular pattern and relationship.

Examples of systems include such things as families, organisations, biological organisms and of course therapeutic systems. Systems are organised in the following ways:

- All systems are subsystems of other systems.
- Change in one part of the system affects the rest of the system. Systems function through process of circularity rather than linear/causality.
- What makes it organise is the way it is organised.
- Boundaries between systems are defined by social interaction.
- Systems maintain stability through change and flexibility. Systems maintain integrity through balancing chaos vs organisation, change vs stability. Processes of feedback correct deviations to bring systems back into life (via feedback loops).
- Therapeutic systems operate on feedback: self-regulating, e.g. a central heating system which regulates itself via feedback between temperature and thermostat and so organising how much heat will be omitted by radiators (Watzlawick et al., 1967). And it follows that
- Parts of the system mutually shape each other.

SOCIAL CONSTRUCTIONISM

According to a social constructionist position knowledge is socially created, emphasising the social and cultural consensually validated perspectives perceived by the observers operating within a given cultural milieu. Therefore categories of knowledge and reality are developed through social relationships and interactions (see table 2). This means that 'mind' is socially constructed through language (Bateson, 1972; Wittgenstein, 1953). 'We are born into the world of stories. A culture is structured around myths, legends, family tales and other stories that have existed since long before we are born and will continue long after we die. We construct a personal identity by aligning ourselves with some of these stories, by "dwelling within" them' (McLeod, 1998: 153). So a soldier during the First World War who refused to get out of his trench would be labelled as a coward or suffering from shell shock whereas nowadays this behaviour may be interpreted as the result of post traumatic stress disorder.

Table 2 Key social constructionist ideas relevant to therapy

One-person psychology – interest and focus on internal drives, constructs.

Two-person psychology – interest and focus lies in relationship between people out of which certain behaviours, actions and meanings then evolve and emerge.

A therapist with a relational orientation is interested in the pattern of communication between people.

Move from Labels as absolutes (He is in denial, he is depressed) to descriptions (the person shows depression, shows resistance in relation to another).

Position of therapist as participant/observer – all members of system bring forth the system/therapist/counsellor part of the observing system.

It is impossible not to be influenced by one's prejudices and beliefs.

How therapists interpret a symptom depends on their social values, ethics and preferences. As the above client examples show, description of a symptom tells us about the observer (in this case the therapist) as much as it tells us about the person being observed (Keeney, 1983). However, we can attempt to take a phenomenological stance, which involves bracketing off[4] our assumptions and taking a stance of curiosity. Being neutral to the outcome of therapy helps therapists to remain flexible in their responses to clients and able to entertain many perspectives and possibilities. This also produces client centred and collaborative relationships. The more aware therapists are of their own beliefs, prejudices and emotional sensitivities, the more they can become aware of how these may play out in their choice of interventions. This will also help them to guard against imposing their own or societal agendas on the client. The anti-psychiatry movement in the 1960s, for example, criticised psychotherapists for acting as agents of social control and using their power to effect change in the direction desired by society. Foucault ([1969] 2002) argued that the criteria upon which we judge mental illness and wellness are based on socially constructed institutions and discourses of objectification. Thus therapists' awareness of how social discourses[5] act as a context for themselves and their clients helps to mitigate against abuses of power, and offer a meta-perspective on issues that the client faces and on the therapeutic relationship itself. 'Relational' in our model therefore means much more than relationship alone as described above.

MEANING AND BEHAVIOUR AS PRODUCTS OF INTERACTIONAL PROCESSES AS WELL AS INTRA-PSYCHIC PROCESSES

Meaning is the product of engagement between people within the context of larger societal discourses that influence all the participants involved. So while we interpret what it is that we experience, see and communicate, this interpretation is itself influenced by the process of relating within relationships. This is important because if we believe that human existence is relational and human beings are mutually dependent on one another, then it follows that we all live within networks of relationships or systems.

Systems are maintained via a process of mutual influencing and feedback between their members. We can never determine what came first; the chicken or the egg. So although we often interpret events in terms of linear/cause and effect (he made her do that because he did this) it is only our punctuation of events that make us see things this way. Gergen and Kaye (1992) suggest that:

> Psychotherapy may be regarded as a process of semiosis; the forging of meaning in the context of collaborative discourse. It is a process during which the meaning of experience

---

[4]This is part of the phenomenological method that attempts to describe experience as it is without using the lens of theory.

[5]Discourse: a term used by Foucault to convey how the meaning of themes, such as power and gender, are socially and linguistically constructed.

is transformed via a fusion of the horizons of the participants ... alternative ways of punctuating experience are developed and a new stance toward experience evolves. (Gergen and Kaye, 1992: 182)

From a relational perspective we regard events as having circular explanations. This is a non-pathologising/non-blaming stance as behaviour is seen within the context of another behaviour. When we see a client for therapy we join a system and coordinate with it. As therapists we bring to the therapeutic encounter the possibility of new meanings, particularly through the exploration of context. There can be no meaning without context. Reframing, for example, is an intervention at the level of meaning where the 'frame' or 'context' is shifted to produce a change in meaning.

Brian, a young adolescent, complains to the therapist:

'My mum is always nagging me about my homework and is always on my case about everything'.

The therapist reframes this:

'Whilst your mum really cares about you the way that she shows this doesn't always feel helpful'.

Here the therapist has reframed the mother's behaviour as 'caring', a possible new explanation that has a more positive connotation than that of 'nagging'. This may offer Brian an alternative 'view' of his mother in relation to him.

When we see meaning as created through interactional processes we become interested in the patterns of behaviour and thinking between the client and others in the client's lives (including ourselves), and how these patterns are more or less useful for the client. We also become interested in the continuity between past and present in the client's narratives. If meaning is a coordination of both action and meaning making processes then when we join with someone in the therapeutic encounter, we are engaging in a process of coordination of our and their meanings, the result of which may be the emergence of new possible meanings. What we cannot know for sure is the outcome of this process and which of the ways that we choose to act (or intervene) may resonate with the client in such a way as to create some difference. Symptoms of behaviour, when taken within the wider context of relationship, can also take on different meanings. The descriptions that the client uses or that we as therapists may use for behaviours or experience will have a powerful impact on our relationships.

INTERSUBJECTIVITY

'It is in the space between inner and outer world, which is also the space between people – the transitional space – that intimate relationships and creativity occur' Winnicott (http://mythosandlogos.com/Winnicott.html). When people interact there is an exchange at a conscious and unconscious level, which constitutes a form of mutual influencing. The space between two people is the space in which meanings coalesce to form a third or shared meaning or joint narrative. Intersubjectivity challenges the idea of a self that is contained and separate from others, and sees selves or subjects as permeable. The theory of intersubjectivity is informed by general systems theory and constitutes a move away from the idea that healthy development involves separation and autonomy, to a view that healthy development is the recognition of the subjectivity of both the child and mother (caregiver) within a context of mutual relatedness (Mitchell, 2000).

So within the RIM we attend to what is happening in the here and now between the client and ourselves. We acknowledge the mutual influencing and coalescing of our two (or more) subjectivities rather than considering ourselves as objective observers. This means we are conscious (and sometimes unconscious) of the effect our clients have on us as well as the effect we may have on our clients. Developing self-awareness helps us as therapists to be attuned to the processes happening in the room with the client (the co-transference (Orange, 2003)) and to be able to utilise this therapeutically in the service of the client.

HOLISM

From a holistic perspective the whole is more than the sum of its parts. This means that we see the client as somebody who is more than a set of symptoms; we are curious and interested in complexity. For example, if a client tells us they have been feeling very anxious lately, we are curious not just about the symptoms of anxiety, but also about how the client feels about the anxiety, what it means to them, how it fits into their lives usefully and not so usefully – what else is going on for them now and in the past and in the future, who else is connected to them and what are the belief systems around worry and anxiety in the client's family of origin. All these questions are ways of becoming curious beyond the client's problem description. These questions bring forth a multiverse of ideas, possible explanations and descriptions. They also elicit the complexity and richness of clients' lives, thus offering greater opportunity for discovering resources and new life enhancing perspectives.

ECOLOGY

> We are always and inevitably part of a wider 'ecology' within political, economic and cultural contexts and that everything in our social lives is connected through our relationships and co-created through and within our communication processes. (Hedges, 2005: 184)

The relational perspective transcends the limiting descriptions of selves as beings bounded by the physical structure of our bodies or individual personalities. We see human beings as inextricably connected to the world in which they live: the environment, the natural world and other beings. We extend our concept of self from this perspective to ecological self. When we do this we have in mind the fact that human beings are part of a wider ecology and always exist within systems and networks of relationship. We all form part of and are contained within the web of life. This view makes us look beyond the individual, in order to extend our thinking and hypotheses, and optimise the possibility for therapeutic exchange. An ecological perspective also encompasses the spiritual and transpersonal domain. This is an essential part of human existence and one that sometimes is neglected in counselling and therapy, but one that may offer a rich source of exploration and therapeutic possibility for clients.

SUMMARY

> The best way to understand persons is not in isolation, but in the context of their relations with others, past and present, internal and external, actual and fantasied. (Mitchell, 2000: 107)

The modernist narrative of therapy is one that embraces the dialectic of pathology and cure.[6] In other words, it assumes that therapists can objectively know the reality of clients and what should be the preferred reality or narrative, and work to achieve this outcome. The postmodern narrative of therapy views the therapeutic encounter as territory in which new meaning can be creatively generated 'between' the participants of the system (therapists and clients). This view embraces the idea of the intersubjective nature of the therapeutic process. Within the RIM therefore we suggest that as therapists we cannot be objective, but are rather participant observers whose beliefs, perspectives, prejudices and cultural/social histories are all brought to bear on what it is we see. The self that determines what is 'real' is intangible. Our perceptions of objects are not necessarily true and accurate representations of reality. We can only know things within the boundaries of our awareness and perception. Within a relational paradigm attention is paid to processes between people that create circumstances and experience, as well as the internal relationships between aspects of self and between mind and body, emotion and cognition.

ACTIVITY

Gergen, a leading social constructionist, once gave participants in a workshop the following exercise: each group was given a term (diagnostic label) such as depression, anorexia, anxiety disorder, Asperger's syndrome, panic disorder. The group were then asked to debate whether they would eliminate this term/label from our social structures and language if they had the possibility to do so.

Imagine that you were involved in this debate: what are the advantages and disadvantages of these constructs as you can see it? Would you decide to keep these terms or get rid of them, how useful are they, what do these terms enable us to do or prevent us from doing?

---

[6]See chapter 2.

This section has given an overview of the meta-theories that underpin our approach. In the next section we go on to discuss further the theoretical thinking we draw upon and these two parts constitute the approach (the first of Burnham's categories) underlying the relational integrative model.

QUESTIONS FOR FURTHER REFLECTION

- What are your own beliefs in relation to the nature of reality?
- How have you come to have these beliefs; what influences how you think about human behaviour, relationships and the nature of reality?
- What are your thoughts about how change occurs in human beings and how human suffering can be relieved?

PART 2

THEORETICAL UNDERPINNINGS

This section introduces aspects of humanistic, psychodynamic and cognitive theoretical approaches that are in line with the unifying theoretical presuppositions discussed in part 1. First we discuss the importance of early relational experience and factors that contribute to developmental processes, as well as insights offered by neuroscience. Next we define the selection of compatible aspects of theory within the three broad schools mentioned above. Finally we discuss seven key domains that form the conceptual heart of the RIM and have been selected as central concepts within the theoretical synthesis of the relational integration.

INTEGRATION OF THE THREE MAIN APPROACHES

Each of the three psychotherapeutic approaches is a broad church incorporating different sub-sections that may differ significantly, while sharing sufficient basic assumptions to belong under the same umbrella. Psychodynamic therapies' basic assumptions, for example, include a belief in the existence of dynamic unconscious processes, as well as the importance of the past, particularly early childhood, in shaping our personality and behaviour. The humanistic therapies emphasise personal growth as well as freedom of choice and the development of creativity. Cognitive behavioural therapies adopt a problem solving approach and focus on how people's thinking affects how they feel about themselves and others, and thus shapes their experience and how they act.

As discussed in part 1 of this chapter, the RIM falls within a postmodern paradigm, according to which there is no one true 'reality' out there; it depends on who does the looking and the lens that is used.

Figure 4 shows three overlapping circles, each circle representing one of the three main approaches of psychotherapy (O'Brien and Houston, 2007): psychodynamic, humanistic and cognitive behavioural.

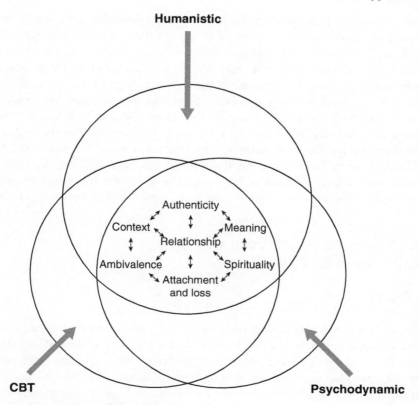

Figure 4 The Relational Integrative Model

There are three distinct areas:

- Areas that are distinct to each of the three approaches, i.e. without overlap.
- Areas of overlap between two approaches – flexible section.
- An area that overlaps all three approaches – our integration.

Figure 4 shows a significant area of overlap between therapeutic approaches. Each also contains an area that is not included within the common area. These outlying areas contain those aspects of theories that are not congruent with the postmodern values, assumptions and presuppositions as set out in the first part of this chapter. However, approaches in existence today owe a debt to those that have gone before; indeed the current models grew out of them. We see current developments therefore in terms of Wilber's (2000) concept of 'transcend and include'. In other words, postmodernist approaches grew out of the modernist approaches to therapy that went before.

The area of overlap between the three types of approach constitutes the theoretical base of the RIM. It includes contemporary developments within the three approaches that help us to understand and conceptualise clients' experiences and actions, as well as the processes that occur between client and therapist. The remaining areas of overlap between two rather than three approaches help create flexibility in the model, so that individual therapists can adapt the model to fit with their particular integration. This is in line with our stance of 'integrating' rather than 'integration' as discussed in chapter 1 and acknowledges that people may differ as to what they feel able to integrate.

Over time there may be a change in the size and shape of the areas of overlap. A therapist may develop more experience in one area and withdraw somewhat from another; or perhaps she focuses more on two of the three approaches, so that the common area includes less of the third approach. The flexibility of the model also means that even for the same therapist it may vary in correspondence to the needs of individual clients. In the same way that a flower may look different depending on the angle from which we view it, how we see and use the RIM may depend on where we, or our clients, are coming from at the time (Faris and van Ooijen, 2009).

DEVELOPMENTAL, RELATIONAL AND NEUROSCIENTIFIC FACTORS

The Brain

During the last two decades neuro-imaging techniques have greatly improved, which has led to important discoveries. We know now that the development of neural pathways in the brain are experience dependent, particularly the experience of a positive affective relationship between caregiver and baby (Siegel, 1999). We also know that brain development is affected adversely by factors such as emotional neglect and chaotic or traumatic stimulation (Gerhardt, 2004).[7] These findings corroborate psychodynamic and attachment-based theory as well as contemporary humanistic and cognitive approaches, according to which the first few years of life are crucial in the development of the ability to understand ourselves and others in terms of inner states, such as thoughts, feelings, opinions, intentions or desires (Gomperts, 2009).

Fundamental to the development of the brain is the development of the ability to regulate states of arousal. In evolutionary terms raw emotional states, such as anger or sadness, have become more complex as human beings started to connect and bond with each other in communities and needed to find ways of controlling behaviours to meet social goals (Siegel, 1999).[8] As babies are initially so utterly dependent, there are during these early years countless (micro) social interactions between them and their primary caregivers, which help the development of the ability to self-soothe and regulate high levels of arousal and emotion.

Brain structures related to survival are already operational at birth. Other structures, particularly those related to the human ability to live in social groups (empathy, the regulation of emotions, the ability to communicate), develop in response to experience.

---

[7]This will be discussed in more detail in chapter 4.

[8]Mammals evolved over the last 200 million years to be sensitive to the needs of their young; this is because the young of insensitive mothers might not survive and thus not pass on their genes (de Waal, 2009).

This has the advantage of making young children very adaptable to the environment into which they are born, but it also means that the early years in any child's life are crucial to future development. In the same way that regular exercise makes our muscles grow, or repetition helps us learn and remember things, frequent and sustained positive interactions between caregiver and child will help the brain to grow and develop its neural structures and pathways. The development of affect regulation as well as mentalisation is an intersubjective process, so if a mother is highly anxious, high states of arousal will be 'grown' in the baby's brain (Schore, 2009). Such children's ability to self-soothe will be severely impaired; they are likely to grow up anxious and out of touch with their own as well as other people's internal worlds (Gomperts, 2009).[9]

What is the Mind?

From a modernist point of view the mind is 'nothing other' than the brain. Johnson (2010: 64), a Jungian analyst, criticises such 'materialistic reductionism'. She argues that the symptoms and some of the neurochemistry that occur in the case of depression following bereavement or a viral infection, for example, might be the same, yet the causes are very different. In both cases there is a correlation between brain function and depression, yet in the case of the former the cause is emotional, whereas for the latter the cause is probably physical. Johnson warns that correlation does not imply causality; two processes may happen to occur together, but this does not imply that one causes the other!

Although the brain and spinal cord are connected with every part of the body, Descartian dualism prevented the full recognition of the mind–body connection. Particularly in the Western world many people are out of touch with their body and appear to see themselves as minds on legs.[10]

Human Beings as Systems

However, as discussed previously, Bateson (1972) recognised that human beings are complex interacting systems, rather than robots steered by an operating system in the brain. He realised that it is impossible for individuals to be conscious of everything that goes on internally, and that it is important to integrate conscious and unconscious knowledge, as well as cognition and emotion. The living world may be conceptualised as a huge system, containing many sub-systems. Human beings (like all living systems) are cognitive systems existing within this larger system (Maturana and Varela, 1998). Within Maturana and Varela's systems approach our minds are seen as

---

[9]According to de Waal (2009) empathy helps us gain information about others, whereas sympathy reflects concern for others and a wish to help. Sympathy is apparently something we have in common with other animals, such as apes, dogs, elephants and even birds.

[10]This can be a limitation from a too narrow implementation of (second wave) CBT; mindfulness and compassion-based CBT approaches, however, aim to help people integrate body, mind, thoughts and emotions.

embodied and constantly influenced by (and influencing) our physical, social, relational and cultural environments. In other words, our embodied minds act across and within many interacting subsystems from the cellular level, right through to social organisation, language, and the coordination of meaning and evolution. They use the term 'structural coupling' for this 'structure determined and structure determining' process (Maturana and Varela, 1998: 75).

A Paradigm Shift

According to Schore (2009), we are in the middle of a paradigm shift, with scientists from a wide range of disciplines working together to integrate current knowledge into a coherent model of human development across the lifespan. Rather than regarding human beings as determined by biology, there is now a growing consensus that relationships with people, as well with as the wider environment, affects the structure and function of the brain.

In 1992 Dan Siegel, the pioneer of 'interpersonal neurobiology', convened a meeting of forty scientists from a wide range of disciplines to study the relationship between the brain and our subjective experience of the mind. It became clear that there was no shared understanding of what was meant by the mind, with some seeing it as 'just the activity of the brain' and others as 'an operating system' or 'our thoughts and feelings' (Siegel, 2010: 52). After much discussion the group accepted the following definition: 'The human mind is a relational and embodied process that regulates the flow of energy and information' (Siegel, 2010: 52). According to Siegel, 'we feel radiant energy when we sit in the sun, we use kinetic energy when we walk on the beach or go for a swim, we utilise neural energy when we think, when we talk, when we listen, when we read' (Siegel, 2010: 52). This definition of the mind is useful as it recognises the holistic nature of human beings, with bodies, minds and emotions.

As soon as we are born (and perhaps even before that), each one of us begins to create our own inner map or framework of the world. This framework is not conscious, yet guides us throughout our lives. It is composed of our earliest feelings and memories, and contains the conclusions we reached when we were very young. It is as if we see everything through tinted glasses (Bradshaw, 1999), as all new experiences pass through the filter of this framework. The good news is that neural structures and functioning are not fixed, as previously assumed, but can be flexible and change throughout life. This flexibility is known as neuroplasticity: the ability of the brain to create new neural connections (Siegel, 2010: 84). The fact that neural pathways continue to grow throughout life also suggests that some of these supposedly hardwired internal working models can be changed (Hudson Allez, 2008). For clients and therapists this inspires hope and confidence.

ATTACHMENT THEORY

Attachment theory was developed by Bowlby, aided by Ainsworth's experiments and longitudinal studies (Ainsworth and Bowlby, 1991). The theory is supported by a great deal of research, including significant new evidence from neuroscience. Schore

(2009) proposes attachment theory as a useful overarching model that can integrate the various disciplines involved in the study of human beings.

According to attachment theory, infants form an attachment with a primary caregiver as part of the developmental journey from dependence through to autonomy, separation and independence. A healthy attachment to a primary caregiver provides the necessary conditions for the development of a secure and self-reliant person and will influence psychological health in later life. In order to form a healthy attachment it is important for the infant to 'experience a warm, intimate, and continuous relationship with his mother (or permanent mother substitute) in which both find satisfaction and enjoyment' (Bowlby, 1951: 13). The importance of context and mutual enjoyment is also an aspect of the RIM's intersubjective approach. As evidence for Bowlby's view we only have to look at the heart-warming sight of a parent and baby enjoying each other's company.

Perhaps an analogy may be made here with the therapeutic relationship: when a good and solid therapeutic relationship has been developed, working together can be enjoyable and survive ruptures (Safran and Muran, 2000). Similarly a child getting angry does not destroy the bond between parent and child.

If children's needs are met with enough consistency and the caregiver's attunement is 'good enough' (Winnicott, 1965a: 145) they will learn to regulate their own emotions and develop a secure base (Bowlby, 1988). Ainsworth et al.'s (1978) research showed that good enough attunement ensures a securely attached child, who, if separated from the mother and left in a room with a stranger, will adapt to her absence after some initial distress. If, however, the mother's attunement has been insufficient or inconsistent, the child cannot learn how to regulate his or her own emotions. Such children will either continue crying and remain highly distressed even on the return of the mother, or will not respond to the mother leaving. Bowlby suggested that the effects of attachment patterns continue throughout life.

A great deal of research has corroborated, consolidated and built on the work of Bowlby and Ainsworth (Stern, 1985; 1995). Crittenden expanded attachment theory into the areas of culture, maturation and developmental context. She usefully points out that it is preferable to speak of 'patterns' or 'differences' rather than 'quality' of attachment, as the latter implies an unhelpful evaluative perspective of good versus bad (Crittenden in Crittenden and Claussen, 2000: 2). She also advocates caution in using and interpreting results from observational studies, as people's past experiences have been shown to influence not only what they see, but also how it is interpreted. Disagreements were apparently found, not only between representatives from different cultures and nationalities, but also between people who had been specifically trained to code observed behaviour (2000: 3).

Crittenden addresses the issue of 'why' human beings behave in a certain way and concludes that from a developmental and evolutionary point of view 'danger, including the need to prepare for and respond to danger, is the central organizing principle around which strategies for self protection are organised' (2000: 2). It is therefore meaningful to ask how the 'the threatened child's strategy reduce(s) the danger' (2000: 7) and to realise that 'all patterns are adaptive in the context in which they are learned' (2000: 9).

Crittenden's view is de-pathologising and indicates that it is important for therapists to understand and value people's adaptive responses. This view is shared by the trauma specialist Babette Rothschild (2000), whose work is discussed in chapter 4.

> ### An Example of Apparent Lack of Attunement
>
> During a train journey I noticed a young woman, who had a baby in a pushchair placed behind her; she could not see him without turning around and the baby could not see her. Although the seat next to her was empty, her other child, a little girl aged about three, sat in the seat opposite next to an older woman who I took to be the grandmother. Throughout the journey the little girl tried to attract the attention of the older woman, standing on her seat, touching the woman's hair and asking her questions. I wondered about the grandmother's lack of response. From time to time her mother would say, 'sit down, you are such a naughty girl', before turning back to her book. At the next stop the older woman got off without saying anything to either the mother or the child and I realised that she was not the grandmother at all but a stranger.
>
> In terms of Crittenden's take on attachment theory, the child may have tried to attract the attention of the older woman in order to reduce the danger she may have felt by being unattended to by her mother.

'Good Enough' Attunement

According to Winnicott (1965a: 145) no caregiver or therapist needs to be perfectly attuned at all times, but 'good enough', which includes the importance of 'necessary failures' as it is through 'ruptures and repair' that the child (and the client) learns about relationships and life (Safran and Muran, 2000; Safran et al., 2002). A recent study compared interactions between mothers and their eight-month-old-babies with levels of distress when those children were adults of thirty-four. High rates of maternal affection were found to be significantly correlated with low rates of adult distress, which suggests that 'early nurturing and warmth have long-lasting positive effects on mental health well into adulthood' (Maselko, 2010: 70).

It is not clear whether we are born as individuals who learn to relate or whether there is an initial 'fusion' between mother and baby, with the baby only gradually learning to differentiate between 'this is me' and 'this is not me'. The latter view is suggested by Winnicott's (1964: 88) famous phrase, 'there is no such thing as an infant'. Although many women report the first few months after giving birth as a period of complete absorption, not all mothers share this experience.

CONTEMPORARY THINKING WITHIN COGNITIVE BEHAVIOURAL, HUMANISTIC/EXISTENTIAL AND PSYCHODYNAMIC APPROACHES

Cognitive Behavioural Approaches

Fundamental to cognitive behavioural approaches is the belief that our thoughts affect the way we feel and act. Many problems, such as anxiety or depression, may therefore be overcome by correcting errors in thinking.

CBT, the youngest of the three main therapeutic approaches, developed in three waves. The view of the first wave was that we can only work with observable behaviour (Watson, 1928); its techniques were based on operant and classical conditioning, with a locus of change behaviour. The second wave, instigated by Aaron Beck, constituted a shift in focus from behaviour to cognitions. Beck collaborated with Kelly (1955), according to whom people develop a cognitive map of the world based on personal constructs. These basic cognitive structures, or patterns of cognitions, evolve via the process of associative linking and distinguishing differences between things, for example between two opposite poles (large–small, happy–sad, etc.) This cognitive process of determining distinctions between events or objects helps to categorise people and events.

Beck later preferred to speak of 'schemata' rather than constructs. He differentiated these from more surface cognitions, such as everyday automatic thoughts (Sanders and Wills, 2003). Beck's ideas were taken up and developed further by Young et al. (2006), who see schemas as deep cognitive patterns or 'life traps' based on assumptions and beliefs, which operate at a level below conscious awareness and over time become self-reinforcing.

The attribution of meaning to behaviour and experience is one of the RIM's core concepts and compatible with contemporary approaches to cognitive behavioural theory.

Importance of Relationship

Whereas the first two waves share a focus on behaviour and/or thought modification, the third wave has a different emphasis. Traditionally CBT focused on technique and problem solving. Now, however, greater emphasis is placed on the therapeutic relationship and a collaborative approach (Fennell, 1989; Kuyken et al., 2009; Sanders and Wills, 2005). Cognitive therapy (CT) has evolved considerably since Beck's original work. It has integrated aspects of Gestalt therapy and mindfulness-based approaches, as well as the concepts of transference and counter transference. While these developments do not constitute a wholesale acceptance of the idea of unconscious processes, they do herald an integrative turn within CBT and illustrate the co-evolution and mutual influencing of ideas across theoretical boundaries.

A Contemplative Turn

Third wave cognitive therapy models constitute a 'contemplative turn' within CBT. They include dialectical behaviour therapy (Linehan, 1993), mindfulness-based stress reduction (Kabat-Zinn, 1990), mindfulness-based cognitive therapy (Segal et al., 2002), compassion-based therapy (Gilbert, 2009a) and acceptance and commitment therapy (Hayes et al., 1999). Rather than changing clients 'faulty' thinking, they aim to help clients create distance between themselves and their thoughts. Mindfulness-based and compassionate-based models offer practical methods that help clients explore their relationship to their thoughts (constructions of meanings and beliefs) and gain awareness that these beliefs are 'constructions' rather than 'fact'. Through the practice of mindfulness clients learn to 'dis-identify' with thoughts as static reality and engage with their thinking in new, creative and more flexible ways. What these therapies have in common, and what makes them particularly influential on the RIM, is an emphasis on working with thoughts by 'non-doing' as well as helping clients to develop internal attunement and affect-regulation, so that people will be able to self-soothe and develop self-compassion (Gilbert, 2009a). As mentioned previously, the use of mindfulness is not exclusive to any one model, although it has become particularly important within CBT.

CONTEMPORARY PSYCHODYNAMIC THEORY AND PRACTICE: FROM 'INTRA-PSYCHIC' TO INTER-RELATIONAL

Psychodynamic theory offers a 'depth' psychology that focuses on the relationship between conscious and unconscious processes. Although classical psychodynamic theory has much to offer, there is an important shift away from 'intra-psychic' explanations, towards 'inter' relational (Mitchell, 2000) and 'inter' subjective (Orange et al., 1997) ways of viewing human experience and development. The contemporary relational psychodynamic approaches grew out of the work of Winnicott, attachment theory, self-psychology (Kohut, 1971) and object relations (Fairbairn, 1958) all of which recognised the importance of early experience in the formation of our internal world. However, it is only within the past fifteen years or so, through the influence of social constructionism, systems theory and intersubjective thinking, that it is realised just how much human beings are embedded in, and constituted by, the system within which they find themselves.

This 'relational turn' (Safran, 2003) has important implications for actual practice. Whereas classical psychodynamic therapists prefer to adopt a 'blank screen' – a way of working that favours therapeutic anonymity, neutrality and abstinence (Mitchell, 1997), relational psychodynamic practitioners offer a therapeutic stance much closer to a humanistic way of working. This is also the reason why 'relationship' is positioned right in the centre of the RIM (see figure 4).

The RIM is particularly influenced by intersubjectivity theory, an important movement within the relational psychodynamic field. Partly based on self-psychology (Kohut, 1971) and general systems theory (see part 1 of this chapter), it sees self-experience as dependent on context and rooted in relatedness (Orange et al., 1997; Stern, 2004). This means that context is crucial to human development and influences the creation of 'organising principles', which like the person centred concept of 'conditions of worth' (Rogers, 1959) or the CBT concept of 'core beliefs' or 'schemata' (Young et al., 2006), are often out of awareness, yet influence our everyday mood and behaviour. Intersubjectivity is sometimes referred to as a 'psychoanalytic phenomenology' (Stolorow et al., 1994: 15), which gives an indication of some of its philosophical influences: phenomenology, hermeneutics, structuralism and social constructivism (Natterson and Friedman, 1995: 38).

Aspects of Jungian psychology are also included within the RIM, as they offer an expanded view of what is happening, which can be very helpful, particularly when things appear stuck. According to the Jungian Knox (2003) it is useful to think in terms of unconscious processes, rather than the 'unconscious'. Like Orange et al. (1997) she regards developmental processes as occurring largely outside our conscious awareness and sees the Jungian concept of the 'transcendent function' (Miller, 2004) as constituting a dynamic process of comparison and integration of conscious and unconscious material.

What the contemporary psychodynamic approaches (as well as contemporary humanistic approaches) included within the RIM have in common is an emphasis on how meaning within therapy is essentially co-constructed between client and therapist, thus leading to continuous internal integration (this will be discussed further in the next chapter).

CONTEMPORARY HUMANISTIC APPROACHES

The humanistic part of the RIM includes current versions of person centred (PCT), existential/phenomenological, dialogic gestalt therapy and core process therapy.[11] Humanistic practitioners share a belief in the equality of all human beings (Rogers, 1980) as well as an emphasis on the importance of the therapeutic relationship. Mearns and Cooper (2005) offer a significant contribution by their stress of the importance of working at 'relational depth'. Like the intersubjectivist approach to psychoanalysis, dialogic gestalt practitioners place importance on what is co-created between client and therapist. They talk about the 'between' where all contact and awareness needs to be grounded and feel that a 'genuine dialogical approach requires a radical paradigm shift away from an individualistic model of the self' (Hycner and Jacobs, 1995: 5).

Similarly a contemporary existential-phenomenological approach regards relationship and intersubjectivity as fundamental to what it means to be human as 'everything that we are, or can be, aware of, all that we reflect on, define or distinguish, is relationally derived' (Spinelli, 2007: 180). This means that how we experience ourselves is not rigid, but dependent on relationship, both with ourselves and others. Mearns and Thorne (2007) have developed a contemporary version of PCT that integrates aspects of other relational therapies. They say that a person's current self-concept is developed through the 'actualising process': a dialogue between the value-free 'drive' of the actualising tendency and the imperative of 'social mediation'.[12] Negative early experiences, such as abuse or

---

[11]Core process therapy integrates person centred and dialogic gestalt methods with Buddhist psychology and mindfulness practice. It aims to gently increase awareness of experience in the moment, and invites people to inquire into their relationship with themselves and others with equanimity and openness.

[12]Interestingly there seems to be an echo here of the Freudian concepts of Id, Ego and Superego, although Rogers's original version of the actualising tendency (1951: 488) was concerned with the maintenance, development and enhancement of the person, rather than with the satisfaction of instinctual drives.

empathic failure (Warner, 2000: 150), may result in a rejection of the social mediation imperative and the development of an 'ego-syntonic' process. Although the function of such a difficult process is self-preservation, it means that the person becomes chronically stuck and is unable to respond and adapt to changing circumstances.

One of the advantages of this contemporary approach to PCT is that its relational aspect may help people to develop a more expanded dialogue between different 'configurations of self' (Mearns and Cooper, 2005: 31), which are defined as sets of thoughts, feelings and behaviours, or organising principles within the self. Mearns and Thorne (2007) appear to have incorporated ideas not unlike a psychodynamic conceptualisation of our internal processes, such as object relations (Fairbairn, 1958), 'representations of interactions that have been generalised or RIGS' (Stern, 1985), internal working models (Bowlby, 1969; 1980) and schemas (Young et al., 2006). This, as well as an emphasis on processes rather than structures, makes this version of PCT particularly suitable for inclusion in the RIM.

A RELATIONAL TURN

As described above, personality (and the way we think) develops through early relational experiences that influence the construction of templates through which each one of us learns to 'be' in the world. These templates can be defined as constituting both assumptions and beliefs about the world, as well as rules that then govern our actions. People from Eastern cultures tend to experience themselves as enmeshed with and constituted by others and may find it hard to think of themselves outside their context. As discussed earlier in this section, in the West, our view of ourselves has been based on the 'Cartesian doctrine of the isolated mind' (Stolorow et al., 2002) and influenced by cultural preferences for individualism and autonomy. We are only just beginning to realise how much we are intertwined with each other. In humanistic, psychodynamic and cognitive circles this has led to a 'relational turn', which has had a profound effect on the way in which therapy is practised. Both gestalt and person centred practitioners define their way of working as 'dialogic', which in practice may be similar to the stance now adopted by relational psychodynamic practitioners. Cognitive therapists increasingly emphasise the importance of a collaborative relationship on the effectiveness of therapy, and attend to such factors as transference, motivation and the working alliance. The current phenomenon of reality TV, texting, Facebook and Twitter are perhaps all an attempt to relate, to be part of the human relational matrix, in a world where intimate and lasting relationships within stable communities are increasingly rare.

As discussed in chapter 1, a relational integrative way of working involves both the inter-relationship between client and therapist, and the intra-relationship within all of us; between our different ways of being. We mentioned in the introduction that the RIM was developed through a recursive process of reflection and discussion. The core concepts emerged from this process and from heuristic research undertaken by one of us into her own practice.

Seven Core Concepts: key themes within the RIM Approach

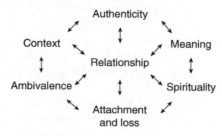

Figure 5   The Relational Heart of the Approach Part of the RIM

The core concepts are trans-theoretical (Mahrer, 1989; McLeod, 2003b), interrelated and interdependent. Although not necessarily all at the same conceptual level, they form a system, which means that change in one of the concepts is assumed to affect all the others. Figure 5 shows the core concepts as a three-dimensional web centred around the concept of relationship. Although many of these concepts are also included in other ways of working, this model explicitly includes all seven as a guide to practice. Context, spirituality and relationship are, for example, included in the multidimensional integrative framework (Lapworth et al., 2001); meaning (making), context and relationship feature strongly in systemic family therapy and narrative therapy (Jones, 1993; Semmler and Williams, 2000); meaning and authenticity are central to the existential/phenomenological approach (van Deurzen and Arnold-Baker, 2005); and the importance of the concepts of relationship, attachment and loss, ambivalence and spirituality are recognised in therapeutic approaches influenced by Buddhism (Sills, 2009; Watson, 2008). The fact that many of the core concepts are also included in other models suggests that they reflect the fundamental issues underlying much human experience, and thus apply to both therapist and client.

Context

As human beings we are always in a context, whether physical, social, economic or emotional, which involves family, friends, colleagues, where we live, where we work, leisure pursuits, etc. Context is connected to one of our presuppositions about the interdependent nature of human existence and may be conceptualised as sets of conditions that occur in ever increasing concentric circles that change depending on where we are and what we are doing. The importance of the emotional, physical and relational context on human development has already been described above. In Western countries, and increasingly so in other parts of the world, continuous social and economic change has become a fact of life.

Practitioners need to pay attention to the external context within which clients are seen, such as, for example, agency, surgery or private practice. The context within which clients live is also important, as this is likely to affect their internal contexts. Within a relational integrative way of working, therapists adopt a reflective stance as well as an attitude of 'empathic-introspective inquiry' (Orange et al., 1997: 89). Each therapeutic approach provides a context that carries its own rules and expectations.[13] A relational integrative practitioner aims to be alive to the multiple layers of context influencing the constantly shifting meanings and occurrences within herself, the client and the inter-subjective field between them. She is free to use her intuition and creativity and, as already foreshadowed by Winnicott (1971), help the client to look inside through play:

> If we can identify the contexts that have led to a particular experiential organisation, we can play with it, question it, and experiment with its reorganisation. (Orange et al., 1997: 90)

The example below (from one of us) illustrates how profoundly human beings are affected by their context:

While travelling in South America I felt very different within myself, almost as if I was not quite me, or not a me I knew well. Although I loved being there, it was strange to walk along streets where nothing felt familiar. No matter how long we stayed some-where, we were always the 'gringos', physically 'sticking out' at least a foot or so above everyone else. As we moved to more Western countries (Buenos Aires, Uruguay) this feeling of 'being strange' lessened. Once back in Europe (Madrid) we could feel from people's responses to us that we were no longer regarded as 'strange'. Perhaps this was due to a shared European identity and sense of belonging: a shared context.

SPIRITUALITY

The core concept of meaning concerns people's struggle to create meaning in their lives. We see spirituality as a search for ultimate meaning (McLeod, 1998: 14), a looking beyond the material and a wish to live ethically. Murdin (2008: 469) suggests that people's interest in spirituality may be a 'search for something beyond everyday experience'; Samuels (2008) defines it as 'beyond the personal'. This take on spirituality is therefore inclusive and not affiliated to any particular movement, ideology or religion. As mentioned in the introduction, the recent interest in mind-fulness suggests a 'contemplative turn' that is influenced by Buddhist thought and practice. For example, Jon Kabat-Zinn's development of mindfulness-based stress reduction (MBSR) has been deeply influenced by his study of Zen Buddhism.

Although some clients do not profess to any interest in spirituality, for others spir-itual beliefs form an intrinsic part of their meaning making or cognitive schema system (Avants and Margolin, 2004) and can be an important, sometimes essential area for exploration. From experience we know that many practitioners regard spir-ituality as an important aspect of our work.

---

[13]Classical psychoanalysis, for example, demanded adherence to rules of abstinence, neutrality and the technique of 'free association'; traditional person centred therapists adopted a non-directive stance, whereas cognitive behavioural therapists had an active teaching role.

At times when I am with a client I realise that I aim towards a more consistently 'transpersonal' way of being (Rowan and Jacobs, 2002), where the client and I are totally open and authentic, and the connection between us feels like something that happens through us and in spite of us, without discernible boundaries. Whenever I am with a client I therefore aim to be with her, in each moment, consciously and unconsciously, with all of me: my body, emotion and mind, so what happens is co-created, and different with every client and in every session.

When we are really 'with' a client, without memory or desire (Bion, [1962] 1984), totally open, allowing ourselves to resonate and respond, there is a sense of 'letting it happen', of 'giving over', but in the context of a holding frame. On the other hand, there also needs to be 'reflection in action' (Schon, 1983) or we would just blurt out anything, therapeutic or not. MacKenna (2008) suggests that Freud referred to himself as 'a completely godless Jew' (Meng and Freud, 1963: 63), but that his concept of 'evenly hovering attention' is an approach to knowledge that seems profoundly mystical. Bion ([1962] 1984) suggested the suspension of desire, memory, sense impressions or understanding in order to gain a sense of an 'ineffable psychic reality' or 'O', which seems reminiscent of prayer (MacKenna, 2008: 479). Both mindfulness and intersubjective approaches to therapy may be seen as going towards the transpersonal and engagement with what Woodcock (2010) calls deep subjectivity, a pre-verbal interior space.

AMBIVALENCE

Change may imply having to let go of what we know, get in touch with painful memories or unpleasant self-knowledge, or taking the risk of jumping into the unknown. This is often the case in depression, which has been described by the poet Gwynneth Lewis (2002) as 'fog over a battlefield'.

I notice red blotches on B's neck and ask, 'How are you feeling right now?' B, 'I feel anxious about coming here, I was not sure whether I wanted to come'. I feel uncomfortable, as if I am a scary schoolteacher to her, I begin to feel a bit hot and wonder whether I am having a hot flush or whether I am resonating with B's anxiety. I take a calming breath and ask, 'What's making you anxious?' B, 'I need to go to the dentist after I leave here. I have not been for ages, so I am scared of what she may find'. I think, Aha, the dentist. It reminds me of Casement who says that clients often talk about the dentist in therapy, but when that happens they may, at the same time, be talking about the therapy. I say, 'I wonder whether coming here feels a bit like going to the dentist?' B, 'Yes, it does a bit. I don't know, perhaps I am afraid of what might come up'.

According to Engle and Arkowitz (2006), reasons for clients' ambivalence regarding change may include misgivings about the process of change itself, or the fear that more may be expected of them. Engle and Arkowitz claim that change is often erratic, irrespective of whether it is about changing 'behaviours, cognitions, views of oneself, or greater awareness or understanding of oneself' (2006: 4). Ambivalence may be expressed by behaving negatively towards the therapist, consistently arriving late, ending the therapy prematurely or, within CBT, not doing homework tasks. It may be an expression of weighing up the pros and cons of change (Miller and Rollnick, 2002), which has been described as the fertile ground of the contemplative stage of change (Prochaska and Diclemente, 1982). Either way some sort of loss is inevitable: the loss of the positives of the current status quo, even though these may be difficult for others to perceive.

This state of ambivalence is often characterised by cognitive dissonance: the contradiction between the way someone may be behaving in the world and their values and goals in life (Festinger et al., 1956). It is also an expression of our difficulty with uncertainty (see also 'meaning' below). The status quo such as it is with all its problems holds more certainty than the uncertainty in the territory of change. One client said, 'Without it I would be in a void. If I cannot predict how things will be and have control over them, then everything is frightening'. It seems that no matter how painful the client's current state, they may prefer it to letting go of the old patterns or schemas, as these give a pseudo security. This is reminiscent of Mandela's assertion that our greatest fear is that we may be more powerful than we can imagine. Sometimes clients leave therapy just as they get in touch with previously unexplored material, which may hold the potential for greater self-awareness. Perhaps the resistance increases in these cases, in order to redress the balance back to the familiar status quo.

ATTACHMENT AND LOSS

My notes of D's session read like a dream, as if the stuff she talks about is really about something else, about some mysterious inner process. This reminds me of Darian Leader's book *Stealing the Mona Lisa* (2002), in which he describes how after the theft in 1911 people flocked to the Louvre to see the empty place. What were they looking for? Did it somehow provide the evidence that it was really lost? What has D lost? I feel lost in my work with her, she feels lost and asks, 'What am I doing with my life? Have I got it right?' What am I picking up unconsciously? Loss of one kind or another is involved in many of the issues clients bring. Often it is not the loss per se that causes pain, but our attachment to what we have lost. The first task of mourning is to 'accept the reality of the loss', which is the first step in the difficult process of letting go (Worden, 2009). Perhaps that is why people flocked to see the empty space where the Mona Lisa had hung; it was difficult to come to terms with its loss until they had seen with their own eyes that it really had gone.

Wahl (2001) states that it is only through letting go of our attachment to past events, past views, past hurts even, that we can receive healing. Indeed it is a fundamental Buddhist concept that all suffering is caused by attachment (Wahl, 2001).[14] Within CBT terms this may be seen as attachment to existing cognitive schemas. Attachment is a dependence on the idea of permanence, the belief that things last which, as the existentialists point out, is ultimately a denial of the fact that our lives are finite and that one day we will die. In order to change we need to let go of that dependence or attachment, which may be difficult or frightening and cause us to feel ambivalent. Thus ambivalence is characterised by a (possibly not conscious) tension between our attachment to that which has a hold on us and our desire for growth.

Wahl argues that in the final analysis the aim of all therapy is the same, 'to help break up archaic patterns of attachment' (Wahl, 2001: 8). The therapist needs the ability to open herself up to clients and help them to let go of attachment and accept what 'is' through developing a stance of bearing witness with equanimity.[15] In other words, as therapists we need to let go of our attachment to wanting clients to change, or wanting to be the one therapist who can help them. This may mean an experiencing of therapy as a 'letting it happen' or 'making the space for it' process, rather than an active striving. In this it is helpful to cultivate a position of 'not knowing' as advocated by Winnicott (Phillips, 1988: 47) and Anderson and Goolishian (1992) and approach each session 'without memory or desire' (Bion, 1970: 70) with an attitude of 'evenly suspended attention' (Freud, [1923] 1955b: 239).

AUTHENTICITY

The concept of authenticity applies not only to clients and therapists, but also to the *relationship* between them. CBT practitioners stress the importance of a good therapeutic relationship and working collaboratively with clients. For humanistic practitioners 'authentic contact' within an 'I-Thou' relationship between client and therapist is 'intrinsically healing' in itself (Buber, [1923] 1958; McLeod, 2003b: 13, 297, 301), a view enshrined in Carl Rogers's 'core conditions' of unconditional positive regard, congruence and empathic understanding (Rogers, 1980: 116) and Mearns and Cooper's concept of relational depth (2005). Its importance is recognised by a 'relational' (Mitchell, 2000) or 'intersubjective' (Stolorow and Atwood, 1992) approach to psychoanalysis. Empathic responding, a cornerstone of all therapies, would seem impossible if it is not coming from an authentic place within the therapist. Ultimately therapy's aim is to help people get in touch with themselves in order to live as authentically as possible, by discarding old habits and conditioned ways of being.

An authentic meeting where both client and therapist are non-defensive and open to each other is more likely to facilitate this than a more formal or distant approach.

---

[14]This view of attachment should not be confused with the word as used in attachment theory by Bowlby (1969), Ainsworth et al. (1978) and others.

[15]This is discussed further in chapter 5 in the section on mindfulness.

Sometimes being true to ourselves or 'finding ourselves' is seen as a narcissistic Western obsession based on an 'individualist' notion of the self, which does not apply to people from a more 'collectivist culture' (McLeod, 2003b: 248). However, in the ancient tradition of Kundalini yoga, which originated in India, people are asked to repeat the words 'sat naam' while practising a particular exercise: 'sat naam' is a Sanskrit phrase which means 'the truth is my identity' (Khalsa, 1996: 24). Also, within Buddhism there is the bodhisattva practice of loving kindness that involves sending/giving/wishing love, compassion, joy and equanimity to others and ourselves, including those with whom we have difficulties or who are enemies (Richo, 2008).

> People are afraid to face the old sadnesses that lurk in their bodies and psyche and that date from failures in their past. They are afraid to face them, but they are plagued by a sense of falseness if they do not, and so they feel stuck. They actually come to therapy not just because they are afraid, but because somewhere within themselves they are searching for a way to go more deeply into that painful place. It is part of our desire for wholeness that we need to connect up with the agonies of the past. (Epstein, 1999: 20–1)

F says, 'I am hoping that eventually I will be able to just be myself, happy and able to engage with people without all this stuff in the way'. F goes on to say that she feels all right on a one-to-one level, but feels self-conscious, as if she is acting, when with a group of people. I have an image in my mind of how that would be and say, 'I have an image of …'. F answers, 'Yes, that is exactly what it is like', and continues talking using the image as her focus.

It seems that F would like to just 'be', in an authentic way, without worrying about what other people may think. People often talk of wearing a mask, in order to be protective of self or to be protective towards others, with the thought that 'if they really knew me as I truly am they would reject me'. This is reminiscent of the concept of a 'false self' that we construct if we find that the real 'me' inside is somehow not acceptable (Winnicott, 1965a), the person centred concept of 'conditions of worth' (Rogers, 1951), the Jungian idea of 'the shadow' (Johnson, 1991; Jung, 1912) or the compensatory behaviours triggered when a cognitive schema is activated (Young et al., 2006). So one task of therapy is to help clients to become more authentic, by letting go of their attachment to a false self or to schema selves (Young et al., 2006).[16]

---

[16]The term 'false self' may sound negative and could be taken as an intention to deceive. It is therefore important to point out that a false self is a response to less than optimal circumstances early on in life and may have developed as a survival strategy. It is not unusual for people who are diagnosed with a personality disorder, for example, to have developed this way of being in order to cope with repeated traumatic experiences, such as physical, sexual or emotional abuse. According to Rothschild (2000) such coping mechanisms or defences should be regarded as resources, rather than as undesirable traits to be got rid of. After all, they helped clients to survive at the time and are often so habitual that they may not even be aware of them. Attachment, in this context, may therefore be out of the client's awareness. We will return to this topic in chapter 4.

However, as this false self or schema has seen them through life up to now, they may feel ambivalent about the therapy. Perhaps the most important task for all of us is to *be* who we are, but before we can do that we first have to learn what that means (Kennedy, 2006). There is no 'it' or 'I' that dwells inside us, rather to 'be who we are' involves a process that has no end – perhaps it is best expressed as a continuous process of becoming (Sills, 2009). Therapy involves therapists and clients naming the reality of what is going on, and bearing it; accepting the truth of what happens, not fighting it, or remaining attached to how we think it should be, or used to be. This does not imply a passive stance, rather it means to 'accept' what is happening and then act appropriately. Once this happens we are liberated from the idea that we are compelled and cannot influence our ways of being but actually have the power of choice.

According to Kennedy (2006) the key to authenticity involves the questions we ask ourselves. He suggests that there is unlikely to be much progress until a client asks herself, 'How have I contributed to my present difficulties?' (Kennedy, 2006: 5). He appears to see authenticity as accepting the truth of what is the case and not to lie, either to others or ourselves.

A prospective client had been talking about feeling unsure whether or not to embark on therapy. I say, 'Perhaps you are afraid that we will get somewhere dangerous and that I will be afraid and out of my depth?' He nodded. I tried to sense within me how I felt. Was I safe enough, unafraid enough, solid enough, to let him go where he was afraid to go? A large part of me wanted to say 'Yes, it is fine, it is safe, I know what that place is like, I have been there. I know that it is ok to go there and be there'. And yet, I just caught an edge of fear, an edge of 'what if this time it is not all right? What if both of us get thrown into the void, the bottomless pit of existential isolation?' And yet, when reflecting on the session afterwards I (and perhaps also the client) had a deep longing to go there. To drop, let be, let go, in the knowledge that it would be all right. Epstein (1999) talks of an inner emptiness that actually, and perhaps paradoxically, has a feeling of connection, a feeling of my personal ego dissolving into the 'all'. Being in touch with that emptiness makes me feel more 'held' in existence, in 'what is', which feels like grace. It reminds me of that 'vast silence in me' that Etty Hillesum wrote about in her diary (Hillesum, 1981: 201).[17]

The above example indicates that authenticity involves the need for therapists to be honest with themselves and accept their positive as well as negative parts. In our attempt to live authentically we are bound to experience anxiety, which van Deurzen and Arnold-Baker (2005: 159) describe as 'as much part of the human existence as the air that we breathe', but which can be faced creatively. In order to help clients to become authentic through a real meeting with their therapist it is therefore necessary that we (the therapists) go through the difficult process of allowing 'the claim of

---

[17]Etty Hillesum was a young Jewish woman, who lived in the Netherlands during the German occupation. She kept a diary from 1941 until her death in Auschwitz in 1943.

truth'[18] upon us, and continue to do so. This is likely to be a never-ending process and we may fall off the wagon again and again. But, as in meditation, the practice is the process, when we fall off we do not have to despair but 'accept' – 'ah that is what has happened' and scramble back up again. Both authenticity and the practice of mindfulness involve a commitment to living consciously in the here and now and a continuous process of beginning, again and again. Being a therapist involves a commitment to a continuous process of becoming – and it never stops.

MEANING

As discussed in part 1, the concept of meaning is central to the way we work,[19] indeed therapy could be described as a meaning making activity. A CBT way of working, for example, may involve helping clients to let go of erroneous conclusions and develop more helpful thinking habits and thus, like humanistic and psychodynamic therapists, help their clients to transform their internal world and meaning making system. Meaning and meaning making can be central to intra-psychic as well as interpersonal processes. In chapter 3 we go on to look at meaning from an interactional perspective. Here we examine meaning as a central aspect of cognitive, existential/phenomenological and psychodynamic approaches. Becker ([1973] 1997), a cultural anthropologist, identifies three levels of meaning, each of which functions as a defence against existential terror: level one, which is rooted in our very early experience; level two, which propels us during the first part of our life; level three, which concerns the soul's purpose.

Level One

We begin to create meaning based on our experience as soon as we are able, probably before we are even born (Piontelli, 1992). Stern's observations of mother–baby interactions showed how mothers help their babies to develop 'an organising perspective about self and others' or system of *meaning*, by 'interpreting all their baby's behaviours in terms of *meanings*' (Stern, 1985: 133–4). Research findings by Bowlby (1969; 1980) and Ainsworth et al. (1978) also indicate how crucial a good mother–infant bond is for the child's healthy development. The internal structures or schemas we develop based on our experiences largely concern how we see ourselves and our relationship to the world and other people. However, we develop these structures when we are too young to know the difference between ourselves and the world, which results in an unconscious belief that 'I am as I am treated' (Hollis, 2005: 47–8). However, the schemas we developed at, say, age four are no longer appropriate at age forty. Within the RIM, we aim to help clients first to become aware of these structures or schemas and then to develop more appropriate ones.

---

[18] The continuous process of unflinching and honest self-reflection and self-exploration.

[19] In chapter 3 we discuss the RIM's 'method', which we see as involving a 'meaning making process'.

Meaning Making as a Defence Against Annihilation

Becker states that our fragility is evident from the moment we are born, naked, help-less and dependent on those who take care of us. Our first line of defence against existential terror is to render it unconscious (Keen, 'Foreword' in Becker, [1973] 1997: xvi). This defence becomes part of our 'character armour', which is expressed in our personality as well as our body (Reich, 1983; Rolf, 1989). In other words, our unconscious conclusion that 'I am as I am treated' may be seen as an adaptation to the world into which we are born.

> Are you familiar with the frightening sensation of melting, the feeling of dissolving into a flowing river, in which the self is annulled by organic liquidation? Everything solid and substantial in you melts away in a wearisome fluidity, and the only thing left is your head … No effort, no hope, no illusion can satisfy you any longer … Since death is immanent in life, almost all of life is an agony. (Cioran, 1992: 16)

Cioran expresses our fragility and fear of annihilation, yet within our Western culture of individualism and self-sufficiency, we tend to deny that fear and the fact that we need connection, mirroring and love in order to survive (Kohut, 1971). When these needs are not sufficiently met in the early stages of our life, we have a range of defence mechanisms at our disposal, including 'identification, displacement, reversal and turning against the self', which possibly develop just after the 'most primitive defences of denial and projection' (Johnson, 1994: 30).[20] Their aim is to help us to continue trusting that our caretakers are good, and deny any signs to the contrary, as they are all that stands between us and existential anxiety (Becker, [1973] 1997).

In addition to hiding our anxiety from ourselves, we also need to hide from others how 'bad' we feel we are, as we fear that they may stop looking after us altogether. We therefore grow up living 'inauthentically'. This is an, often unconscious, attempt at a solution, a way of coping that helped us survive at the time. But the cost can be high. We live our lives terrified that others may discover who we really are, and work hard at trying to do the things we hope will make others like us. As we are not true to ourselves, we are never quite sure whether we are getting it right. Clients often talk of 'feeling a fraud' and of fearing being 'found out'. When things go wrong we may feel that we have been rumbled, are bad and do not deserve the good things in life.

Level Two

Whereas the meaning making at level one is largely unconscious, the meaning crea-tion at the next level is a semi-conscious adaptation to the wider context. Up to the age of forty or so the meaning of our lives tends to be bound up with a career path, success, recognition, getting married and having children, all of which is, however, influenced by the first level of unconscious meaning and may be compensatory for early lack.

---

[20]See also Gilbert (2009a: 309) on 'self attacking'.

> Jim, a man in his late thirties, had compensated for his emotionally deprived childhood by working hard and developing a successful business in retail. However, his company collapsed during an economic down turn and he became depressed. He told his therapist, 'I feel lost, nothing seems to mean anything anymore, I no longer know what life is about'.

Cultures, societies and religions are systems of *meaning*, which help us make sense of the world. It seems that almost any external structures, such as consumerism, sport, work or being thin, that tell us what life is about, can become a religion if it is used as a defence against existential terror. Any threats to that *meaning* are therefore strenuously opposed, which may explain why people in organisations are often so opposed to change.

Level Three

Many clients come to therapy around the age of forty. This may be because, like Jim in the above example, their system of meaning has collapsed. Others may feel that they have achieved many of the things they had set out to achieve (get married, have children, a good career) and yet feel somehow dissatisfied – hence the well-known concept of the 'midlife crisis'.

Level three meaning concerns the question 'what is my life's ultimate purpose?' According to the Jungian Hollis (2005) at some point during the second half of life we may, consciously or subconsciously, wish to work through previously unrecognised issues and problems. By now we may be strong enough to do so and have sufficient evidence of self-defeating, repetitive patterns (Hollis, 2005). 'The first step towards not being unconsciously influenced by something (is) to become conscious of it' (Dass, 2000: 13). The task within therapy therefore is to help people bring their internal meaning or schema systems to conscious awareness, in order to make sense of any problematic experiences (Cooper and McLeod, 2007: 138) and help them begin to formulate new *meanings* and possibilities.

Some of us experience a loss of meaning on getting older (Dass, 2000), particularly if we are forced to retire and there is a loss of the (level two) long-held roles. Here the task is to accept what is, let go of our attachment to what we have lost and allow the soul to be born into its own full awareness (Dass, 2000: 57). In previous centuries religion provided level three meaning, but in our increasingly secular society, there are also other sources of meaning. Vaidhyanathan (2007), for example, wrote about how when he was a student the lectures by the existentialist philosopher Solomon literally saved his life:

> By the end of the semester I had pledged to savour every breath and sunrise as the only rational reaction to the soulless absurdity of the universe, as Albert Camus (through Solomon) had advised. I had accepted responsibility for my free will, as Jean-Paul Sartre (through Solomon) commanded. Solomon was clear that a passionless life was not worth living. (Vaidhyanathan, 2007: 31)

To be fully human we need to be in contact with our own soul (Hollis, 1998) as without soul we are lost and our lives become meaningless. Following his experiences in a Nazi concentration camp, Frankl (1987: 110), who later developed logotherapy, asserts, 'one should not search for an abstract meaning of life'. He writes:

> Ultimately man should not ask what the meaning of his life is, but rather he must recognise that it is *he* who is asked. In a word, each man is questioned by life; and he can only answer to life by *answering for* his own life; to life he can only respond by being responsible. (1987: 111)

In other words, there is no pre-set meaning of life; it is up to us how we live our life and what meaning we give it. Within the context of the RIM we aim to help clients take responsibility for their lives by being honest with themselves (authenticity), being prepared to let go of previously held beliefs and schemas (attachment and loss), acknowledging their ambivalence and engaging in self-exploration through relationship.

No matter what the circumstances of our lives are, we are always free to choose how to respond to them. From a CBT point of view it is not so much events themselves that upset us, but the meaning we give those events. Within the RIM we strive to help people realise that different meanings are possible and that the meaning we choose is ultimately our own responsibility.

RELATIONSHIP

L, the middle child of a large family, was mainly looked after by his older brothers and sisters, as his parents were always occupied with the latest baby. Although rationally he understands that his parents probably felt overwhelmed by the demands of so many children, he remains adamant that there is something fundamentally wrong with him, or his parents would have cared for him more. As an adult he has few friends and relationships never last long. For the first few months of the therapy I concentrate on developing the relationship between us, which takes longer than I am used to. Despite my efforts to be friendly and relaxed the atmosphere in the room tends to feel rather formal.

This concept involves relationship with ourselves and others, as well as the therapeutic relationship. At the first level of meaning making (see above) we tend to draw the conclusion 'I am as I am treated', which indicates that how we see the world and ourselves is rooted in our relationships from the very beginning. Therefore it is hardly surprising that the issues people bring to therapy often concern relationships, if not with others then with the environment or with different parts of themselves. The crisis may be one that is co-constructed between people. However, it may be experienced first when the context of an intimate relationship triggers, or resonates with, early childhood relational patterns or schemas. The therapeutic relationship provides a microcosm within which intra- as well as inter-personal issues can be addressed. Sands (2000) describes how important it is for her as a client to work with a therapist who is prepared to have a real (rather than a transference) relationship and authentic dialogue with her. Within the RIM we therefore aim to be authentically present while paying attention to, and working with, what clients and therapists co-create in the intersubjective field between them. This is reminiscent of Mearns and Cooper's concept of 'relational depth', which they define as:

> A state of profound contact and engagement between two people, in which each person is fully real with the Other, and able to understand and value the Other's experiences at a high level. (2005: xii)

Working in an intersubjective/relational and collaborative way means that as therapists we can be profoundly affected by our work. This is not always easy, as strange things can happen in that co-created space, particularly around the edges. A contemplative position can help us in that moment-by-moment awareness that is needed in this way of working. One therapist said:

> When I am working at relational depth I feel that I can rest in that space, as there is nowhere else I need to be and nothing else I need to do. All that is needed is to be fully present, here and now.

DIFFERENT LENSES

The three approaches that form part of the RIM may be seen as different lenses through which we look at the world. Each focuses on a different aspect of human experience; what we focus on determines what we see. Where the focus or the emphasis of the work lies depends on what speaks to the client and what appears appropriate. However, change in one aspect of human experience may affect others too; in terms of systems theory, change in one part of the system is likely to affect all others. Perhaps there can also be a sense of a particular approach not being appropriate, or not enough. For example, to a client who is not psychologically minded an emphasis on unconscious processes may seem meaningless and frustrating. Equally clients who want to get in touch with aspects of themselves that they are not consciously aware of, may find an emphasis on thinking and conscious experience irksome and missing the point. Each therapeutic approach looks at human experience through a different lens and offers a partial explanation. Taken together, however, the blend of approaches within the RIM constitutes a dynamic system that offers a way of working that is sensitive to the needs of the client.

Integrative therapy can help promote change at different levels: internally, externally or a combination. Where the focus is placed depends on what is appropriate and desired by the client. It is also important to remain mindful of the phenomenon of resistance and, as discussed above, ambivalence: of wanting to change and fearing it at the same time. Whereas changes made in clients' external circumstances and relationships can be very positive, such change may be more long-lasting if a corresponding change happens internally – at a conscious and unconscious level. Sometimes this can take time; on the other hand rapid change in therapy is not necessarily a superficial flight into health. It can be both sudden and profound (Watzlawick et al., 1967). The Palo Alto group of brief therapists, for example, take an interactional approach that focuses on patterns of communication between people and the definition of relationship between therapist and client. They were interested in how change takes place and what happens in therapeutic conversations, rather than in theories of growth, understanding or insight (see chapter 3).

Although understanding and insight alone are not always enough, they can help people to accept themselves: 'so that is why I am as I am, that is why I react like that, no wonder given my experience, how could it be otherwise?' Also, being seen and accepted by another can be very healing, which is why a good therapeutic relationship is so crucial. Telling the therapist things that they may never have talked about before and still feeling accepted, without conditions or judgement, is helpful in bringing about a client's self-acceptance. 'I have told her everything and she still thinks that I am ok, could it be that I really am ok?'

At the end of a successful therapy therefore, clients may feel that something has changed without being able to say exactly what or how. So the person is still the same, but his internal world and/or his relational world has changed. In terms of object relations theory this means that the relationships between the client's internal objects have been changed; in terms of attachment theory, that unhelpful forms of attachment have been let go of in favour of more helpful ways of relating; from a Winnicottian (1965b) point of view some layers of a false self have been peeled away so that the person can be more authentic; from a person centred point of view, some of the client's conditions of worth have been jettisoned and he has learnt that he is acceptable without those conditions, and from a contemporary-based cognitive approach (such as schema, mindfulness or compassion-based therapy), the person has learnt to dis-identify with his thoughts and be more compassionate towards himself.

However, it should not be forgotten that human beings are complicated and complete self-realisation or actualisation may take a lifetime, if it is achieved at all. From a humanistic perspective we are always in a process of becoming, there is no point at which we say – 'right, now I am fully realised, there is absolutely nothing else in this life or beyond it that I do not understand'. Equally it is sometimes in the coordination of action between client and therapist and as a result of taking an interactional view of difficulties that problems may 'dissolve'.

SUMMARY

The store of theoretical ideas that we have selected to synthesise in this chapter provides the rationale as well as the definition of our use of the term 'relational' to describe our model. It was not our intention to provide a detailed account of those theories, however, further information may be found in the suggestions for further reading below.

To summarise:

1. 'Relational' implies that human beings are embedded within social networks. The problems and difficulties that people bring to therapy are products of relational experience explicitly and implicitly, internal and external. The core concepts link to the model's relational heart, which means that they cannot be defined without referring to the relational: attachment, context, meaning, etc. – all are products of relational processes rather than individual processes alone. If relatedness forms the backdrop of human experience including human suffering, then it follows that relational solutions may be needed.
2. The therapeutic relationship itself can offer a fertile ground within which change and healing can occur. The invitation to clients is to entertain relational explanations and solutions for their difficulties – together these can then open up choice, freedom, possibility and a way out of the constraints of individualist, potentially pathologising explanations.

Having discussed the RIM's approach, we turn to its method in the next chapter.

QUESTIONS FOR FURTHER REFLECTION AND DISCUSSION

- What was your experience of childhood? Can you identify your own attachment style? How does this relate to your parents' childhood? What impact do you think your attachment style has on your current relationships?
- Can you identify some templates (schemas, organising principles, internal working models, etc.) for yourself?
- Do you feel more or less attracted to any of the three approaches we have discussed. Do you know why that is?
- Thinking over your work with clients, can you identify any of the seven core concepts in your work with them?

FURTHER READING

Bateson, G. (1980) *Mind and Nature – a Necessary Unity*. Glasgow: Fontana/Collins.
Capra. F. (1996) *The Tao of Physics*. New York: Fontana.
De Young, P. A. (2003) *Relational Psychotherapy, a Primer*. London: Brunner-Routledge.
Hayley, J. (1963) *Strategies of Psychotherapy*. New York: Grune and Stratton.
Hedges, F. (2005) *An Introduction to Systemic Therapy with Individuals: A Social Constructionist Approach*. London: Palgrave Macmillan.
Jones, E. (1993) *Family Systems Therapy: Developments in the Milan-systemic Therapies*. London: John Wiley.
Kabat-Zinn, J. (1990) *Full Catastrophe Living*. New York: Delta.
Mearns D. and Thorne, B. (2007) 'Recent developments in person-centred Theory', in *Person-centred Counselling in Action* (3rd edn). London: Sage. pp. 19–41.
Orange, D. (1995) *Emotional Understanding: Studies in Psychoanalytic Epistemology*. New York and London: The Guilford Press.
Watson, G. (2008) *Beyond Happiness: Deepening the Dialogue between Buddhism, Psychotherapy and the Mind Sciences*. London: Karnac.

3

Method

In this chapter we discuss how explorative conversation of past, present and potential futures provides a structure for the unpacking of relationships between experience and meaning making, in order to generate therapeutic possibilities, insight and the potential for change. We draw on communication theory and Coordinated Management of Meaning (CMM) (Cronen and Pearce, 1985), systemic notions of recursivity and feedback (Boscolo and Bertrando, 1992) and temporal frameworks for practice (Menninger's Triangle of Insight, 1958: 148 and Lapworth et al.'s Framework of the Self, 2001) to form a framework or method for practice which we call TIME: the Temporal Framework of Insight, Meaning making and Experience. TIME acts as a framework for conceptualising the therapeutic process. We describe how language is central to meaning making processes and the vehicle for the reinterpretation and construction of new meanings. We define the nature of the reciprocal relationship between experience, the interpretation of the experience and the emergent action or behaviour.

A TEMPORAL FRAMEWORK FOR INSIGHT, MEANING MAKING AND EXPERIENCE

Outside client factors the therapeutic relationship is generally regarded as the largest contributing factor to therapeutic outcome, and considered by many to be more significant than orientation or technique (Cooper, 2009). Yet many therapists privilege technique over relational factors in their estimation of what effects change in the therapeutic endeavour (Timulak, 2008). However, we wonder whether therapists choose a theoretical orientation with its concurrent techniques that best fits their values, beliefs and ideas about change. Working from a paradigm or philosophical orientation that intuitively feels right will probably best enable them to act in the most congruent manner. This is likely to benefit and enhance the construction of a beneficial therapeutic relationship.

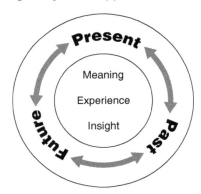

Figure 6 TIME: A Framework for Practice

> What defines us as systemic is our interest in context and the way that meaning is socially constructed, contextually defined and is therefore capable of being changed. (Jones and Asen (2000) quoted in Hedges, 2005: 47)

The above quote points to the interplay between experience and meaning making. In the TIME method we pay attention to the interplay between experience, meaning and insight. Experience, meaning and insight are domains that are related and act upon each other in reciprocal pathways. Experience and how we interpret it influences how we make sense of the world and how we derive meaning for our existence. Insight and learning may be seen as products of the ways in which we make sense of and interpret experience. They also entail our gaining awareness of hitherto unknown or hidden aspects of ourselves. Insight and understanding influence how we construct meaning and our current and future experiencing. These three serve as cornerstones of the therapeutic process and guide our action as we continue to elaborate and evolve meanings together with our clients, create experiences and new patterns in and outside of the therapy room, and co-generate new insights.

These three dimensions of experience, meaning and insight reoccur and can be seen as mutually evolving: past experience and beliefs will influence how we make sense of current and future experience. These experiences, beliefs (meanings) and insights (learning) affect how we will act now and will influence what we experience and how we make sense of these experiences in the future. Likewise present beliefs, experiences and insights offer us new interpretations of the past. These three dimensions impact on action and patterns of behaviour. We suggest that these dimensions are key to the therapeutic process and may be seen as the clay with which we work.[1]

> Do not think that an action or a word is its own sufficient definition. I believe that an action or the label put on an experience must always be seen ... in context. (Bateson (1972) quoted in Hedges (2005: 47)

---

[1]Interestingly, potters use a metaphor in which the right hand is said to be the corrective hand (the hand that steadies the pot), metaphorically the hand of reason, and the left hand is said to be the intuitive, creative and non-rational hand (the hand that shapes and moulds the pot).

TIME is based on the assumptions discussed above. It provides a structure that maps approach and interventions onto a temporal framework that provides a coherent and integrated method of working.

LANDSCAPE

Therapy is like a landscape in which clients and therapists journey together. Lakoff and Johnson (1980) suggest that we live our lives by metaphors that are embedded in our language. The metaphor of the journey is often used in spiritual, educational or personal development quests as well as in the therapeutic domain. Psychotherapy, the arts, literature and mythologies abound with the conceptual metaphor of life as journey and include the symbolism of paths, pathways, searches, quests, horizons or thresholds. We cover ground, we lose our way, we find the path, we have a vision, a horizon in sight. Clients may say I have lost my way, I need to find a new path, I am going around in circles, I don't know where I am going, I feel lost.

The landscape through which we journey includes the dimensions of time and relationship. In therapy we can choose at any time to look at the territory behind for reference points to determine where we are and how we have come to be here. Looking at the territory behind us provides us with a picture of what we have already done, explored, accomplished, the challenges we have survived and also reveals where we have taken a turn off a path that may have led to difficulties, obstacles and dead ends.[2] The landscape we have come through also tells us how our constructs and frameworks for living have evolved and grown.

From where we (client and therapist) stand we can observe the ground underfoot, the relational domain, the context that shapes our current experience; the landscape of the 'here and now'. Looking ahead we see the choices available to us, the uncharted territory, and the ground that has not been covered and that we cannot therefore fully know, but perhaps can imagine. This future landscape is one of imagination; it contains horizons, a vision of goals as well as hope and expectation within the risk of the unknown.

The therapist often acts as a guide to help the client look at the opportunities or possibilities ahead. Bill O'Hanlon (1999) calls this 'Possibility land'. With a therapist as travel guide or co–explorer, the client's vision may turn to parts of the horizon hitherto not seen. The bedrock of this landscape is the relational field. This is not unlike a tourist, who uses her guidebooks and maps to help her to make her own discoveries and to experience the place in a uniquely subjective way.

Certain parts of the landscape may feel more comfortable than others. Depending on orientation the therapist may be particularly interested in the territory of the past, in order to find explanations and insight into the client's current experience. Clients may also like to focus on their past experience. On other occasions both therapist and client may wish to look more towards the future. Hope and expectation are often characteristics of this future focus. Clients want something different for themselves and may expect therapists to guide them towards a particular future. Therapists

---

[2]This is why regular evaluation may be helpful, see chapter 5.

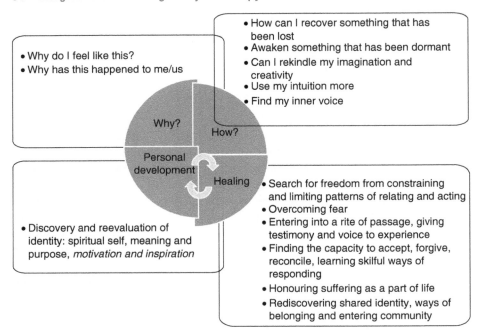

Why do I feel like this?
Why has this happened to me/us

How can I recover something that has been lost
Awaken something that has been dormant
Can I rekindle my imagination and creativity
Use my intuition more
Find my inner voice

Why?

How?

Personal development

Healing

Discovery and reevaluation of identity: spiritual self, meaning and purpose, *motivation and inspiration*

Search for freedom from constraining and limiting patterns of relating and acting
Overcoming fear
Entering into a rite of passage, giving testimony and voice to experience
Finding the capacity to accept, forgive, reconcile, learning skilful ways of responding
Honouring suffering as a part of life
Rediscovering shared identity, ways of belonging and entering community

Figure 7 The Therapeutic Journey

may also drive towards particular outcomes and future goals. We shall discuss in more detail how this may influence and shape expectation and influence how we then meet the client. Therapists, when asking the client about the future, may operate from their own preferred time frame asking for example, 'If you were to think six months ahead ...' (Burnham, 2005).

Anne says, 'I don't trust anyone anymore'. I think: what has happened to change her trust in people? Was there a time (in the past) when she was more trusting? She is not sure whether she can trust me (present), she is not sure whether she will be able to trust others again or even if she wants to be able to (future).

I ask, 'When did you last feel that you were able to trust anyone?' She looks down; her face is sombre (I feel she may say that it has been a long time ago), 'It's as if I have disappeared, I'm not myself anymore, I don't feel myself'.

Time is an integral part of the therapeutic landscape. 'There is no form of psycho-therapy that does not find itself working in time and on time' (Boscolo and Bertrando, 1992). Time is not fixed and absolute but a construction. Think for a moment of an experience you have had of time 'flying' when you are having fun and 'dragging' when you are bored. Boscolo and Bertrando (1992) offer an elegant exploration of the nature and use of time in the therapeutic context. They suggest that therapist and client renegotiate, re-vision and co-create the past and future in therapy. They quote St Augustine:

> From what I have said it is abundantly clear that neither the future and the past exist ... It might be correct to say that there are three times, a present of past things, a present of present things and a present of future things ... the present of past things is the memory; the present of present things is direct perception and the present of future things is expectation. (*Confessionum, Libri XIII*)

Boscolo and Bertrando propose that the past defines current meanings, but is itself defined by the present, so that past and present act upon each other. The expectation of possibilities in the future will also impose an influence on the present. They suggest that all problems however, can only be situated in the present: past problems are a memory, future problems a possibility. As we will discuss in chapter 4, the practice of mindfulness may help clients to be more in the present and to see past and future in perspective.

> Clients undergoing therapy almost always have a linear conception of time, a historical conception according to which the past determines the present and imposes insuperable constraints on the future. (Boscolo and Bertrando, 1992: 2)

Using Boscolo and Bertrando's framework, present meaning and behaviour form the first avenue for exploration in therapy; the 'here and now', following which it may be beneficial to explore the present that may already have begun to change, because it is being explored from a different vantage point. It is helpful to start with an exploration of meaning and behaviour in the present (Stern, 2004), and then enquire into what has already changed since the client decided to come to therapy. Sometimes clients' decision to address a problem by seeking therapy can in itself begin to create a change.

STORIES

The relational and systemic assumptions in the RIM make us interested in patterns and in examining patterns of action, meaning and relationship over time. Stories that we tell about our lives are a way of organising events and experiences in a coherent sequential narrative, and tend to powerfully influence our sense of self and our identities. Stories and narratives are not fixed, but sit in relationship between the narrator and the audience, even if that audience is oneself. They bring forth different figure/ ground configurations as different details or aspects are recalled or emphasised. The discourse within which the story sits shapes its meaning and the organisation of relationships. An interactional perspective implies circularity; the recursive nature of past and present means that present creates the past and past creates the present.

This is important as it frees the therapist and client from a deterministic notion of the past creating the present.[3] However, if we ignore the past we are in danger of

---

[3]The Western mind tends to be linear, which is not necessarily the case for other cultures. Linear thinking – the idea of cause and effect – is often associated with a modernist perspective A non-linear way of working is postmodern!

de-contextualising the present. In interactions between couples, families or parents and children it is often the case that one person will say that the other's behaviour 'causes' their response.

From a relational and interactional view of human behaviour (Ruesch and Bateson, 1951) we see people's behaviour and the meanings derived from it as interdependent. In other words meaning is co-created from moment to moment through the continuing process of mutual response to feedback between parties. This mutual reciprocal responding is defined by circular rather than linear explanations. Circularity defines behaviour and meaning as located within a system and as a co-construction of that system. Language, however, tends to uphold linear assumptions: 'I did this because he did that' tends to close down dialogue and stops us looking for other options.

Within a circular view we look for patterns and multiple perspectives in interaction and communication (Watzlawick et al., 1967). When freed from this linear causal connection we can consider each session as a story in and of itself rather than a progression. Often this is the beginning of our therapeutic journey; to explore the meanings and actions of the present, and widen this exploration to include relationships in the present and significant systems in the person's life. Following this we may explore the past to learn how the patterns influencing the current problems may have evolved. But not only this; in exploring the past we also begin to co-construct possible new stories of the past.

The Therapy Journey

Like the hero who, returning home after a journey, is not the same person who left; he needs to integrate his experiences into a new sense of self, which will change his relationships with those he had left behind (Campbell, 1949).

Exploration of the Present

Jane, a woman in her mid 40s, talks about her difficulty in forming a significant intimate relationship with a man. Although she has had various infatuations and crushes on men, she has never truly entered into an intimate relationship. She has had two serious depressions; panic attacks and anxiety keep her in a state of fear and prevent her from entering into the complex and terrifying world of intimate relationships. Her fear of rejection and annihilation makes her extremely guarded near men and gives a message that reads 'stay away'.

Exploration of Her Past

This reveals a strict family background. Mother and father were not affectionate, had high expectations of their children, frowned upon displays of emotion and disapproved of crying. Jane describes her mother as fragile, her father puts her down when she shows emotion; he is verbally aggressive although not abusive to mother, and insists that all emotion must be contained. Jane is a sensitive child and was admonished when she showed fear or cried.

Exploration of what she knows of the histories of mother's and father's childhoods: paternal grandfather was violent towards his children. Jane's father had not been allowed to cry or he would be humiliated and punished. Jane's mother's father committed suicide – no one really spoke to her about it and her own mother never talked about her father again.

Re-storying of the Past (Restored, Re-visioned)

The new perspective: that Jane's parents' relational responses to her and her siblings may be a result of their own traumatic upbringing, reframes Jane's interpretation of her parents' behaviours towards her as more than a reflection of their feelings about her alone. It provides a benign perspective, affording room for a more compassionate view, while not denying Jane's hurt, nor the notion that she deserved to have had a kinder, more loving upbringing. Jane's belief that it is her fault, that she is in some way responsible for her parents' cold response to her, has shifted to one in which she can entertain the idea that their inability to express or tolerate emotion is due to their own experiences.

MEANING AND COMMUNICATION

Words do not have any inherent meaning, they only make sense when we know the context in which they are used. (Wittgenstein, 1953, quoted in Hedges, 2005: 47)

Deconstructing Meaning

In chapter 2 we discussed meaning at the level of approach. Here we talk about meaning making as part of the therapeutic method.

Meaning is fundamental to the human condition. As Frankl ([1946] 2004) has so potently argued, people cannot survive without meaning. This is true at a macro and micro level. At a macro level we need to have a sense of how we fit in to the ecosystems of which we are a part. Meaning is essentially a product of relationship: relationship with others, with the environment and with the ecosystems within which we reside. Meaning is therefore not limited to the mind but is also enshrined in the body; hence the usefulness of body psychotherapy and mindfulness practices. The discussion on relational depth (chapter 2) included the importance for therapists to 'be with' clients with mind, body and emotion. Indeed, it is often through our bodies that we may get a sense of what is going on for a client – consciously and unconsciously. Meaning is not limited to our mind, but is embodied in our bio-psycho-social adaptation to our changing environment (Vygotsky, 1978). It is multifaceted, multidimensional and constitutes a language, not as something that we merely use to label objects and experience, but as something that we live. Our emotional, gestural, embodied and sensory experience lives and is enacted within language. Therefore language is not limited to words, syntax and grammar but is the totality of our psycho-linguistic and cognitive interactions (Faris, 2010).

Communication, Messages and Frames

In an evolving theory about communication coming from a ten-year study of paradox in communication, Bateson and his colleagues at Palo Alto became interested in the relationship between a message and the message that frames it (Watzlawick et al., 1968). In other words, people signal how a message is to be received and understood because of the message that precedes it which offers a particular frame.

Messages are qualified by other messages, which are called meta-communicative messages. If I frown and scowl at you while saying 'welcome I am glad to see you', the frown qualifies the words that I speak and the message you pick up is that I am not pleased to see you at all. These meta-communicative messages are often implicit and analogue (non-verbal), but they are crucial in that they signal the meaning of subsequent messages. How we label or frame a situation will determine how a message will be understood. An example of this is that of film or theatre.

Relevance to Therapy

Imagine a person who displays a set of symptoms such as lethargy, listlessness and crying. These are interpreted by us and defined according to our perception of them, so we may describe and attribute meaning to them, which then generate a label such as 'depression', 'laziness' or something else. These descriptions convey meaning and are often reified as if they were real states rather than constructs (Hayley, 1981; Hedges, 2005). The effect such labelling has is that it can diminish or close down the possibility of generating other descriptions and alternative meanings. An allied concept is that of punctuation. This is a concept used in systemic therapy to describe how sequences of events can be 'punctuated' ('organised, selected, privileged and highlighted' (Jones, 1993: 7)) in specific ways that generate particular meanings. Consider these two statements:

> A group of students was asked by their English professor to put the correct punctuation into the following sentence:

> 'Woman without her man is nothing'.

> The men wrote: 'Woman, without her man, is nothing'.

> The women wrote: 'Woman! Without her, man is nothing'.

> Similarly, 'Eats, shoots and leaves' means something different from 'Eats shoots and leaves'.

These are literal examples of the way in which our choice of punctuation alters meaning. We can extend the metaphor of punctuation to include the way a modernist worldview splits self from other and subject from object.[4] Within a relational paradigm there

---

[4]See chapter 2.

is no split between subject and object. Rather there is continuity between the interior world of the person and the exterior surrounding world (Sampson, 2009); both are contained within and connected to the ecosphere.

> Psychotherapy may be thought of as a process of semiosis – the forging of meaning in the context of collaborative discourse. It is a process during which the meaning of experience is transformed via a fusion of the horizons of the participants … alternative ways of punctuating experience are developed and a new stance toward experience evolves. (Gergen and Kaye, 1992: 182)

This statement and the focus on meaning implies a focus on language as the vehicle for meaning making, so that therapy can be said to provide a forum for the re-evaluation of meaning, and can help us (client and counsellor) to explore experience from many differing perspectives taking into consideration the context and relational field in which behaviour is situated.

Communicators, including therapists and clients, may find themselves using different understandings of the context or may emphasise a particular frame of reference. One person may be operating from the frame of reference: 'we are friends' and within that frame make a joke about their friend's ethnicity. The friend, however, may by default be operating from a stronger frame of reference in their lives, which is culturally determined to privilege the family life script, which implies that a criticism of your ethnicity is a criticism of your family. Therefore they do not understand their friend's humour as a gesture of friendly intimacy within the framework of a solid friendship relationship, but redefine their boundary by withdrawing into a position that can best be described as 'you cannot trust outsiders but only your family'.

This kind of frame slippage similarly occurs in therapy. The client says that they feel misunderstood by their family. The therapist responds by asking the client to tell her more about their family, working from a framework of 'I need to understand this person's context'. However, the client hears the question as a criticism, and interprets it as: 'She is more interested in my family's perspective than in mine'. This is not, however, overtly discussed, yet manifests through defensiveness and closed suspicious behaviour on the part of the client.[5] The framing of messages may also differ between cultures. Within some cultures, for example, it is impolite to have eye contact with people in authority. This lack of eye contact might easily be misunderstood. When working with all clients, including those from different cultures, it is therefore important for therapists to explore such differences in the framing of messages to avoid general confusion and the possibility of the client feeling judged or misunderstood.

Coordinated Management of Meaning (CMM)

CMM is a practical model for making sense of complex communication patterns (Cronen and Pearce, 1985). Cronen and Pearce offer a framework for examining the influence of context (societal/cultural/political/historical) on the co-creation of

---

[5]We discuss the therapeutic frame later in this chapter.

meaning. They describe problems as emerging out of a system: they call this a problem-determined system. If the problem emerged in conversations (descriptions and explanations) between members of the system that had coalesced around it, it could be dissolved through the creation of new meanings via conversation (language). This involves a change from the perspective of the therapist as a person who intervenes (possibly covertly) and is an observer, to one in which the therapist becomes a part of the therapeutic system (intersubjective perspective) and facilitates a conversation in which they hope new meanings and alternative narratives will evolve which will bring about change.

CMM is a way of understanding and thinking about communication in terms of general rules (Cronen and Pearce, 1985). The model also suggests that communication is a type of action, i.e. a 'doing' or performing. We do not just communicate 'about' but, as with social constructionism, the communication in itself serves to create our social worlds. We attempt to make meaning of our lives through communication and we need to develop coherent narratives in order to do so. So we need to manage the multitude of meanings that we have and coordinate these meanings with others. Our stories need to merge with the stories of others, we need to be able to identify with the stories of others and our mutual stories need to mesh together in some coherent way. The creation of interwoven stories that create meaning through and via language happens at a number of levels from macro to micro: at the level of culture, relationship, episode and speech act. As therapists we can avoid misunderstandings and improve our coordination with the client by 'talking about talking' (Burnham, 2005), for example: 'I notice that when I asked you to tell me more about your family you seemed to be uncomfortable with this and I wondered what you thought about my asking you this question'.

People come together and coordinate activities and meanings with each other. As we coordinate routines, standards and norms develop; beliefs and values emerge, thus creating a way of being together. Therapy offers a new forum for these processes to occur. With reference to the previous discussion about monitoring and modifying, meaning making processes are like a coordinated dance between therapist and client. CMM may be used within the TIME method. It gives useful directions regarding the use of questions, reflections and reframing, in order to explore, construct and deconstruct meaning as a coordinated activity between client and therapist. CMM is useful to ascertain how different levels of context influence the meanings that are ascribed to events and experiences. So to deconstruct a given event, we are interested in looking at the speech acts (mother says, 'You disappoint me'), the episode itself (argument with mother), relationship (closeness and distance between mother, attachment to mother, this relationship in the context of the family), cultural influences (roles of mother, how children should behave, gender roles, etc), which will all exert an influence on the meanings that have evolved.

EXPERIENCE

Different theories employ a variety of ways to talk about the sense of self. A relational point of view suggests that the subject or sense of self is a product of intersubjective experience. As discussed previously, self is a construct that arises out of collective action and experience. In other words, the subject interacts with the other and out of that interaction the self continues to emerge and evolve. From Buddhist and post-modern perspectives there is no such thing as a self. It may therefore be more useful to talk of self-processes, self-states and aspects of self or even a 'multitude of selves'. Stern (1985) sees our sense of self as partly made up of representations of interactions that have been generalised (RIGS) of relational experience. Object relationists, on the other hand, see the self as containing internal objects or part objects, which are aspects of other people (usually caregivers, e.g. the authoritarian father, the critical mother) that are internalised. Paul Gilbert (2009b) recognises that how we see our-selves reflected in the minds of the other influences our experience of ourselves. These become internalised and make up part of our belief and value system and contribute to creating our unique subjective frames of reference and our experience. While not exactly alike, all these terms refer to self as partly constructed by aspects of relationship and experience that become internalised. The construction of mean-ing evokes certain experiences that either reinforce and reaffirm those constructions or bring them into question. This frame becomes the lens through which the world is seen and influences the meaning given to future possible experience. Much of this internalised experience is laid down at a young age, yet has a powerful influence on how meaning is created out of experience throughout life.

In therapy we unpack (deconstruct) experience, including the experience in the room, and at the same time we generate new experience. How therapists respond to clients then also becomes part of the internal landscape of the client's self. In other words, the client comes to experience and see herself reflected in the 'mind' of the therapist. The experience of self is always located in time. The only time in which we exist is now. We do not exist in the past and we do not exist in the future. As discussed above, the past is the present experience of recalling what has been. The future is the present experience of our imagining what is to become. How we expe-rience the present (in mind and body) will be dependent upon what arises within our field of awareness.

DEFINING THE PROBLEM

The client brings into the therapy room their understanding and expectation of the therapeutic process. The client's understanding of how they are supposed to behave is framed by what they are aware of in the here and now. For example: a client whose present configuration of awareness is dominated by their memories of the past as the reason for their current distress may believe that they are required by the therapist to retell the story of what has happened to them. Significant others in this person's life may also share this belief and in their present interactions with the client focus on interactions that emphasise the narration of the past.

Client's message: I am coming here for you to cure me – you need to fix the problem (meaning: my definition of self is one in which I am the victim of circum-stances and have no power to determine and make things change, I also take no responsibility for this – others must take responsibility for me).

Different therapists will respond differently to this client. One therapist may accept the client's way of being by encouraging him to tell the story of the past but in listening to the story seek to elicit recollections of the client's resilience, triumphs and successes as well as acknowledgement of what he has suffered.

Another therapist may focus on what the client is doing 'here and now' in the therapy room. All the therapist's behaviours and responses are focused on facilitating self-awareness (insight) in the client. The gestalt therapist for example will frustrate all attempts by the client to get the therapist to take responsibility for 'making things better'. Eventually the client runs out of strategies. This leads to an impasse: existentialist therapists refer to this as an 'existential vacuum' or 'existential crisis'. The client is now thrown back on his own resources and it is out of this existential spaciousness that an opportunity for the client's own resourceful insight may emerge. It is awareness in the here and now itself that holds the potential for healing. The more the client attempts to escape into the past or into the future the more the therapist brings them back to their awareness of what they are doing now. It is important to emphasise that there is no criticism or judgement from the therapist. The therapist accepts whatever the client is doing, but invites him to be aware of what he is doing as fully and as completely as possible (Perls et al., 1951). Victor Frankl (1972) describes Goethe's statement below as 'the essential maxim and most important motto of any psychotherapeutic project'.

> When we treat man as he is, we make him worse than he is; when we treat him as if he already were what he potentially could be, we make him what he should be. (Goethe, quoted in Frankl, 1972)

Existentialist therapists invite clients to relate authentically to one another (see chapter 2) and to take full responsibility for how they are choosing to be 'here and now'. Questions as to how clients are finding meaning in their life are central to the therapeutic relationship. The therapist takes no responsibility for what clients may choose. Existentialist therapists are transparent in their emotional responses to clients and share their own reflections and thinking, but take care not to impose their views on clients. We integrate both gestalt and existentialist ideas into the RIM as they offer us elegant and useful guidelines for working with the here and now.

SAFETY AND RISK

The need to provide a safe and boundaried environment is a reoccurring and important theme in most therapeutic literature; Bion talks of 'containment', Winnicott of a 'holding environment', Bowlby of a 'secure base' (Raval and Maltby, 2005). It is the job of the therapist to create an environment that is safe enough, but what does this actually mean? When clients come to therapy they are looking for something to shift or change, for present conditions to improve, yet at the same time they may feel ambivalent about change.[6] This ambivalence is normal (Prochaska and Diclemente, 1982) as the status quo involves negotiating the territories of uncertainty and entering into the domain of risk.

---

[6]As discussed in part 2 of chapter 2, ambivalence is one of the RIM's core concepts.

The use of mythology to illuminate the client's process is a technique often employed by Jungian therapists. The therapeutic journey may be compared to the hero's journey in mythology, an example of which is that of Theseus going into the labyrinth to slay the Minotaur, or when the Knights of the Round Table go in search of the Holy Grail. These journeys are also rites of passage, entailing transformation of some kind and a deliberate venture into the unknown, which inevitably hold some risk. Often the client is looking for 'safe certainty' (Mason, 1993), a 'no risk' strategy for change.[7] However, creating a space that can contain safe uncertainty is both more realistic and more likely to generate creative possibilities for the client. The therapist's task is to create a therapeutic environment and conditions for change and healing. The therapeutic method therefore includes the task of establishing therapeutic conditions and a context[8] (also a core concept) in which transformation becomes possible (Cecchin, 1992). Rogers (1957) famously coined six conditions that he regarded to be necessary and sufficient to create such an environment.

As mentioned earlier, research shows that the therapeutic relationship is the second most important factor in determining outcome after client and 'extra therapeutic' factors (Cooper, 2009: 56). How do therapists position themselves in relation to people who have different life experience, orientations and beliefs? Which 'prejudices' (in the sense that Gadamer (1975) uses this term of favoured or preferred views) become the highest context markers that organise our own sense of our self as well as our sense of how others should be, and how do we know where the boundaries are between our own beliefs and those of others? How do we negotiate these territories/boundaries? How do we bring into question our own ideas that we believe to be true? When we ask ourselves these questions we adopt a stance of self-reflexivity, we acknowledge that we are irrevocably part of whatever ensues with the client (Jones, 2003). Maturana and Varela (1998) suggest that what we know or perceive is 'structure determined', so that a message or an event will resonate or not in the recipient dependent on the receiver's 'structure'. In other words, what we say has to fit with the client's being in order to make a connection. It has to be received at a threshold at which it can make a difference. Therapists may be required to meet certain outcomes, e.g. if a client goes to an alcohol agency she expects that the agency's agenda is to help her stop drinking. Sometimes such outcomes do not fit the goals of the clients. If the therapist is 'married' to a particular outcome this may narrow the therapy's focus and restrict options.

Sometimes therapy is likened to a laboratory in which the experimentation and investigation in the therapeutic encounter and relationship can be generalised to other contexts. When we consider the present of the client we are interested in considering not only the client's intra-psychic conscious and unconscious experience, but also the external world of the client and how he or she fits into other systems.

Within the therapeutic context we may negotiate how to establish a footing from which we can go on: how are we going to be together? What is the frame or footing upon which we will be meeting? How close or distant can or should we be? Who decides or brings these things into question? Everything is up for

---

[7]We say more about risk in chapter 5.

[8]Context is one of the RIM's core concepts – see part 1 of chapter 2.

negotiation; ultimately it depends on whether we accept the definition enough in order to be able to engage in dialogue (Fruggeri, 2010; McNamee and Gergen, 1999).

Below is an example of the kinds of questions one can ask when exploring context. In this case the therapist is exploring and deconstructing the contexts that surround the client's experience of worry. Fred comes to therapy complaining of the distress his constant worrying causes him.

Questions from the therapist to Fred:

- If you were worried about something what would it be?
- How come it is important for you not to be worried? (Present orientation exploring the meaning of worry.)
- When you are worried who do you talk to, who else has worries, who do they talk to when they are worried? (Present and past orientation.)
- How does worry impose itself on your life – usefully, destructively? (Present orientation – exploration of experience.)
- If worry were to disappear from your life what would you miss about it, how would things change, what would become possible, no longer possible? (Future orientation, exploration of meaning, experience and possible insight/awareness.)

The contexts and multiple perspectives that influence the therapist and client are illustrated in the diagram below and may serve to guide the therapist's thinking about her position and the contexts that may be influencing her and her choices of interventions.

- How are you (the client) responding to me now? (Feedback.)
- What am I noticing about my response to you, my thoughts about what is happening? (Stance of curiosity, attunement.)
- How are my beliefs influencing my responses? (Including gendered, political and cultural beliefs, for example.)
- What am I sensing in my body, where do I feel the push and the pull, resistance, opening, softening, tension?
- How is the client responding to me, how am I responding to the client?

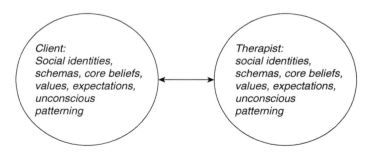

Figure 8   Self-Reflexivity of the Therapist

A systemic orientation and formulation in TIME means paying attention to and try-ing to understand the systems within which the client lives and operates (which of course includes the therapeutic system – client/counsellor/referrer or other helping professionals or significant persons who may attend counselling with the client). It is useful to take a stance of curiosity. This helps us to remain open to new information and not to formulate a fixed picture of the client – it can be helpful to 'not under-stand too quickly' (Anderson and Goolishian, 1988; Cecchin, 1992; Winnicott, 1953).

- What brought you to counselling at this time? Who suggested you come? Why did they think it might be useful? Who else thought it would be a good idea? (Present.)
- Who else is concerned about these issues? What other concerns do they have? (Unpacking meaning.)
- Who is most concerned?
- If the problem were to go away who would notice first? Who would notice that you no longer had the problem? What difference would that make, good or bad? (Future focus and orientation – meaning, experience, relational frame of the problem.)

INSIGHT

Insight signifies a process of gaining awareness and of self-discovery. The *Collins English Dictionary* defines it as: 'the ability to perceive clearly or deeply; penetration, a penetration and often sudden understanding of a complex situation or problem'. Insight therapies (e.g. psychodynamic or humanistic therapies) see insight as the ingredient that brings about change, wellbeing and growth. Exploring context, relational factors, deconstruct-ing meaning and engaging in a new experience of relationship with the therapist or with new behaviours may contribute to insight. Gaining insight into our patterns of relating with others as well as insight into our internal and automatic patterns of responding to life is extremely useful although not necessarily sufficient to bring about change.

It can, however, facilitate a new awareness of an inner subjective feeling whose meaning has hitherto eluded us, or the acquisition of a new understanding of our-selves in relation to our behaviours, relationships and of the multiple contexts that we inhabit and the ways in which they influence us. Taking its meaning as awareness (or awakening), then from the mindfulness perspective awareness constitutes paying attention to mind and body in the present moment, one's thoughts and one's sur-roundings. As we have suggested above we believe that insight constitutes a vital third component of the activity and processes that occur in therapy.

The figure and table below summarise briefly how we conceptualise working with past, present and future as well as therapeutic and relational processes within the TIME method.

SUMMARY

The Temporal Framework for Insight Meaning-making and Experience (TIME) offers a framework for practice and gives us a means of navigating the territory of change within the therapeutic relationship. What this then looks like in practice is expanded upon in the next chapter where we move on to discuss technique, the third section of Burnham's categorisation. These techniques help to forge the thera-peutic alliance and can be thought of as the tools of the TIME framework.

Past
- exploration of pattern, meaning and experience in the past
- redefining, restorying, reframing, co-evolving new definitions, frames of reference, insight, creating a new relationship with the past rather than changing the past, although this in itself can arguably change the past as we perceive it from the present

Present
- exploration of current reality for the client, what is the experience in the 'here and now' of the therapy room, outside the therapy room, in the client's relationship with the therapist, with others, their environment, their social networks, acknowledgement of aspects of self denied and preferred, giving voice to these aspects or parts of self, honouring the being mode
- in the therapy: processes of experimentation, feedback, attunement, reparenting, holding and containment, a safe haven, transference and countertransference, encountering each other, the intersubjective field, the therapeutic relationship

Future
- hopes, dreams, goals, expectations, horizons and limitations
- entertaining possibilities, choices, hypothetical futures entering the domain of the future through dreaming, envisioning, what if .... then......

Figure 9   Application of the Temporal Framework for Insight Meaning-making and Experience (TIME)

Table 3   The Therapeutic Process and Relationship within the Temporal Framework for Insight Meaning-making and Experience (TIME)

Establishing an agenda for therapy	Meeting the client in the 'here and now', attending to co-transference, definitions of relationship, patterns of relating, working with intersubjective experience	Inviting new perspectives, multiple views, introducing circular epistemology forging new meanings, co-constructing new narratives, challenging the status quo	Using appropriate self-disclosure, bearing witness to the client's story, evoking the client's strengths and resources, normalising the client's experience where appropriate

QUESTIONS FOR FURTHER REFLECTION AND DISCUSSION

- What are the social identities that you bring with you into your work?
- Using the metaphor of story, what would be the story you would tell of your life and what frames of reference have you derived from experiencing this story?

FURTHER READING

Boscolo, L. and Bertrando, P. (1992) 'The reflexive loop of past, present and future in systemic therapy and consultation', *Family Process*, 31 (2): 119–30.

Burnham, J. (2005) 'Relational reflexivity: a tool for socially constructing therapeutic relationships', in Flaskas, C., Mason, B. and Perlesz, A. (eds), *The Space Between: Experience, Context, and Process in the Therapeutic Relationship*. London: Karnac.

Cecchin, G. (1992) 'Constructing therapeutic possibilities', in McNamee, S. and Gergen, K. (eds), *Therapy as Social Construction*. London: Sage. pp. 86–95.

Cronen, V. E., Johnson, K., M. and Lannamann, J. W. (1982) 'Paradoxes, double binds, and reflexive loops: an alternative theoretical perspective', *Family Process*, 20: 91–112.

4

Technique: The RIM in Practice

Chapter 2 contained a discussion of the relationship between theoretical approach and the conceptualisation of clients' problems, which in turn will influence the interventions that are made. In part 1 of this chapter we first clarify our practical therapeutic stance before setting out how to work in a relational integrative way with clients presenting with a variety of problems. These include trauma, abuse, loss, relationship and identity issues, eating disorders, alcohol addiction and anxiety and depression. In part 2 we offer two case studies, which show how the RIM may be used in brief and open-ended therapy.

PART 1

APPLICATION TO SPECIFIC PROBLEMS

In our work with clients we have multiple choices regarding what we do, say or bring into the encounter at any given time. We also have hypotheses about the nature of problems that clients bring, be it anxiety, depression or issues relating to trauma, relationship concerns or addictions.

Problem definition forms part of the context of therapy and helps to establish a certain set of meanings (between client and therapist – or between clients and their context) that are open to acceptance or challenge. From an intersubjective perspective the definition of clients' problems is likely to have evolved as a co-construction between them and others and may differ from the definition offered by the therapist. Clients may say, 'You are here to solve my problems' or, 'You are the expert and must tell me what to do'. Both these definitions of the therapeutic relationship make practitioners responsible for solving clients' problems, rather than for creating a context in which difficulties may be dissolved. Thus we may enter into a process of negotiation, within which definitions of relationship are offered, accepted, rejected or reframed as part of the therapeutic process.

When we meet a client for the first time we are influenced by our experience of working with clients who have similar problems, as well as the associations we make between our knowledge, beliefs and experience. In chapter 3 we discussed how therapists are part of the meaning making system in therapy; occasionally we may therefore unwittingly contribute to a problem's continuation or to the creation of new problems (Jones, 2003).

THERAPEUTIC STANCE

Previously we discussed our orientation and preferred 'lens'. Here we will explore further how we may think about clients' difficulties as well as the resulting interventions. Below we outline a number of assumptions and discuss our preferred stance regarding our practice with clients.

Resource Focused

Our stance regarding our practice with clients is resource focused rather than deficit-based. This means that we help clients access or rediscover resources and skills, with the aim of opening up new choices and possibilities.

Bertrando (2006) suggests that therapy may be effective due to either *understanding* or *influencing*. The understanding pathway to transformation grew from the insight therapies[1] and implies that change occurs when clients gain insight into their difficulties. Understanding also involves understanding the contexts that contribute to the evolution and maintenance of the client's difficulties.

Understanding Context

A young man in a psychiatric unit diagnosed with encopresis, smeared himself with his own faeces. The team of professionals on the ward urgently tried many interventions, including behavioural rewards and token systems to encourage him to stop this behaviour; all to no avail. It was only when they asked themselves, 'In what context would it make absolute sense for him to be behaving this way' that they began to think differently: smearing yourself with faeces has the effect of keeping people away. Why might he want to keep people away? Is this to keep himself safe? Has something happened to him that has made him afraid of people coming near him? These questions led to the discovery that the young man had been abused by other boys within the unit. Once there was an understanding for the context of the behaviour the team could talk to the young man about alternative ways of keeping himself safe (Cecchin et al., 1992: 34).

---

[1]Insight therapies are commonly understood to be those therapies whose criteria for change are contingent upon the client gaining insight into their difficulties. These include psychodynamic as well as humanistic therapies.

The therapist's attempt to understand the client's experience is the cornerstone of empathy and regarded as therapeutic in and of itself. As the client experiences the genuine interest and regard of the therapist (Rogers, 1961) a sense of self-worth is engendered in the client: 'I am worthy of being listened to'.

Other approaches privilege the use of influence by the therapist to bring about change; through, for example, the use of exercises, behavioural experiments or homework. At a level of meaning making this may include the use of reframing, interpretation or, in its most directive form, telling the client what to do or giving advice. Therapies that fall within this category include behavioural therapies, cognitive therapies, Ericksonian hypnosis, neurolinguistic programming and solution focused brief therapy. Bertrando (2006), however, suggests that one cannot influence without having understanding. He claims that a client's experience of being understood is a kind of influence in itself; therefore the two processes are mutually constitutive of each other.

If an understanding stance is regarded as less directive and an influencing stance as more directive, then it may be said that in general the insight therapies and person centred approaches fall within the understanding end of the spectrum, while cognitive behavioural, Ericksonian hypnosis, solution focused and mindfulness-based approaches fall more towards the influencing end of the spectrum. In the RIM we may position ourselves differently along the continuum from understanding to influencing, depending on what is happening in the therapy at a given time. During an exploration of the experience of loss with a client, the work may fall more within the arena of understanding. In a discussion of a client's motivation to change a particular behaviour, on the other hand, we could be regarded as having positioned ourselves more towards the influencing mode. We do not see this positioning as governed by a set of therapy rules, but by what seems most therapeutically useful. The client's response acts as feedback that will guide our choices and enable us to become more, rather than less, useful to the client.

Neutrality to Outcome

Therapists may perturb clients' meaning making systems, but the effect of the perturbation is unpredictable. However, there has to be enough 'fit' between the clients' actions and beliefs and those introduced by therapists. If there is not enough 'news of difference', then it is unlikely that the clients' beliefs or patterns of relating and acting will change.

Cultivating Curiosity

Curiosity enables us to remain ever open to new information. It also guides us to ask questions that may help to elicit new information and understandings, or uncover/discover crucial information that was not known, or was out of the client's and/or therapist's awareness. This includes a curiosity about our own responses to the client and what they might mean; do we become tired, bored, anxious or tense in the presence of the client, or at particular moments in the session?

Multiple Views

As discussed previously any situation may be understood in a number of different ways. We invite clients into a process in which they can begin to entertain a number of new and different ways of seeing their situation. By asking relational and contextual questions we invite the client to consider relational explanations. This means that we seek a non-linear and non-causal understanding of the complex web of association and connection that produces a particular configuration of difficulty.

3D Observation

This requires us to be attentive to clients' verbal and non-verbal feedback, as well as our own intuition, bodily responses, sensations and hunches. Our clients and ourselves are like participants in a dance of co-transference (Orange, 1995). We also need to be skilled observers of possible patterns across contexts. For example, how the client negotiates cancellations, lateness or payment. We treat these observations as useful information about relational dynamics that help us attune to the client's frames of reference and enable us to make useful therapeutic interventions

LANGUAGES, THOUGHTS AND MEANING MAKING

In the West, consciousness cognitions and thinking tends to be identified with the mind. Links are assumed between people's cognitions and language, but it is acknowledged that language cannot provide a definitive guide to someone's thinking (Smith and Osborn, 2003). Language offers an interpretation of thinking that is then further interpreted by the listener. What emerges is a version of an experience that is co-constructed, in language, between therapist and client. There is a recursive link between experience and the language used to describe it, in that experience also shapes the choice of language used. On the other hand language itself defines and can be said to shape experience (Willig, 2001).[2] Attendance to all aspect of communication, including the language the client uses, is helpful to the identification of themes, patterns and key frames of reference, which we can then use to optimise our work with the client.

BEING AND DOING

The concept of relationship is at the heart of the RIM. It involves people's relationship with their inner world and their relationships with others, which includes the therapist. Clarkson (2003) identifies five aspects of the therapeutic relationship that come into play at different times: the working alliance, transference and countertransference,

---

[2]This is consistent with social constructionist epistemology.

reparative, person-to-person and transpersonal aspects. The creation of a relationship is not so much about trying to meet as about removing obstacles, as 'doing' too much can get in the way of empathic dialogue. It is often better to wait, create a space, and whatever needs to be said will come. Sometimes all that is needed is silence. So a good relationship involves being able to 'meet' clients by being attuned to where they are, so we can be there too.

Within the current therapy world there appears to be a tension between being and doing. It is generally accepted that the therapeutic relationship is more important than theoretical approach. At the same time there is also a belief that some therapies are more effective than others, which consequently receive more funding and provision. Perhaps this tension is an inescapable part of therapy; it is about relationship or how we *are* together *and* it is about what we do, how the client and the therapist work together. The latter inevitably involves specific ways of working, as well as certain techniques.

'Being With' a Client

'Being with' a client involves a special kind of intimacy (Rogers, 1951), which is different from being with a friend or partner. Freud talked about adopting an attitude of 'evenly hovering attention'; Bion ([1962] 1984) and Bollas (1995) speak of the therapist being in a 'reverie', which we see as akin to the mindfulness state of being fully awake in the present moment (Stern, 2004).

The intersubjective nature of the therapy process means that client and therapist cannot help but affect each other, both consciously and unconsciously. This means that in order to be with the other we also need to be with ourselves and our own felt sense, so that we can notice subtle shifts in how we are. We may feel changes in our body, in our feelings and emotions, and how we are generally, from moment to moment, and then reflect on what this might mean. Schon (1983) calls this 'reflection in action', to distinguish it from 'reflection on action', which we do later, when we write our notes or talk about our work in supervision. Our reflection may lead to a tentative enquiry of the client, 'When you said … I felt … and I wonder'. This way of 'being with' pays attention to our own and the other's phenomenological experience, thus incorporating a relational ethic or ethic of care (Slote, 2007). Intersubjectively each of us enters the other's world, we engage in each other's phenomenological field (Benner and Wrubel, 1989) in order to really 'meet'. Mearns and Cooper (2005: xii) call this 'working at relational depth'. So we do not meet the other through a preconceived diagnosis or theoretical glasses. Rather we attempt – and it can only ever be an attempt – to really meet the person 'as they are'. We may not always succeed, sometimes we get it wrong; it is the aim, the willingness to be open to the other – and not being afraid to fail – that is important. We are finite and fallible human beings and sometimes get preoccupied or sidetracked, so that we 'miss' the other person. When this kind of rupture does happen it is important to acknowledge it immediately; in fact we should always look out for the effect our interventions have on clients.

TRAUMA, ABUSE, LOSS AND BEREAVEMENT

Many people who seek therapy have had some kind of traumatic experience. Perhaps it was a discrete event, a series of events or developmental trauma, such as ongoing neglect, lack of attunement or abuse. All types of trauma are about something that was not supposed to happen and involve the *loss* of trust in a benevolent world. Abuse, whether physical, emotional or sexual, are types of trauma; bereavement is often traumatic too. Working with severely traumatised people is a specialised area, so it is important for therapists to know their limitations and when they need to refer clients on. Here the focus is on how the RIM is used in the context of trauma generally. We also add some examples from our work with bereaved clients and people who have been abused.

Emotions and the Brain

The brain is our 'nerve centre' with messages travelling continuously from body to brain and vice versa. At this very moment your brain is busy processing what you are reading, facilitated by information received from the body! The brain has three main sections: the brain stem, the limbic system and the cerebral cortex. The brain stem is mature at birth and regulates basic body functions such as heart rate and breathing. The limbic system is concerned with survival instincts and reflexes, and contains the hypothalamus, which regulates body temperature, nutrition, hydration, rest and balance. The limbic system also houses the hippocampus and amygdala, which process information from the body before passing it on to the cerebral cortex. The amygdala responds automatically to events with a high emotional charge; the hippocampus makes sense of the experience and is involved with conscious memory. Whereas the amygdala is mature at birth, the hippocampus does not mature until a child is about three, which explains why we do not remember much from before that time. All higher mental functions, such as speech, thought and memory, are orchestrated by the cerebral cortex. The right cortex appears to receive sensory and emotionally charged information from the amygdala, whereas the left cortex is concerned with language and has more connection with the hippocampus. Schore (2003) argues that it is particularly the orbitofrontal cortex of the right hemisphere that is affected by the interactions between infant and caregiver. The processing of emotion plays an important part in the way we attribute meaning to events.

STRESS AND TRAUMA

Stressful events prompt the release of stress hormones, which disable hippocampal functioning, but do not affect the amygdala. This is why conscious memory of highly stressed situations is often impaired, although it is held unconsciously and can get 'triggered' by events that have some similarity with the original experience. When this happens we may fall back on the habitual way of responding we learnt at the time, without necessarily 'knowing' why we are doing so.

As I open the door to Sheila, it is as if a large ball of pain hits me right in the stomach. I feel shaken and need to ground myself by breathing slowly and deeply and telling myself, 'This is not my pain'. My experience is in sharp contrast to Sheila's appearance of a well-dressed and confident woman in her mid-fifties whose manner is friendly and businesslike. She says that a colleague had referred her, as there are some issues she needs to work through. As Sheila talks she gives no hint of the pain and shock I am still feeling. I wonder what is causing me to feel like this when Sheila does not seem to feel like that at all? My experience tells me that she may have built some defences against whatever has happened to her and that I need to go slowly and carefully at her pace.

In severe trauma there may be 'structural dissociation', a division inside the person between the parts that engage in normal everyday life and the parts that are fixated on the trauma (Nijenhuis et al., 2004). Eventually the client may be helped to integrate traumatic memories and thus re-integrate body and mind. This may, however, be a slow process and needs to proceed at a pace that the client can tolerate without being retraumatised.

Preventing Vicarious Stress and Trauma

The above experience may be explained by the existence of mirror neurons (Rizzolatti and Arbib, 1998), brain cells that reflect the activity of another's brain cells, and probably underlie the capacity for empathy. The intersubjective stance of the RIM has relationship and empathy at its heart, but this does not imply a complete immersion. In order to prevent ourselves from getting lost in the other's experience, it is useful to engage in 'shuttling', in and out of the client's phenomenological field. A 'mindful' stance is helpful here,[3] so that we are aware of 'now I am going in ... now I am going out'. Rothschild (2006) suggests a number of strategies that help prevent us from getting lost, so that we can remain present and in relationship with the client.

Between Sessions

Awareness of our own issues and history is crucial. Clients' stories may trigger memories of our own, which can be helpful or unhelpful, depending on how well we know ourselves. This is one of the reasons why personal therapy is often required during training.

Sometimes we may find that we mentally carry our clients around. It helps to imagine putting all their distressing material in a container, which is left behind in a filing cabinet or wherever is suitable.

---

[3]Mindfulness is discussed later in this chapter.

Our work can be difficult and distressing. It is therefore important to look after ourselves, indeed self-care is one of the BACP's (2007) ethical requirements. Rest, relaxation and regular exercise help reduce stress and enable us to feel better and think more clearly.

During Sessions

During sessions we aim to be totally present and aware of what is happening in our body so that we can take action if we feel under stress. The arousal reducing strategies below are also taught to clients:

- *Breathing.* Breathe calmly and regularly in order to prevent stress from building up too much, which would interfere with the capacity to think clearly.
- *Dual awareness.* Here we deliberately focus on the external surroundings to remind ourselves of the 'here and now', which will take us away from our own history, our 'there and then' (Rothschild, 2006: 175).
- *Controlling self-talk.* This is based on the CBT maxim that how we think affects how we feel. In the above example I might have thought, 'I am competent, I am fine, I can do this', or whatever would be helpful.
- *Reducing identification.* In the above example I was able to 'dis'-identify myself from my client by saying 'this is not my pain'.
- *Grounding.* We can ground ourselves by being aware of our feet firmly planted on the ground; by feeling our arms or legs and mentally saying, 'This is me, this is my edge, what is outside is not me' (Rothschild, 2006).

Further Strategies to Teach to Clients

The aim of these strategies is to bring down arousal, teach the client to self-soothe and facilitate the integration of the split off parts of their experience. The various methods also aim to integrate the left brain, which is focused on language, with the right brain, which is involved with emotion and non-language activities. The ultimate aim is to help clients create a new narrative, incorporating their past, present and future.

- *Resourcing* helps calm the nervous system sufficiently for the hippocampus to function, so people can engage in the therapy. Physical resourcing or body awareness is particularly useful (Rothschild, 2000: 88) and helps integrate it with cognition and emotion. I may ask, 'When you do x, where in your body do you feel good?' or 'When you think about your "safe person", what do you feel in your body?' Resourcing helps clients to stay grounded in their body sensations. The aim is to prevent overwhelm, make the therapy safe and strengthen the therapeutic relationship.
- *Anchoring* is related to resourcing and integrates cognition and emotion. 'Tell me again about this cottage by the lake where you spent your summer holidays, what kind of roof did it have?' Once the client's arousal has subsided it is helpful to

explain what you just did and why; not only will this relational way of working strengthen the therapeutic alliance, it will also facilitate the client to integrate the work the two of you are doing together. There are two kinds of anchor: a specific one for work on a specific issue; and a generic one that can be used any time. This may be found by asking the client, 'What would be a good topic for us to switch to when things get overwhelming?' (Rothschild, 2000). Some clients may find this difficult, in which case we can be on the look out for what might make them feel better. For example, 'I noticed how different you looked just now when you talked about that field you used to play in. You looked alive and smiling'.

- *Dialoguing* is where the therapist (or the client) can dialogue with the inner child – how old are you? How are you feeling? What do you need? What would help you? Working with the inner child *and* the adult helps clients integrate different self-states. The combination of right brain activities, such as drawing or painting, with talking creates a bridge between experience and language. This is particularly useful with very early trauma that happened before the age of three, when neither language nor conscious memory structures are fully developed.

The 'Threat System' (Gilbert, 2010)

Initially Nancy talked about problems she was having at work but gradually she relaxed into the therapy and began to say more about her life generally. Divorced with a teenage son she was finding it hard to cope and often felt irritable and depressed.

One day she came in saying:

'I don't know whether I want to talk about this, I was going to do it last week, but chickened out'.

Therapist: 'What might help you?'

Nancy: 'I don't know, I am scared'.

I notice that Nancy looks pale and is breathing fast and ask, 'What is happening right now?'

Nancy: 'I feel fuzzy, I cannot think properly'.

The autonomic nervous system (ANS) has two complementary branches: the sympathetic branch, which is involved in the fight/flight response; and the parasympathetic branch, which is active during rest and relaxation. Our immediate response to danger is fight or flight; this is a normal response of what Gilbert (2010) calls the 'threat system'. The ANS is mobilised in case of threat, but once it has passed, returns to its normal balanced state.

Nancy was showing signs of sympathetic hyper-arousal. I sensed that Nancy might have experienced some kind of trauma and felt that it would be unwise to work with her while in this state as that could be retraumatising. I therefore asked her to take a few deep breaths and plant her feet firmly on the floor, while I did the same. I said that I did want to hear what she had to say,[4] but that there was no hurry. First I would teach her strategies to help her feel more in control, so that she would not get overwhelmed. I explained that she would be able to use these strategies outside the sessions too, whenever she felt the need. Nancy nodded, her colour was coming back and her breathing was returning to normal.

It is advisable to take a brief history of the client in the first session as part of the assessment, which may help prevent us being taken unawares. I usually say that I like to know who I have sitting in front of me. In order to begin to develop a therapeutic relationship I also encourage them to ask me any questions they may have about the therapy. Rothschild (2000) advocates asking for a synopsis, titles or headlines rather than complete narratives of events. This helps to get a 3D picture of clients and see them in the context of their lives. The way in which people talk about themselves may give an indication of possible trauma. For example if, as in the case of Sheila, the trauma has been dissociated from, they may talk about it with a complete absence of feeling as if they were reading the weather report. This provides important information we may wish to hold in mind. We may also begin to wonder about any defence strategies the client needed to develop, but which may now be affecting her relationships negatively.

All therapy, but particularly therapy with traumatised people, needs to be within the context of a safe, attuned relationship; we must take care that the person does not get overwhelmed, which could be retraumatising. In the example above, Nancy's 'threat system' was activated, which happens when (consciously or unconsciously) we perceive a threat (Gilbert, 2010). The natural response to a threat is fight or flight, or if we can do neither, freeze. The fight/flight system works very fast, there is no time to think or reflect because when we are in danger we need to act immediately. The threat system is unable to distinguish between actual threats happening now, and the memory of threats.

When I noticed Nancy getting overwhelmed I helped her to bring herself down from the high state of arousal, which is not unlike a caregiver soothing an upset baby – over time the baby learns to self-soothe when it feels upset. Once Nancy felt calm again she told me that she had been worried about something we discussed a few weeks before. If trauma remains unprocessed and unintegrated it remains 'free floating'. Therefore, if something in the current situation triggers the memory of a traumatic event, our threat system gets activated and the whole body gets ready to run or fight. A boyfriend had tried to strangle Nancy when she talked to him about something she

---

[4] I felt it was important to say that I did want to hear her story as otherwise Nancy might feel that it would be too much for me and lose confidence in the therapy.

was unhappy about. All she remembers is his hands around her throat and then 'waking up' by someone calling her name. Nancy had been unable to get away, but was saved as one of her flatmates had walked in on them. So when Nancy was about to talk to me about something she was not happy about, the memory of what happened with the boyfriend caused her threat system to immediately jump into action.

> Nancy later says that she had been afraid that I would jump up from my chair and attack her. I empathise and say that given the frightening experience she had told me about, I am not surprised that she feels like that. 'So you don't think I am going mad?' she asks. 'Not at all', I say, 'it is a normal response' (meaning). I then briefly explain about the threat system, how it can get triggered and teach her a few strategies she can use herself when needed.

It is important to respect people's defences as these have helped them to survive up to now (Rothschild, 2000); we therefore need to work at their pace (relationship, attunement). We may ask, 'How have you survived up to now?' and validate their strategies, which may help them value themselves and the way they coped more (relationship, meaning). We may say: 'So these strategies have been very useful to you, but it sounds as if you now want to develop different ones?' When I noticed that Nancy showed signs of high arousal I realised that it was necessary to 'put on the brakes' (Rothschild in Oakes, 2002: 22). It is useful to help people figure out what works best to bring down their own arousal, as this will make them feel more in control.

> Nancy's eyes look vacant, I have the impression that she is switching off. I ask, 'Tell me about that park you used to go to with your grandfather, did it have a lot of big trees?' Nancy's colour returns, she looks more animated and says, 'Yes, there were lots of trees. I particularly liked a large chestnut tree as it had a low branch with a swing on it'.

Here I helped Nancy come out of 'overwhelm' by asking her about her 'safe place' (Gilbert, 2010; Rothschild, 2000). I could also have asked her about a 'safe person' – 'What was the colour of your teacher Shelley's hair?' Safe places or people can be real or imaginary and are agreed with the client beforehand. In order to bring a client out of overwhelm the questions need to be specific rather than general, as this enlists the non-traumatised part of the brain. Clients can also be taught to use this technique for themselves; the beauty of it is that they can do it anywhere at any time.

Over time Nancy and I worked on understanding her early experiences, how they had affected her relationships with men, how they were affecting her in her current life and how she might want to do things differently in the future (meaning). Initially she found it hard to let go of her attachment to the idea that 'everything is my fault; there is something wrong with me' and accept that 'yes, it really was that bad, I was not well looked after, and it was not my fault'. As long as Nancy believed that it was actually her fault she did not have to face the 'loss' of the belief that things had been all right really and that abusive relationships had not been that bad. Like Nancy, clients may be ambivalent about the therapy, appearing to really engage one week, and then be highly critical of the therapy the next. This happens particularly when the trauma or deprivation happened at an early age, before the hippocampus was fully developed. Such clients may rationally understand that they were not to blame, but be unable to 'feel' it (Gilbert, 2010). Through mindfulness- and compassion-based practices Nancy was able to get in touch with the 'felt sense' of her experience, and utilise the various strategies and resources I had taught her, to prevent herself from switching off or dissociating when her threat system was activated. This enabled both of us to engage with our authentic experience in the moment with an attitude of curiosity and equanimity. In other words, Nancy developed non-attachment, the ability to accept 'what is', and was gradually able to dis-identify with her traumatic experiences and integrate them into her life's story.

SEXUAL ABUSE

Sexual abuse has been defined as 'any form of coerced sexual interaction between an individual and person in a position of power over that individual' (Dolan, 1991: 1). The most damaging effects are sustained when: violence and coercion are involved; the abuser is a trusted family member; and it goes on for a long period. There are many reasons why people may not be able to tell anyone what is going on at the time. Denial and repression are often used as coping mechanisms, which allows people to function in the world.

> Michelle tells me that when she was in hospital for a routine operation she was asked to undress in a small room that reminded her of the room at her grandparents' house where she was abused. Anyone who has been abused can be taken off guard when something in the current situation triggers a memory. As happened with Michelle, the threat system may be activated and as far as the emotional mind is concerned, the abuse is happening now. Michelle was too frightened to tell anyone that her grandfather abused her for most of her childhood, and had carried the shame and secrecy with her for a long time, afraid that people would reject her if they knew. Michelle has few close friends and although she is unhappy in her current relationship, does not want to leave, as she is afraid of being alone. She tells me, 'I have never been treated well, so I must be bad. My grandfather said I was bad. There must be something very wrong with me. I don't know what it is, but others can see it, that is why I got abused'.

This was how Michelle created meaning out of her experience. She coped by splitting the good grandfather who was kind and played with her, from the bad grandfather who abused her at night. 'The child attempts to control the troublesome object in its world by mentally splitting the object into good and bad aspects and then taking in or internalising the bad object' (St Clair, 1996: 56). She lived her life with a false self (Winnicott, 1965a), pretending to be someone without problems. In effect she thought, 'I must not let others see what I am like or they will reject me or treat me badly'. Michelle lived in fear of being found out, was frequently depressed and in the past had made a number of suicide attempts. She came to therapy as, 'I don't want to carry on living like this'. As she had never been able to talk about the abuse it remained unprocessed and could not be integrated in her life. It was sitting there like a heavy meal that could not be digested.

As she tells me about her history I am struck by the way she talks about the abuse, without any feeling, as if it had happened to someone else. As the therapy goes on I notice that she has a tendency to go blank, probably not unlike the way she dissociated during the abuse. After a while I might ask, 'What is happening Michelle?' She is not always aware what has just happened, but over time realises that she goes blank when there is a danger of 'feeling'. So the dissociation offers a retreat from the danger of experiencing disturbing emotions and memories. I feel it is important to create a warm and caring but non-intrusive relationship with Michelle. I tell her that there is no hurry and that we will go at her pace. I carefully introduce Michelle to mindfulness, which she is only able to do for a few minutes at a time. However, it helps her to get more in touch with her body and to notice when she begins to blank out. She then uses one of the grounding strategies I have taught her, or imagines herself in her safe place.

At the beginning Michelle is ambivalent about the therapy, and I often feel that she may run out of the room at any time. I share this sense with her, which contributes to the development of the therapeutic relationship as it helps her to feel more fully understood. Sexual abuse is a betrayal of relationship that makes the world an unsafe place. For a while Michelle is always late and then tries to stay longer to make up the time. We explore this and she begins to realise that through the abuse her boundaries were shattered, she genuinely does not always understand where her boundaries are supposed to be, so has to keep testing (meaning). It is therefore important for me to be clear about the boundaries of the therapy. For example, initially she often wants to change the time or day of her session, and sometimes makes inappropriate requests, such as a character reference for a job application. It is hard for Michelle to let go of her attachment to her belief that the abuse is her fault. After we have been working for more than a year she says, 'If it was my fault then I don't need to acknowledge that my grandfather was at fault for abusing me and that my grandmother and my parents must have known'. As children we need our parents to be good, even when we know that they are not. Michelle remains ambivalent about the therapy for a long time, frequently wants to end soon, only to change her mind the following week.

LOSS

Each loss is unique; our reaction to separation or death is never the same and cannot be predicted. Some well-known grief models appear to imply that the process of mourning follows a predictable trajectory with defined stages or tasks (Kübler Ross, 1970; Worden, 2009). In our experience, however, it often resembles a tangled knot, with people lurching from one state to another and back again, even within a single day. Neimeyer (2001) and other postmodern writers criticise stages or tasks theories as based on a modernist framework that values order, structure and predictability, and implies that grief is a passive process, the ultimate aim of which is to 'let go'. According to Dual Process Theory (Stroebe and Schut, 1999) the bereaved person may experience a tension between agonising pain and the wish to engage in activities that provide a relief from this pain. This may well be why during wakes or funeral receptions there is often laughter as well as tears. In contrast to a stages view of grief, Stroebe and Schut see both forces as operating simultaneously. They say that both forces facilitate each other: periods of deep pain should not therefore be seen as complicated grief, or an inability to 'move on', but as enabling people to fully express their feelings, whereas an engagement in other activities helps with the rebuilding of the structure of their lives.

Tasks of Mourning (Worden, 2009)

1   To accept the reality of the loss.
2   To experience the pain of grief.
3   To adjust to a world without the deceased: externally, internally and spiritually.
4   To find an enduring connection with the deceased in the midst of embarking on a new life.[5]

The four tasks may be engaged with in any order. Worden's concept of 'tasks' of mourning is reminiscent of Freud, who speaks of 'the work which mourning performs' ([1923] 1955a: 253).

Stages of Grief – based on People's Behaviour Following a Loss (Kübler Ross, 2009)

1   Denial.
2   Anger.
3   Bargaining.
4   Depression.
5   Acceptance.

We agree with some of the above criticisms, but prefer a stance that 'transcends and includes' earlier models as they do contain useful realisations (Wilber, 2000). Worden's

---

[5]Initially Worden saw the fourth task as: to emotionally relocate the deceased and move on with life (Worden, 2001).

first task, for example, involves the need to 'accept the reality of the loss', which appears similar to Kübler Ross's stage of depression and implies that grief 'work' or mourning, cannot be started until that acceptance has been achieved (attachment), which can take days, weeks, months, sometimes even years. People may say, 'Rationally I knew he was dead, but emotionally I could not get my head around it'. The second task of mourning involves, 'To work through the pain of grief'. This means that there is no short cut; the pain must be felt. It is through being awake to that pain, with compassion, that therapists can help their clients do the same. Purkiss (2010), a psychotherapist, poignantly writes how despite years of therapy and being familiar with models of mourning, she felt it difficult to create meaning out of her experiences and integrate them. What helped was to allow herself to be with the darkness. She quotes Lewis (1961: 29) who wrote, 'there is nothing we can do with suffering except to suffer it'. Not only is this similar to a Buddhist position, it also suggests a being alive to the pain of grief.

> Naomi's brother died around this time of year. I sense a great deal of disturbance under the surface, but put this on the back burner, as we have not yet built up a strong enough relationship. I feel that first and foremost I need to just 'be' there (Rogers, 1980) as she is extremely distressed. Naomi says, 'I cannot talk about him to anyone, they all expect me to be ok now, but I miss him terribly, every day'.

According to research in neuroscience our attachment to a person is like an addiction. Separation and loss may therefore be compared to coming off heroin, as the brain is flooded with the hormone acetylcholine (Panksepp, 2004). The experience of grief may be particularly painful or difficult when the relationship with the deceased was problematic, or if the loss was sudden, unexpected, untimely, or the death was due to violence. There is a current trend to offer immediate counselling following a disaster, when people are still in shock and unlikely to fully comprehend the reality of the loss. Although this may be useful for some people, according to Worden (2009: 8) this is crisis intervention rather than grief counselling.

When someone has died, there is a loss of the kind of relationship we had with the person. Freud (and initially Worden too) assumed that eventually we need to withdraw emotional energy from the deceased in order to re-invest it in a relationship with a living person. Worden's recent modification of the fourth task, however, implies the importance of enduring relationship and recognises that we experience ourselves through relationship with others, even if they are no longer alive. Their death modifies rather than erases that relationship, hence our need to process our internal relationship with the deceased. Having processed the loss, we can be open to other relationships, while maintaining an internal relationship with the one who died and 'find a way to make [that] loss a part of one's life' (Leader, 2008: 99).

Traditional cultures often maintain relationships with the dead through honouring their ancestors. In Mexico there is the annual Day of the Dead (Dia de los Muertos), when those who died are remembered and celebrated publicly! Similar remembrances occur in Asian and African cultures, a practice that seems to say, 'Yes we know you have died, but we have not forgotten you. We live our lives, but we do honour our dead and we do this with and in communion with others. We honour our dead together'. The public nature of these festivals demonstrates the importance of sharing grief and mourning, something not generally recognised in Western countries. The need to share mourning may explain the huge public outpouring of grief after the death of Princess Diana in 1997; it offered a context for people to share and express their private emotions.

Klass et al. (1996) developed a postmodern theory of Continuing Bonds. They are critical of earlier models' focus on 'letting go' of the relationship with the deceased. They regard such a view as based on a misguided Western and modernist emphasis on individuality, that does not recognise that we are all part of and constituted by our relational contexts. The theory holds that we continue our relationship with those who have died, so that we do not 'get over' a bereavement, but incorporate (integrate) this changed relationship into our lives. This theory feels intuitively right. Years after her child died, V wrote a poem entitled 'Connected, through invisible thread'. For V this expressed the ongoing bittersweet connection that she felt she had with her child.

Contextual Factors

Context is an important factor in our experience of grief. The experience of mourning may be difficult in so-called disenfranchised grief (Doka, 2001), when the context is such that the grief cannot be shared, or the relationship is not recognised, as in the case of an affair. The bereaved person may not be able to attend the funeral and is thus deprived both from partaking in an important ritual and from sharing their grief with others.

It may be hard (and lonely) to mourn a loss that is not recognised by society, such as a miscarriage or abortion. After a miscarriage a woman may be advised to 'try again', which denies the actual loss that has taken place. Abortion tends to be seen as the person's choice; however for many people this choice is not made lightly and they may feel conflicted about it. This applies to men as well as women.

> Roger told his partner that he was not ready to start a family and was not prepared for the sense of guilt and grief he experienced after she had an abortion.
>
> Paul was delighted when his girlfriend got pregnant and was devastated when she had an abortion without telling him. He said, 'How could she do this, I would have done anything for her, now I've lost everything'.

Other losses may be hard to speak about (such as suicide or AIDS), perhaps because of shame and/or guilt, or a sense that it is not acceptable to talk about it. 'You are the only person I can talk to', Graham tells his therapist regarding his brother's suicide, 'People just don't seem to want to hear about it'.

The above examples demonstrate the context of a bereavement; how it is seen in the person's family, social group or culture is highly relevant to the person's ability to adapt to the loss. If people are unable to share their grief with others they may be forced to wear a mask and pretend that they are fine (authenticity). Therapists can help clients talk about their loss and explore their thoughts, feelings and any other reactions and experiences. Particularly in the case of disenfranchised or unrecognised grief, where people were deprived from the ritual of a funeral, therapists can help clients devise their own ritual to commemorate the deceased person and say good-bye. Examples of ritual include burning a candle, playing some music, letting go of a balloon, or throwing a bottle into the sea with a message. If a person is religious it can also be helpful to involve a person connected to the church.

Mourning has its own rhythm and is not something that can be hurried along, we need to be prepared to accompany people in that process and help them make sense of what they are experiencing (meaning, spirituality). As much of mourning happens at an unconscious level we need to be aware of the co-transference[6] that arises and listen to what is created between client and therapist. Useful methods include dialogue, art, moment-by-moment attention and working with dreams. According to Leader (2008) there is no need to interpret dreams about mourning; it is usually sufficient to help the client pay attention to them and associate to the symbols contained within.

> After her mother died Alison has several dreams in which she tries to follow a shadowy person through a door, but before she does so the door slams shut.

Later losses, even if these do not involve bereavement, may bring back earlier losses, causing people to go through a period of intense grief for the earlier loss. In terms of neuroscience, the more recent experience may trigger the 'threat system' to be on red alert. David says, 'It has happened before, so it will probably happen again' and although he agrees that the evidence does not really support this, he 'feels' it to be true. It can be helpful to explain to clients that this is a normal reaction, as people are sometimes afraid that they are going mad.

Painting can also be a powerful aid in helping us to grieve and mourn:

> I had seen many reproductions of Picasso's Guernica, but nothing had prepared me for the impact of the raw emotion of the real thing. I stood transfixed for at least thirty minutes, tears streaming down my face, while the crowd ambled past me. I did not consciously think of any particular loss, yet identified with the mother holding her dead baby, the horse braying in terror. It spoke to me directly at a deep level.

---

[6]Within the RIM we use the term co-transference, rather than transference and countertransference. This is because, from an intersubjective point of view, therapist and client are deeply influenced by each other. It is often impossible to separate transference and countertransference as they are 'two faces of the same dynamic' (Orange, 1995: 67).

After we have lost someone, it often feels as if life has lost its meaning. According to Niemeyer (2001: xi) grief involves highly individual processes of meaning making and meaning reconstruction. In therapy it is important to pay attention to the implications of a loss, and 'the patterns and processes by which loss is negotiated in (clients') families and (their) wider social contexts'.

> The pain of loss and separation is one of life's great givens, an inevitable consequence of the loves and attachments of our lives (Purkiss, 2010: 39).

The work of grief is greatly helped by being able to talk with others who are familiar with the 'darkness' through their own experience. (Klass et al., 1996).

DEPRESSION

In the West we often seek to relieve or try and end suffering by *doing* something, by changing the conditions in which suffering arises; for example by improving self-worth or self-confidence, learning to regulate emotional and cognitive responses or changing the way we act in the world (Gilbert, 2005). People seek therapy either to get rid of, or to attain something (qualities, skills, relationships, experiences) (Moore, 1992). Alternatively we could learn to embrace and accept whatever is happening, even if this includes embracing experiences of suffering (Moore, 1992).

> Jane felt flat, numb and immune to all joy. She woke each morning with a hollow, empty sensation in the pit of her stomach and anxiety fluttering around her and in her chest. She told herself to get a grip and pull herself together, that she had no reason to feel this way and that it was stupid, but no matter how much she admonished herself, she was unable to shift her mood.

We tend to fear suffering and want to reject, deny, ignore and avoid it, or push it away. However, if we allow ourselves to listen and tune into the message of such difficult experiences, they can offer opportunities for growth and learning. Moore (1992) sees suffering as part of the human condition; it cannot therefore be eliminated from our lives, a view that echoes the philosophies of the East and is taken up by third wave cognitive therapies (we list all the CTs in chapter 3). From a RIM perspective both *doing* something to alleviate suffering, and *being with* and accepting suffering, are not incompatible.

Mindfulness-based approaches aim to help people develop the skills of:

- Being able to tolerate and accept both pleasant and unpleasant experiences non-judgementally.
- Cultivating evenly focused attention or equanimity.
- Caring for the wellbeing of self and others through the development of an attitude of kindness.

Recently one of us asked a client whether he ever felt kindness towards himself: 'Oh no!' he replied. A brief silence followed as what he had just said settled in his awareness. When clients are asked what advice they would give to a friend in a similar situation, they often give a compassionate response, which they have not been able to apply to themselves.

> In order to operate from a safe base, we need to have a good enough sense of ourselves and others; an 'all rightness' from which to act in the world. (Bowlby, 1969)

From a relational perspective symptoms of depression are understood as a consequence of interactional as well as intra-psychic processes. The context of relationship in the past as well as in the here and now and cultural contexts will contribute to the development of such symptoms (Jones and Asen, 2000).

> Jane's husband is very concerned about her. Every time she is quiet he will ask whether she is alright. I ask Jane what he is concerned about. She replies that he doesn't know how to deal with her when she is like this. I ask what the effect of his questions have on her. Jane replies that she knows he cares, but his questions make her feel monitored. She also believes that he likes her less when she is this way. Because she can't change her mood, this makes her feel more inadequate and her response is to withdraw further into herself. At other times he tries to cheer her up, which is also an unsuccessful strategy. She feels he wants her to get better, so that she can get back to work. He is concerned about money and worries about the bills. This makes her feel guilty and at the same time under pressure to get herself better. She doesn't think he can possibly understand what she feels like and yet longs for him to automatically know how she is feeling. I ask, 'If he were here and I were to ask him how he feels about your depression, what do you think he would say?' She tearfully replies, 'He will say he wants the old Jane back'.

> Positive feelings in minds of others create positive feelings in us. (Gilbert, 2009c)

If at some point there have been experiences in which the person feels there have been no positive feelings in the minds of others towards them, for example where there has been hostility, abuse or neglect of any kind, then this will often result in the person developing self-attacking and self-critical tendencies or high levels of shame. This may be as a result of internalising the attitude and/or voice of the abusive neglectful carer or finding an explanation as a child that, 'I must deserve this treatment because I am not good enough' and carrying this belief into adulthood. If this shame-based belief or critical mode has been laid down at some earlier stage of the person's development and is deeply ingrained then clients can find it very difficult to feel compassion or kindness towards themselves.

Although Jane acknowledges that her husband cares about her, he renders her helpless and weak in her mind: 'If he worries about me then I am not ok'.

Compassion-based therapy (Gilbert, 2009b) attempts to help teach clients to learn how to develop kind and compassionate feelings towards themselves and others. The nature of this approach is non-pathologising in as far as it suggests that people have developed coping mechanisms and have become sensitised to situations or triggers that evolved out of managing experiences in the past, and that these strategies are now redundant as the context has changed. Developing compassionate and kindly feelings will activate and strengthen the part of the emotion regulation system that is self-soothing[7] (Gilbert, 2009b).

Depression and anxiety are often characterised by self-attacking thinking and low self-esteem. Often clients have a sense of alienation from themselves.

> Jane tells me she has not felt herself for a while. She used to be cheerful, energetic and sociable. Now she is reluctant to go out and is less trusting than she was before, which is not like her. I ask her when last she felt like 'herself'. She recalls a time a year ago, when during a beach holiday she had a sense of freedom and contentment.

It can be useful for clients to learn to direct their attention away from the negative to other aspects of experience. Clients may be helped to remember or identify strengths, resources and positive qualities, as well as successful ways in which they have managed situations in the past. This strategy also calls on clients' resilience. Third wave cognitive strategies help people to find a balance between the tendencies to seek pleasure and avoid pain. Like the sutra teachings of the Buddha, the middle way involves finding a path between the extremes of aversion and attachment; between seeking and striving for goals, be they material, spiritual, relational or emotional, or avoiding and withdrawing from pain or suffering. These approaches also focus on the 'process' of thinking more than on the content of our thoughts (Gilbert 2009b; Mace, 2008; Segal et al., 2002). So while correction of less than useful strategies or ways of thinking can be useful to achieve change, mindfulness-based approaches encourage clients to notice and 'be' with experience as it arises in the moment. So mindfulness is not a problem solving approach in the way of traditional cognitive behavioural therapy. Rather it involves a 'letting go' of the need to solve problems instantly (Segal et al., 2002: 159).

Segal et al. (2002) distinguish between the doing mode and the being mode of mind. In the doing mode, the mind processes discrepancies between actual states and desired states. This is often a characteristic of depression, where the perceived discrepancy between one's actual state and a desired state is very large. This perceived discrepancy triggers negative automatic thoughts, which in turn trigger an action to redress this difference. People who are depressed therefore tend to go over things in their mind, in order to reduce the discrepancy: so called ruminative thinking (Segal et al., 2002). Thoughts in this mode take on the characteristic of facts, whereas in the being mode they are experienced as mental events that come into and pass out of our awareness. In the being mode thoughts are less likely to activate people towards

---

[7]See chapter 3.

doing something, as they are less identified and more detached from them. This de-centred perspective means that people are less driven by their thoughts. It allows the cultivation of detachment from previous attachment to certain patterns of responding. For example, if a self-attacking or critical negative automatic thought enters in being mode, this will not trigger a sequence or spiral of ruminative thinking and action, but will merely be labelled and then let go of.

> I want to explore with Jane her possible attachment to her default negative automatic responding and her depressive symptoms. I ask Jane to imagine that the depressive symptoms have disappeared and then ask if there is anything she would miss about them going, what might be the downside of the depression lifting, what effect would it have on her relationship and who would notice first that her mood had changed. This sequence of questions is also an exploration of the losses and gains for Jane of potential change in the status quo.

The mental maps or schemas that we have constructed over time are also made up of patterns of association. So if someone frowns, we associate this non-verbal behaviour with negative mood, anger, irritation, puzzlement or perhaps concentration. Over a lifetime we construct a complex network of associations and meanings that create tendencies in our way of interpreting the world and in our thinking. We also create tendencies in the way that we interpret somatic/body signals, so increased heart rate may signal fear for one of us and excitement for another. Our perception becomes patterned, or to put it another way, we develop default and automatic ways of perceiving and responding. These are often reinforced by a relational default pattern, like the way that Jane and her husband respond to each other, to reinforce and maintain Jane's depressive symptoms. Within the RIM we attempt to perturb this default automatic response in a number of ways, including helping clients to have an awareness of their associative tendencies or pattern of responses. One way of doing this is to invite clients to become their own observer. For example, I may ask Jane to notice over the next week the times when she feels that the depressive symptoms are less acute. In this observational task there is no pressure on Jane to do anything about her experience, except to subtly change her relationship to it, as she becomes an observer. She is also invited to notice when the symptoms are less acute, rather than when they are strong. This takes her perception away from the default mode of thinking, which is to be on red alert for the depressive mood. We attempt to change this slightly by being on the alert for the improved mood. This task may generate insight and a new awareness in the client while exerting an influence on the pattern itself.

Alternatively I may deliberately ask Jane to practice different behaviours, even if initially these feel awkward and a little uncomfortable. When people are experiencing depressive symptoms they become very sensitive to triggers, both somatic and cognitive. Statistics suggest that 13 million working days are lost in the UK because of depression, anxiety and stress related difficulties alone. It is estimated that 1:6 people will suffer from some emotional/psychological difficulties that could be categorised as a mental health problem at some time in their lives.[8] We are now at a point in our understanding where relational explanations of suffering in human experience are coming to the fore. As discussed in previous chapters the relational paradigm proposes that patterns of thinking, believing and acting are governed by relational templates (Stern, 1985).

Beck (1976) found that depressed patients tended to have particular ways of thinking about and interpreting experience, as well as a greater tendency than others to negatively evaluate events. This negative interpretation of events was largely automatic and habitual and seemed to have a strong effect on the mood of the person. He believed that if you could alter people's habitual ways of thinking through retraining and practice, then this would in turn improve their mood (Wills, 2008).

WHAT ARE THOUGHTS AND WHERE DO THEY COME FROM?

Stop for a moment and see what happens if you try to empty your mind of thoughts. What is it that happens as you focus your attention on the mind? You may notice that you have a stream of thoughts one after the other. Thoughts are mental events (Segal et al., 2002) constituted of an internal monologue or internal 'voice' as well as images, sequences of images, daydreaming, contemplation, reflection. They make up the activity of conscious mind. Our thoughts are the means by which we process information and interpret events, be they feelings, bodily sensations or events external to us such as other people's behaviours or actions. Our thoughts act as the mechanism by which we evaluate, judge, monitor and reflect on our experience. Over time we develop patterns of thinking informed by our beliefs about the world. At the same time thoughts contribute to the development of our beliefs and to the ways in which we make sense of life. These patterns of thinking can be thought of as habitual and are mostly out of awareness. Jon Kabat-Zinn likens this to being on 'automatic pilot' (Kabat-Zinn, 1990; Segal et al., 2002). Automatic thinking can govern not only our behaviour but also our moods and experience. Thoughts are the ways in which we interpret things. Thoughts make up our assumptions, like having a script or commentary running through our lives, and they play a huge part in influencing our experience at all levels: emotional, cognitive, behavioural and spiritual. From very early on we begin to develop patterns of thinking, sometimes described as schemas (Beck, 1976; Young et al., 2006), core beliefs, internal working models (Bowlby, 1969), or RIGS (Stern, 1985) and because they start to develop early in experience and pre-verbally they are largely implicit and unconscious. According to Young we develop coping mechanisms to compensate for the consequences of theses schemas. Beck (1976) proposes that we develop assumptions based on these schemas from which we then develop rules for living. From a psychodynamic perspective these would be called organising principles (Stolorow and Atwood, 1992). Carl Rogers also described something similar, which he called 'conditions of worth' (Rogers, 1961). A client recently described this as the 'scaffolding' on which she has built her life.

---

[8]Mental Health Foundation, www.mentalhealth.org.uk/help-information/mental-health-statistics/UK-worldwide (accessed 25 April 2011).

Mindfulness-based cognitive strategies within the relational integrative model enable us to work with all the seven core concepts and in particular authenticity and attachment. The practices of mindfulness allow clients to really tune into themselves in a deeply authentic way, to come back to a more genuine sense of self without the need to continue to adopt a mask or 'false self', as well as to learn to dis-identify from self-critical, attacking and negative patterns of thinking, which will have the effect of giving a greater sense of choice to how they then act and relate.

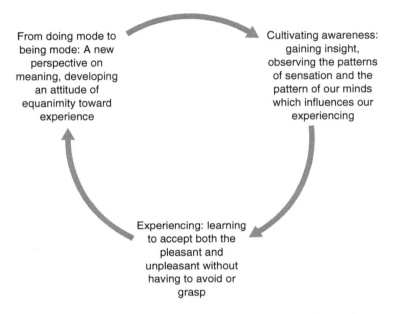

From doing mode to being mode: A new perspective on meaning, developing an attitude of equanimity toward experience

Cultivating awareness: gaining insight, observing the patterns of sensation and the pattern of our minds which influences our experiencing

Experiencing: learning to accept both the pleasant and unpleasant without having to avoid or grasp

Figure 10   Meaning, Insight and Experience from a Mindfulness-based Perspective

Monitoring, evaluating and modifying are useful concepts for how we might work at a number of levels. We can facilitate the client's ability to monitor their thinking, which in itself may serve to modify beliefs and behaviours thereby changing experience. We believe it is possible to embrace aspects of traditional cognitive behavioural therapy and contemplative cognitive approaches even though they operate in different ways. We see working with thoughts as essential to meaning making. The question is whether to modify thoughts or to accept them as they are and essentially cultivate an ability to 'detach' from them. We feel both are useful approaches and as always context will guide which feels most therapeutically useful at any given time. As discussed in chapter 2, we attempt to steer clear of certainty about the right way of being, so are careful to avoid terminology that may be potentially pathologising. We tend not to talk about cognitive distortions, but do see certain ways of thinking or identifying with thoughts as less useful. From this perspective we can invite clients to explore the legitimacy of their own beliefs, without imposing our values or judgements onto the clients thinking patterns or process. This is consistent with the idea of guided discovery and Socratic dialogue, which enable the client to explore and challenge their own automatic thinking patterns and the assumptions that underpin them.

Socratic dialogue entails asking exploratory and analytical questions that facilitate examination of assumptions around a particular theme or core belief (Padesky, 1993). Reflective and empathic listening are part of a guided discovery process.

SOCRATIC DIALOGUE IN THE RELATIONAL INTEGRATIVE MODEL

Although Socratic dialogue is an important part of CBT, it is not unique to this approach. Its originator was Socrates, a teacher of philosophy in ancient Greece, who used questioning and dialogue to guide his students to come to the conclusion or realisation of something he wanted them to learn or grasp. This style of enquiry became known as the Socratic method. Socratic dialogue can also be described as a technique or process that enhances critical thinking skills. Critical thinking is the process we use to reflect on, assess and judge the assumptions underlying our own and others' ideas and actions.

There is much debate (Padesky, 1993) in the psychotherapy field as to whether the intention behind Socratic dialogue is to lead the client to a particular view held by the therapist, or to facilitate a focused examination and exploration of a theme or issue that the client is bringing. We do not believe that leading a client to an outcome that is coming from our frame of reference is useful, and therefore prefer to use Socratic dialogue in an open-ended way as a process to explore and examine meanings, beliefs and assumptions. Similarly, Padesky argues that guided discovery should be utilised not to change a client's mind, but to allow the client to explore and reflect on their thoughts and behaviours:

> In the best cognitive therapy, there is no answer. There are only good questions that guide the discovery of a million different answers. (Padesky, 1993: 4)

Socratic dialogue aims to elicit themes and identify more clearly how clients make sense of the world. When we listen for clients' patterns of thinking and ways of making sense of things, we need to remain curious about the relational contexts that have influenced their construction. Thus Socratic dialogue helps to 'unpack' (deconstruct) the layers of meaning and examine and explore the processes by which patterns of thought and belief are constructed. In this process new ideas or ways of thinking about something may emerge or be 'discovered' by the client (hence the term guided discovery).

We also believe, however, that change can occur by becoming aware of ways of thinking or cultivating new 'modes of mind' through mindful awareness (Segal et al., 2002). When we are able to do this we are becoming the observer of our thoughts and less identified with them. At this point we change from believing our thoughts are facts to seeing our thoughts as mental events (Segal et al., 2002). In this sense we re-condition the conditioned mind through a process of reflection on our understanding of events. As discussed earlier our interpretation of events will influence our mood and behaviour; one interpretation is not necessarily more valid than any other. When we examine 'the unexamined life' there is the potential to become free of our conditioned responses and modes of mind and more impartial or neutral to our thinking responses to events.

Key Concepts in Mindfulness Approaches

- Mindfulness approaches constitute a movement away from a focus on content of cognitions to a focus on process of cognitions where, for example, the emphasis on changing negative automatic thoughts moves to attending to the way all experience is processed.
- Cultivating neutral attention (turning towards the unpleasant as well as the pleasant – not recoiling).
- Mace (2008) describes the practice of mindfulness as having the effect of resetting an internal clock to go back to an earlier phase of clinical history, for example, in relation to depression to a time before the onset of depression.
- Moment to moment non-judgemental awareness cultivated by paying attention.
- Non-instrumental dimension of meditation, inhabiting the present moment.
- Importance of the notion of de-centring in relation to depression, anxiety, stress and particularly in relation to relapse signatures. Teasdale (1988) proposes the Differential Activation Hypothesis suggesting that people who have experienced a depressive episode are more sensitised to possible triggers such as life events or stress (also see Jones and Asen, 2000).
- Latent body memory of depression and anxiety – embodiment in general of psychological distress and trauma that triggers repeating patterns. Mindfulness practices weaken the links between things that have become associated so that the pattern is not activated. Wherever people use chemical means to regulate high states of arousal and difficult emotions, which themselves are chemical reactions in the system (Pert, 1999), mindfulness may be a useful way of working therapeutically.

Case Study: Depression and Anxiety

Therapists and clients cannot but contribute to a conversation in a particular way that is dependent on their own personal histories, culture, etc. (Cecchin, 1992). This selection is also constrained by the response of other members of the system. So the conversation is mutually evolving and, at the same time, constrained by each member. Therefore choosing to select a particular interpretation does not ensure a predictable outcome. And it is impossible to avoid a particular stance. Therapists, however, can take responsibility for their position by making it overt and offer it as their interpretation rather than as absolute truth. Putting their interpretation into a cultural context and elucidating the alternative interpretations available can achieve this. It allows the therapist to become irreverent to any particular truth including his or her own while acknowledging that each therapist brings into the therapeutic domain their own constructions of truth, privileged discourses, histories and cultural influences.

> However, since it is impossible not to take a stand, it is exactly this reflexive loop between taking a stand and immediately thereafter putting this stand in a larger context that creates the 'becoming' and not the 'being' of a therapist. (Cecchin, 1992: 93)

These views confirm that one cannot not influence, but acknowledge a need to be mindful of the dangers of strategising and instrumentality. They constitute an ethical and political position that seeks to avoid the possibility of the therapist becoming co-opted into the position of social controller or agent of social control. In this case study we see how the therapist facilitates a process of guided discovery, which includes the occasional use of Socratic dialogue and questions in order to unpack meanings and beliefs.

> Jim came to therapy via an employee assistance programme having lost all enthusiasm for work. He had felt low in mood for some time and could not understand why he was feeling this way, as the change in mood and his recent experience of anxiety seemed to have come out of the blue.

One of the therapist's tasks is to create an atmosphere of discovery. The client is invited into a space in which news of difference can be generated. Using the TIME method as a guide to the therapeutic process, the therapist listens to Jim's story with 'floating attention' (Foulkes, 1964) allowing herself to hear 'between the lines' for themes and key associations that Jim might be making. Taking a 'not knowing' position (Anderson and Goolishian, 1992) also facilitates this floating curiosity so that the therapist does not attach too strongly to any particular ideas or hypothesis about Jim's experience but remains open to multiple explanations. She also 'listens in' to the heart of what is being said and not said, listening to the language of Jim's non-verbal behaviour and notices his lack of eye contact, the fleeting appearance of a frown and distress on his face as he speaks. She notices herself feeling tense and wonders what this may mean, adding it to the information that is made available through the process of inquiry. She asks open questions to begin to explore the layers of context that may be significant in furnishing possible explanations as well as potential resources in relation to Jim's depressive symptoms. She asks Jim when he first remembered starting to feel this way, and when the last time was that he felt differently from the way he feels now. By asking these questions she tries to locate the history of the problem or difficulties as Jim sees them, locating them in time, as well as checking out with Jim his understanding and interpretation of his situation.

> Jim started to feel down following his father's death two years ago. He has been happily married for twenty-five years. He has always enjoyed his job although work pressure in the last couple of years has made it increasingly hard to achieve his work tasks in the way he would like and this has become a source of frustration and dissatisfaction. He feels that he was always being asked to achieve more with fewer resources. Jim decided to seek therapy after an incident at work during a meeting, when he suddenly felt overwhelmed by feelings of anxiety. His heart was racing and palms were sweating and he had a strong urge to leave the meeting. He was afraid that this would happen again.

The therapist, using the technique of guided discovery, began to ask some questions to help the client make an appraisal of the level of threat that actually existed.

Therapist: If it were to happen again, what would be the worst thing about that?

Jim: That people would notice and I would feel ashamed.

Therapist: If they did notice, what would that mean to you?

Jim: They would think that I am not coping, that I can't take the pressure.

Therapist: You would worry that they would judge you in some way.

Jim: Yes that they would think that I was weak, that I couldn't take it. I have always been the one that people come to when they are struggling.

Therapist: So this would be new and different for you and you would worry that they thought less of you in some way.

The therapist decides to explore the history of this idea.

Therapist: When did you first get the idea that you needed to be the strong one?

Jim: (there is a pause as he reflects) I remember when I was about eleven years old. My mum had been ill; I'm not sure whether perhaps she was suffering from depression. My dad, he looked after all of us, me and my two younger brothers, and I remember one day him saying to me, 'We have to be the strong ones Jim'. He never complained, he just got on with things – I think he got anxious and worried but he never grumbled about anything.

The therapist pursues the theme of weakness and strength.

Therapist: You really admired him for that. He was a bit like a hero to you. So your dad invited you into a pact: you two had been the 'strong ones' looking after the others. In what other ways are you like your dad?

The therapist uses the metaphor of the 'pact' to give a name to this alliance between father and son and then asks a relational question to explore the similarities and differences between them.

Jim: Well I guess we both can be stubborn and like to get things right. He never criticised but you knew if he was disappointed in you. I am a bit the same in that way.

Therapist: So if people were to see that you were not getting things right all the time or that you were not coping, that would be hard for you?

Jim: Yes, and yet logically I know you can't get everything right all the time.

The therapist notices that the client has introduced the voice of the 'logical self'.

Therapist: So the part of you, the logical part, knows that things can't be perfect all the time and yet there is another part of you that feels differently. Tell me about that part of you.

Jim: Well I always like things to be right. I don't like to make mistakes, it makes me feel … incapable and weak if I make mistakes.

The therapist tentatively offers an alternative perspective on mistakes and asks:

Therapist: Is it possible to learn anything without making mistakes?

Jim: No I guess you are right, we all have to learn by our mistakes but I still can't shake that feeling.

Therapist: So if you were to make a mistake how would that non-logical part of you respond? If it had a voice what would it say?

Jim: It would say, 'You're stupid, get a grip, don't be such an idiot!'

Therapist: So this is quite a harsh voice, a kind of 'pull your socks up' voice?

Jim: Yes, I get disappointed in myself.

The therapist picks up the theme of disappointment, which Jim has already mentioned, in order to try to understand and unpack its meaning and significance in Jim's life.

Therapist: Is disappointment a feeling you have had before?

Jim: (pauses for a moment) Yes it is a familiar feeling; I have felt disappointed at times, most of all when my dad died. I was so disappointed that I hadn't been able to tell him how much I loved him.

At this point Jim has tears in his eyes and shields his face with his hand. The therapist leaves some silence to give Jim space before offering an acknowledgement of the welling up of emotion. She feels a deep sadness on Jim's behalf at this point.

In the next part of the session the therapist explores the story surrounding Jim's father's death. Jim is able to express some of his feelings of loss and grief, which he had held inside until then, not wanting to upset his brothers or other family members by showing them his sadness. In subsequent sessions the therapist asks Jim about his thoughts and beliefs about dying. It becomes clear that Jim's father's death has suddenly made him aware of his own mortality, making him question the purpose of his life and what the future holds. The therapist reframes this existential fear as part of the life cycle and offers the idea that perhaps Jim is entering into a new phase of his life. Jim then discloses his fear and sense of responsibility about now being the oldest generation. The theme of being strong comes up again and the therapist utilises this to explore with Jim the validity of this idea now that Jim and his brothers are adults. Jim expresses relief as he comes to acknowledge that being the 'strong one' may no longer be necessary and that it was not an injunction from his father that he had to fulfil for the rest of his life. After this significant realisation and insight Jim begins to experience an improvement in mood. At times he still feels anxious and the therapist introduces mindfulness approaches to Jim. He starts to practice the three-minute breathing space during work when things get hectic and regularly does a body scan at home. He begins to notice that he is able to tolerate some anxiety without pushing it away or feeling panicky. He speaks more to his brothers about his father's death and shares his concerns and worries with his wife, who is supportive. They make plans to do more activities and Jim takes up sailing again, which he had enjoyed doing with his father as a young boy.

SELF-HARM: ADDICTIONS, EATING DISORDERS AND SELF-HARM

We use the overall category of self-harm as the sets of behaviours in these categories of difficulty can all have a harmful effect. Self-harming behaviours often arise because clients attempt to find a chemical solution to unwanted emotions or levels of arousal. Other methods of self-regulation may not be working or effective (Miller and Brown, 1991). The solution is to find something that has the effect of self-soothing by helping to regulate emotion or deal with unbearable feelings. Starving oneself, cutting, drinking, taking drugs, can produce a change in body chemistry that appears, in the short-term, to alleviate the unwanted symptoms, thoughts or emotions. Engaging in such behaviours can help to avoid situations or feelings that are intolerable. Because they are particularly successful they are used again and become part of a pattern of association between aspects of experience, e.g. I feel angry and upset, so I will have a drink, which temporarily calms me down and takes the edge off. I feel upset and the thoughts I have are that I am useless and worthless, so I cut myself and this gives me a moment of calm and relief (Gerhardt, 2004).

   As discussed previously, when people have had early trauma as infants or suffered from neglect, they will have experienced levels of cortisol that are toxic in the system. As adults their levels of cortisol in the brain will be regularly elevated, making it harder to reduce high levels of arousal, as the chemical pathways for reducing cortisol are less well established (Luecken, 1998).[9] The therapeutic approach taken towards addictive disorders or behaviours has often been one of confrontation and coercion (e.g. Alcoholics Anonymous 12 step philosophy, forced re-feeding for anorexia), in which the client is made aware of the terrible consequences of their addiction on their health and relationships. This method sits alongside the general negative connotation of addictions, general societal disapproval and a commonly held belief that if only people tried harder they could overcome the addiction. A confrontational strategy is underpinned by the idea that people will be motivated by negative factors, e.g. the threat of ill health. This has been strongly challenged by therapies such as motivational interviewing, which suggests that people are best persuaded by their own arguments for change, and solution focused brief therapy and systemic approaches, which take the view that people are more likely to change under a positive connotation (Cecchin, 1992; Miller and Rollnick, 2002). For example, if I believe that change will bring a perceived benefit then I am more likely to do it than if I believe that changing my behaviour will mean I can avoid a negative consequence.

---

[9]Research suggests that high levels of cortisol are found in people suffering from anorexia nervosa (Redei et al., 1995).

   Addictive behaviours are hard to change, as they become a deeply entrenched behavioural coping mechanism that has benefits for the client. If we fail to acknowledge the benefits then we are missing one side of the equation in the cost benefit analysis of change. Following Miller and Rollnick (2002), we believe the task of the therapist is to look for leverage in this equation by asking questions about the pros and cons of the current situation for the client and by eliciting the client's own concerns about the negative consequences of the behaviour. It would be easy for therapists to point out what these consequences are, but we know that this would be directive instruction and is usually less effective. A process of guided discovery, using open questions, helps the client to explore their own relationship to these behaviours. Clients usually have become very attached to this way of being, it has become familiar territory and, as discussed in previous chapters, change means breaking the bonds of this attachment and holds many potential risks for the client. Ambivalence is the prevalent emotion; resistance is a key defence and acts as a barrier to change. Sometimes this is captured in the voice of the addiction, the 'anorexic voice' (Treasure and Schmidt, 2008). When the therapist attempts to understand the benefits of the self-harm or addiction this can lower barriers and defences and the client may then feel able to voice their concerns about the behaviour. Unlike solution focused brief therapy where the focus stays on solutions rather than problems, we agree with Miller and Rollnick (2002) on the importance of paying attention to both sides. One way of helping the client to articulate their ambivalence to the behaviour is by inviting the client to write a letter to the addiction, e.g. writing a letter to anorexia (Treasure and Schmidt, 2008). Another intervention is to change the pattern surrounding the symptomatic behaviour; Cade (Cade and O'Hanlon, 1993) describes his work with a young female client with bulimia where, instead of encouraging the girl to stop making herself sick, he intervened at the level of pattern by negotiating with her that she would have to change her clothes each time she was going to make herself sick. Often it can be useful to involve significant others either in the therapy or to invite their voices into the therapeutic room by asking questions about their opinion in relation to the addiction or self-harm. Asking exploratory questions and using reflective listening to deliberately highlight and develop the discrepancy between the client's internal voice that is pro health and the voice of addiction can also be a valuable method to increase the importance of change in the mind of the client (Miller and Rollnick, 2002).

Addictive Behaviours

- Solution to painful or difficult emotion, initially the task of the therapist is to explore the history of the behaviour.
- Exploring the relationship and attachment to the addiction; understanding the nature of ambivalence about change in order to find leverage in the cost benefit analysis.
- Externalising the behaviour, guided discovery, examining values, widening the context.

Case Study: Self-harm and Bulimia

Jenny is thirty-two and has come to therapy because of unhappiness and frustration with the way she relates to people and how she manages her life. She moved to Oxford to take up an academic university post having lived in the north of England for most of her life. She has found the work load and pressure hard to manage and at times overwhelming. She feels isolated and lonely; due to the demands of work she has not been able to establish friendships. At times she feels exhausted and at one point she found the pressure too much and had to return to her parental home for a break and was signed off sick with stress. Jenny admits she is a perfectionist and can't tolerate making mistakes. She has begun to feel increasingly anxious just before lectures as she fears that the students will judge her negatively.

I notice in the first session that Jenny is very self-critical and wonder where this internal critic comes from. I notice a theme of perfectionism and judgement of herself, and fear of being judged by others.

We explore together some of the history of her career in academia.

Jenny: My father is an academic and my parents both went to Oxford University and talked about it with great fondness. They were very pleased when I got a post here.

Therapist: What is it that they told you about their time in Oxford?

Jenny: They always said it was a golden time. They had very high hopes to take up university posts when my dad got a job in a different university. My mother found it hard to settle there and then couldn't find a job herself. She was very bitter about this and then became pregnant with my older sister so never actually pursued an academic career.

Therapist: It sounds like that has been a disappointment for her. What is it that she most hopes for you?

Jenny: I think she would like me to pursue the career that she never had.

Therapist: Who is most interested in this career, you or your mother?

Jenny: Oh I think I am. (She pauses) I mean, you know, she wants me to be happy ... I am glad that I am doing this because I know it makes her happy.

Jenny's words reveal confusion about the theme of happiness and career and whether it is her mother or herself who is motivated by her career choice.

Therapist: Who is most likely to notice when you are happy?

Jenny: Probably my dad if I am at home. He is a bit like me, quieter than my sister and my mum. He is also more likely to notice if I'm unhappy.

Therapist:	And how do your sister and mother respond when you are unhappy?
Jenny:	Well my sister is usually busy so we don't see each other much. My mum will start to encourage me to do things, get a boyfriend, get a different job; she comes up with solutions and it doesn't help.
Therapist:	What would you rather she did?
Jenny:	I wish for once that she would just listen and be supportive. I always feel that she is on my case and nothing I can do will satisfy her.
Therapist:	So you would like her approval. What would happen if you gave up wanting her approval, how would that change things, if at all?
Jenny:	Maybe I could relax, I could do what I wanted to do, I wouldn't have this constant feeling that I am not quite getting it right, or achieving enough.
Therapist:	This part of you that has that feeling that you are not quite getting it right, if you had to name this part of yourself what would you call it?
Jenny:	(pauses for a moment) I think I would call it … the harsh doubter.

Later I ask:

| Therapist: | Would your mother be surprised that you feel she doesn't approve of you? |

We explore whether Jenny thinks there is a link between the pressure her mother appears to put on Jenny and her own experience after having left Oxford. In this way we are looking for different perspectives on Jenny's mother's behaviour.

Therapist:	The harsh doubter – can you tell me a little more about her
Jenny:	Well when she is at her most vociferous she tells me I will never amount to much, that I will never be in a relationship and that I'm incompetent.
Therapist:	Yes, I see what you mean by harsh!! So when this voice is the stronger voice how do you respond?
Jenny:	(pauses and hesitates before saying) Well in the past I used to cut myself and then that changed and kind of got tangled up with food and eating.
Therapist:	Ok, so the harsh doubter used to have the effect of making you self-harm by cutting, but that has changed recently?

I have a number of choices at this point. I could ask about the pros and cons of the self-harm, what made her stop, etc., which would be an exploration of the past, and then could link it to what is happening now and how they are linked or not in terms of pattern and meaning for Jenny. Instead I explore what is happening now in relation to the harsh doubter. Jenny reveals that for the last ten years she has struggled with bulimia. She describes it as a companion.

| Therapist: | Is bulimia more of a friend or an acquaintance or would you describe it differently? |

Jenny: Sometimes it is a friend and at other times an enemy. Sometimes it has so much control over me that I seem to lose myself and it takes over.

Personification of aspects of self has a long and rich history in the field of psychotherapy. Perls et al. (1951), Assagioli (1965) and others brought this into the field of therapeutic work by naming the parts of selves and addressing them directly in therapy. Michael White (1988) introduced the technique of externalisation which 'encourages a person to objectify and at times to personify, the problems they experience as oppressive' (Lee and Littlejohns, 2007: 3). Here the therapist begins to use externalising techniques to invite the client to explore the possibilities of a new relationship with bulimia and one in which the possibility of separating herself from bulimia may be entertained. Eating disorders and other self-harm behaviours often have the effect of focusing the individual (and their families) on the here and now; the current meal, the avoidance of food in this moment, the next drink, the next fix, so that envisioning the future or looking to the past for alternative models of being can become rare. It can be useful with all issues of self-harm to reflect on times before the self-harm behaviour appeared and also to enter into conversations about hypothetical futures: when the self-harm has gone, what would be different, what are the fears about this for the individual as well as the possible opportunities, how will their relationship to others change if the self-harm behaviour leaves? At this point broader issues such as life goals and values that are of importance to the client (Eisler, 2005) may be explored. This inevitably leads to a shift from the present focus to a future oriented conversation. Future oriented questions such as asking the client to imagine how they would manage food and eating related issues if they become a parent, or to imagine how they would like to tell the story of how they recovered from the self-harm behaviour in ten or twenty years hence can engage the client in an imaginary (as yet) alternative future of life without the self-harm behaviour (Eisler, 2005). Guilt, fear and blame, however, are persistent themes that often arise in the therapy and it is important to continue to help the client to identify their resources and strengths to counter these more negative influences. As with all the case examples and specific issues that we have talked about in this chapter, hope and hopelessness form part of the landscape. At times it is important for the therapist to take up the hope when the client appears to have lost all hope. The therapist can declare this openly and be both respectful of the client's beliefs about change while also keeping the voice of hope alive within the therapeutic system (Flaskas, 2007).

Jenny reflects on her relationship to bulimia and also explores with me dreams that she has for herself, things she holds dear. Later in the therapy we discuss the possibility that bulimia keeps her close to her family while she is living her mother's dream and we look at the possibilities of what might happen if she were to live her own dreams, deconstructing the ideas of responsibility and loyalty in relation to this hypothesis. Jenny has a conversation with her mother in which they are able to discuss these themes and after this Jenny's mood and confidence improve. She begins to make plans for the future and maintains a perspective on her work. She becomes less anxious and bulimia slowly disappears from her life as she starts to make some new friends.

BRIEF SUMMARY

These case studies illustrate how the RIM can be adapted to a wide variety of difficulties that clients bring. The pacing and emphasis differs depending on what is appropriate and useful for a particular client.

PART 2

THE RIM IN PRACTICE – THE PROCESS OF THERAPY

This section takes the form of two annotated case studies that illustrate how the model is used in short-term and more open-ended therapy.

LONG-TERM, OPEN-ENDED THERAPY

And you find yourself suddenly forty

And you ask yourself 'what have I done?'

And you wonder 'where am I going?'

(Els van Ooijen)

ANDREW

I open the door to a tall man wearing a grey suit and polished black shoes. He spends a few moments checking his phone before switching it off. I greet him, explain the structure of the session and invite him to tell me what brings him here and what he is looking for.

Andrew:	I went to see my GP because I thought I was having a heart attack, so I had some tests. She said my heart is fine and that it sounded like panic attacks, so she referred me to the counsellor at the practice. I saw him four times and it was really good.
Therapist:	It helped you cope with the panic attacks?
Andrew:	Yes, it did, but he thought that I could do with longer-term work and gave me your name.
Therapist:	So this is about more than panic attacks?
Andrew:	Yes, I'm stuck, I do feel slightly better than I did, but I'm still quite depressed, I don't know what my life is about anymore. He thought it would be good to have some help to sort it all out.

During a First Session I Like to Find Out About:

- The reason for seeking therapy and why now?
- The client's hopes, aims, ultimate goal.
- Any previous therapy? When? Why? How long? What kind? How was it? What was helpful/not helpful? How did it end?
- Any other help, e.g. GP, psychiatrist, social worker, community psychiatric nurse? Any medication or other medical treatments?
- Many of these questions tend to get answered by just letting the client tell me why they have come.

Andrew tells me that he has been feeling depressed for a while. Now forty-two, he met his wife Lucy at university. They have been married for fifteen years. Lucy has a high-powered job in finance and does not want children. Andrew says that if he had been married to someone who wanted kids he would have had them, but that he is not particularly bothered.

Andrew: I feel that we are just going through the motions; I don't think Lucy loves me anymore and I am just waiting for her to tell me that she wants a divorce.

Therapist: What about you, how do you feel about Lucy?

Andrew: I don't know, I feel confused. I love Lucy, but we both work long hours so don't see that much of each other. Lucy tells me that I am irritable when I am at home so she does not want to spend time with me. I don't know, I just … (he stares into space).

I wait but Andrew appears frozen, I sense that he has blanked out, so I ask gently:

Therapist: What's happening Andrew?

After a few moments he says:

Andrew: I don't know; I lost track.

In the periods between clients I practise a few minutes of mindfulness so that I can be fully present with the next person. As Andrew talks I monitor my thoughts, feelings and physical sensations and become aware of a sense of pain and sadness. I know that 'blanking' can be a sign of stress or trauma, so I ask:

Therapist: I was just wondering what it is like for you to be here, talking to a complete stranger? (Inviting client to focus on here and now.)

Andrew: Oh, it's fine, I feel I have got to do this, but I am not very good with feelings. The counsellor thought it might be good for me to do some work on myself, but I don't know really. Maybe this is just how I am.

Andrew smiles and his face comes alive. I find this encouraging as it tells me something about the state of his depression; it suggests that there is some 'life' inside him.

He tells me more about himself, his family and problems he is having at work. I ask how he will help the therapy process, how he might (perhaps unwittingly) sabotage it and what we might both need to watch out for (checking self-awareness, openness, inviting client into relationship).

> Andrew: Oh, I really do want to do this, but I do find it hard. The relationship counsellor we saw a few years ago said that I'm very good at talking about stuff, but crap at expressing how I feel.

I say that we should both watch for that and tell each other when we notice it happening. I warm to Andrew and say that I would like to work with him. We make an appointment for the following week and I give him my contract, which explains that the therapy process is not always easy and can be painful at times. This is important, as not everyone understands what therapy entails. I ask him to read the contract at his leisure at home and say that we can go over it next time to make sure that it is clear.

Over the next few sessions I gradually learn more about Andrew. He remembers little from before the age of seven, but knows that he was eight weeks premature and in an incubator for several weeks. I produce a bowl containing stones of various shapes and sizes and ask him to choose one to represent him as a child and place it on the floor between us. Next I ask him to choose stones for the significant people in his life at the time and place them where it seems appropriate. Andrew chooses a small, grey stone for himself and places two slightly bigger stones side by side a little distance away, to represent his six-years-older brother and three-years-younger sister. For his parents he chooses two larger stones and places them on the other side. Then he picks up an irregularly shaped blue stone and places it between the two large stones and the small grey stone.

'That's my grandfather,' he says.

We sit back and look. I comment on the distances between the stones. He tells me that as a child he felt unimportant and in the shadow of his brother:

> Andrew: Mark was brilliant at sport, they are still going on about it.
> Therapist: You sound angry. (Here and now reflection.)

This seems to surprise him, but he says:

> Andrew: Not really, it's just how it is.

I decide to 'put this on the backburner' for now, as it is early days, and ask about his grandfather.

> Andrew: He was great; he used to take me fishing and tell me stories. He was also the only one who supported my going to university, now he's gone; he died when I was at university.

I am beginning to get a sense of Andrew as the middle child from a working-class family, squeezed between his siblings, and perhaps not getting much attention. His parents had a shop and were always busy. After school Andrew used to go to an aunt who lived nearby, but he did not like it there as she was very house proud and did not allow him to touch anything. His brother and sister left school at sixteen, but Andrew stayed on for 'A' levels and then went to university.

> Andrew: My dad thought this was a complete waste of time, he only agreed because my maths teacher said it would help me to get a good job. To my dad that means earning lots of money so that you can provide for your wife and children. I have got a good job, but he thinks I'm a failure as my brother earns a lot more than me. His wife does not work and they have three kids. Maybe they are right.

I sense a lot of sadness and say:

> Therapist: What's that like for you to have done so well, but for your family not to value it? (Empathy, reframe, inviting client to focus on feelings.)
> Andrew: Well, that's just how it is, isn't it; they're not going to change.
> Therapist: I am sorry that your family does not realise how well you have done, that feels really difficult. (Empathic reflection, I do not want to 'blame' or 'judge' the parents.)
> Andrew: (shrugs) Well, it's fine. What really bothers me at the moment is work.

Privately I note that Andrew appears to suppress his feelings without knowing that he is doing so; this defence has probably been there a long time and was developed for good reason. I sense that we will need to work slowly and trust that these defences will unravel gradually as our relationship develops. In other words, the work may well entail a parallel process between the development of the therapeutic relationship and Andrew's relationship with his internal world.

Andrew is a middle manager in a large IT company. The firm has not been doing well and Andrew has been told that he needs to let go of half his team.

> Andrew: That's when I started getting the panic attacks, I felt frightened and out of control.

Case Conceptualisation

Andrew was born prematurely and spent the first few weeks of his life in an incubator. This early trauma was exacerbated through his mother's inability to bond with him. Chronic lack of attunement and insufficient mirroring has left Andrew with deep wounds. His paternal grandfather loved him unconditionally and thus provided some of his needs for attunement, mirroring and idealisation (Kohut, 1977), which probably helped him to create an affable and competent persona (false self/authenticity), make friends and get married. However, gradually his wounds began to show in his relationship with Lucy. She became unhappy with his lack of communication and a few years ago they had relationship counselling. His current work situation is very stressful, he

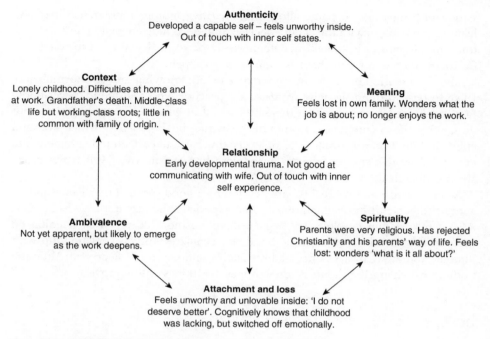

Authenticity
Developed a capable self – feels unworthy inside.
Out of touch with inner self states.

Context
Lonely childhood. Difficulties at home and
at work. Grandfather's death. Middle-class
life but working-class roots; little in
common with family of origin.

Meaning
Feels lost in own family. Wonders what the
job is about; no longer enjoys the work.

Relationship
Early developmental trauma. Not good at
communicating with wife. Out of touch with inner
self experience.

Ambivalence
Not yet apparent, but likely to emerge
as the work deepens.

Spirituality
Parents were very religious. Has rejected
Christianity and his parents' way of life. Feels
lost: wonders 'what is it all about?'

Attachment and loss
Feels unworthy and unlovable inside: 'I do not
deserve better'. Cognitively knows that childhood
was lacking, but switched off emotionally.

Figure 11   Conceptualisation of case study using Core Concepts

feels out of his depth and fears losing his job. Both issues are likely to trigger early feelings of worthlessness as well as anger, but at the moment he is not aware of this.

According to Orange et al. (1997: 70) the caregiver's sensitivity to the child or 'affect attunement' is crucial in the 'organisation of self experience'. To develop a healthy sense of self we need our caretakers to be attuned to us, in order to have the experience of reciprocity in the relationship. However, a consistent failure in mirroring, attunement and responsiveness (Kohut, 1971; Orange et al., 1997: 79), may result in an unconscious relational template according to which the child's needs and feelings are not important. This seems to be the case with Andrew and would explain his lack of communication with Lucy. He says he has tried talking with her, but that most of the time he is not aware of what he is feeling, and thinks that she wants something of him that he cannot give. Stolorow and Atwood (1992: 54) explain how trauma and the absence of an 'affect-integrating, containing and modulating intersubjective context' can cause a child to dissociate himself from intolerable painful affect. I think that this may well be the case for Andrew and wonder whether I am holding these feelings for him, particularly as during every session I am aware of severe emotional pain somewhere deep inside my chest.

As Andrew gets in touch with his inner experience he may become more depressed and find it hard to accept 'the reality of the loss' (Worden, 2009) both of his grandfather and of what he never had. Sometimes this leads clients to leave prematurely through a 'flight into health' (thank you so much, I feel so much better, etc.), or they may show their ambivalence through coming late, getting the time wrong or 'forgetting' to come altogether. Negative mother transference may also happen at this stage, with the client experiencing me as judgemental or 'just not getting him'. Ruptures in the alliance might easily occur, so I will need to watch out for them and try to repair them as soon as they happen.

There is a tension between the importance of 'not knowing' and case formulation. I like to bear in mind the wise words of a supervisor who told me to 'never know first and never know best'. I am therefore careful in what I share with Andrew, but do say that the circumstances around his premature birth may have had a profound effect on him. I have a strong sense of a very tiny baby all curled up in a huge white desert. I share this co-transferential image with him and he says, 'Well, it was probably just like that'.

As the months go on I feel we are developing a good therapeutic alliance and he appears to benefit from being listened to, an experience he may not have had before. As our relationship develops, we begin to explore more deeply what is going on between us. The closer therapeutic bond also facilitates Andrew's relationship with himself. Andrew is always punctual, likes talking and seems less depressed. Although nothing has changed at home Andrew hopes that things will improve.

Dreams

Dreams are an important part of relational integrative therapy. I usually ask Andrew what he thinks the dream is about, before getting him to associate to its various elements. I tell him that it does not matter if the meaning does not become clear, as the process of paying attention to what is going on in his internal world is in itself helpful (Bollas, 1995: 53–54). I also say that dreams provide useful metaphors that make it possible for us to talk about his inner processes. Initially Andrew has many dreams in which he is either not present at all, or only as an observer. He has trouble connecting to anything in the dreams, but says that there is something familiar about the feel of not being important enough to be part of the action. When we have been working together for thirteen months he has the following dream:

> I'm doing (or have done) a lot of work on an empty house even though I haven't bought it yet. Someone points out that despite all the work I'll still have to have a survey done. Then I'm with a lot of other people in a house that seems to be a community. I'm part of a small group that is arriving in this community. At one point I'm travelling towards it and I've taken a drug. I'm warning the people that I'm with that at some point I will start repeating things that I have heard during the first phase of the drug's action. After I arrive I am still slightly isolated from the rest of the community, in a kitchen (like the one at my parents' home). I have to deal with some bees, which I do by attracting them with a tray of melted chocolate. When I go to check next door (where some of the people are) the bees have embedded themselves very neatly in this chocolate. I want a drink from a bottle of whisky I have brought, but Lucy has put everything away and I have to

retrieve it from the back of a cupboard directly above the tray of bees, which makes me slightly nervous. An image of a bearded man called Gregori appears in the room, which it seems he is projecting from somewhere outside the house. Back in the kitchen is another tray with something like marshmallow. A group of maggots are making valleys through this tray but I am pleased to see that they are sticking together. I close the sliding plastic door to keep the bees in but Gregori arrives. I say that I just want to communicate and he shouts 'Moi aussi!!' so I let him in.

Therapist: What was the overall feeling of the dream?

Andrew: Being disconnected, on the outside, the action is somewhere else. People are having a good time somewhere else, but I'm not there.

Therapist: What do you make of the work on an empty house?

Andrew: I have a feeling of not really owning it yet. If it is to do with myself – I guess I have not yet come into my own.

Andrew then talks about the survey, which he sees as letting someone in 'to poke into the corners and find all the mouldy bits that aren't quite right'.

Therapist: What are you aware of as you hear yourself say that?

Andrew: There's probably still stuff around that I'm not comfortable revealing to anyone.

Together we reflect that this part of the dream feels like a comment on the therapy.

Andrew's associations to community are 'inward looking and not very integrated with the rest of society', which might refer to old relational templates. I wonder whether the new community is a reference to the work being done in therapy where the 'truth' may be spoken, insights may occur, but they are temporary and not yet integrated. Then action shifts to the kitchen, a place where food is transformed into something that can be taken in and digested, and where, Andrew says, 'everyone ends up at parties'. He says the kitchen at his parents' home is 'not very big and not very cosy, with hard chairs and a cement floor, not a place where you want so spend a lot of time'. This may point to an unconscious recognition that his internal world needs to be transformed and made more relational. I ask him to speak as if he is the swarm of bees and he says:

Andrew: We're quite far from our hive and it is night time now, so it is hard to get back, so we're going to hang out in this kitchen and there's this tray of sweet smelling chocolate laid out, so we go and investigate that. It's quite sticky, but it's nice.

Therapist: And they have 'embedded themselves very neatly'.

Andrew: Yes, bees are very organised.

I wonder whether the therapy feels like that, something that could be dangerous, that could sting – something that lasts beyond the session. I wonder whether there is an unconscious wish to put the bees (the therapy) out of action – but they do not die – and stay there. Later in the dream Andrew does not want to let them out, which suggests ambivalence: he does *and* does not want the 'news of difference' the therapy is providing.

Regarding Gregori, Andrew associates him with menace, but also wisdom and, because he speaks French, with good food and sophistication. After we have pondered on the dream for a while I ask Andrew what he makes of the dream now.

> Andrew: It all feels a bit ambivalent, I'm trying to join this community and at the same time I'm under the influence of this menacing figure. I'm in the kitchen, but the food seems to be wasted. And there is this dangerous character who can impart wisdom so I let him in, but it is all sort of non-committal.
>
> Therapist: Yes, and bees can sting, so they are a bit dangerous … and this dangerous character – you let him in, and you also take care to keep the bees in the kitchen. Overall there seems to be an openness to let in something new.

With hindsight it is clear that the dream marks a turning point in Andrew's therapy, it indicates that movement is beginning to happen in his internal world.

Co-transference

Andrew has been coming for eighteen months and is remembering more and more of his childhood. Now a divorce seems likely he fears that his father will regard him as even more of a failure. I say that we cannot undo the past; but together we can perhaps acknowledge it for what it was, the effect it had and make links to what is happening now (TIME). I hope that I can help him see how the future need not be predetermined by the past, although this will not be easy.

As human beings we constantly try to make sense of our experience, but can easily be fooled into creating the wrong meaning, particularly if the current creation is based on past experience. Intellectually Andrew knows that a divorce does not make him a failure and that it is not 'all his fault', but emotionally that is exactly what he believes. We spend quite some time 'deconstructing' that emotional meaning and decoupling his father's view of success from how Andrew feels about himself, but do not get very far.

One of the aims of the therapy is to help him create a new meaning that fits the now rather than the past and is therefore more appropriate and helpful. However, one day I feel that I am not working well, and wonder whether this is true or whether I am picking something up from Andrew (co-transference). Andrew talks about wanting to speak with his father, but says:

> Andrew: What's the point, he won't listen and will probably get angry. I want to do it but I probably won't.

I notice that as soon as he lets himself engage with doing something, the negative part comes in and says, 'No, what's the point. It has never worked in the past, why would it work now?' 'Yes', Andrew says, 'and that part is stronger'. When it is time to leave he says, 'It was hard today'. I feel that he has engaged well with the therapy and say, 'Yes, you have worked hard', but I wonder whether he believes it.

Afterwards I worry that he may feel the therapy is going nowhere and will ring me to say that he is not coming back. I realise that I am probably feeling what he is feeling, useless, not effective, unable to change things (ambivalent). I realise my feelings may be a result of negative transference, remind myself that I had been expecting this and discuss Andrew in supervision. This helps me feel more grounded and able to let Andrew's anger in, I am no longer afraid.

In the next session I say, 'I have been thinking about our last session, how was it for you?'

Andrew: Well it was good to talk about what is on my mind, but it did not change anything.
Therapist: You sound frustrated. (Here and now reflection, acknowledgement of his feelings, attempt at repair of rupture (Safran and Muran, 2000).)
Andrew: (raising voice) Of course I am bloody frustrated. I have been coming here for more than a year now and I feel no better.

I am taken aback, but also excited, as this is the first time that Andrew has expressed any frustration; he is always so pleasant and polite. I say:

You're angry – great! How does it feel? (Acknowledgement of his feelings; attempt at repair of rupture.)

Andrew looks at me in surprise, then bursts out laughing, 'This is like a comedy show, I am this client that is being really difficult and you say … do you know that sketch? … where whatever the client says the therapist answers with, 'Well, that is not surprising, of course you feel like murdering me, I have no time today though, would next Tuesday suit you?'

I laugh too as I know the sketch he is referring to. We talk some more about its content and what it might mean in terms of the therapeutic relationship. Andrew's creative use of the comedy sketch has enabled us to repair the connection between us; his reaction suggests that he is becoming more 'alive', and at the same time holding himself more lightly. I decide to introduce Andrew to the technique of focusing, to help him gain access to his inner felt sense (Gendlin, 1979).

Therapist: Are you up for trying something a bit different?
Andrew: Sure.
Therapist: Ok, close your eyes and take a few slow, deep breaths. Just relax and see if you can get a sense of how you are feeling inside.

Initially Andrew does not understand what I mean, but then says that he feels pressure in his stomach.

Therapist:	A sense of pressure, if you could see it, what would it look like?
Andrew:	Ehm, this is weird … but it feels like a small furry creature, it is inside me, all rolled up in a ball.
Therapist:	A small furry creature, rolled up in a ball … see if you can stay with that … just focus on it.
Andrew:	I feel constricted here (moves his hands over the solar plexus) as if I cannot breathe properly.
Therapist:	A sense of constriction … see if you can just stay with that … without doing anything.
Andrew:	Actually, it seems to come out of its ball, I can breathe a bit more (takes a deep breath).

The constriction suggests a lack of connection between head and heart. Andrew often says that 'there must be something fundamentally wrong with me or they would love me more' – even though rationally he understands that this is not true. It did not feel appropriate to me to try focusing earlier in the therapy, as I was afraid that the lack of eye contact might cause him to feel rejected (this can happen with clients who have a history of feeling neglected or abandoned). When the relationship is strong enough focusing can be a powerful tool to help people get in touch with their inner experience and express what they are feeling. Through it Andrew is gradually able to become more integrated with his sense of self. As he gets more in touch with his own inner world, more memories surface and I feel less sadness and pain. This illustrates the intersubjective and contextual nature of our experience: I have been holding his pain for him, but when he is able to feel it (take it back) there is no longer a need for me to do so.

From an existentialist point of view we create our own meaning, even though we may not be consciously aware that we have done so. However, this does mean that we are free to create a new meaning, although that can be hard. For Andrew, that meaning is bound up with who he feels himself to be: 'I am a failure, it is all my fault, if only I had … etc.'. Such negative thinking makes the neural pathways involved stronger and stronger. For clients like Andrew it does not really work to argue with this meaning or to disprove it by looking for contradictory evidence. Mindfulness, however, can create a distance between the person and his thoughts, so that he can begin to dis-identify himself from the thoughts, develop self-compassion and create a new meaning. Because of Andrew's positive engagement with focusing, itself a meditative technique, I decide to introduce Andrew to mindfulness. For a few weeks we practise it in the session. When Andrew agrees to practise at home, I give him a CD with instructions. Initially he finds it difficult, but one day he tells me that he has started to attend weekly meditations at a local centre.

Andrew:	Having those people around me feels supportive, quite different to doing it by myself. I like the discussion we have afterwards, it is good to realise that many of us are having the same difficulties – our minds wander, we bring it back, etc.

Andrew finds it particularly helpful to see his experience as a constant flow or river, the river of experience – to watch his thoughts as 'leaves on a river', they come and go continuously. The river is always there, but it is continuously changing. As the ancient Greek philosopher Heraclites said: 'You cannot step into the same river twice for other waters are continually flowing in'. Andrew learns to observe his thoughts with equanimity and when the rumination starts to say to himself – 'Oh there I go again' – eventually without further engagement with it.

A few years into the therapy Andrew realises that it is possible to be happy. This is a revelation. A few months after his divorce, during an evening with friends, he suddenly realised, 'I am happy'. During the three and a half years that Andrew and I worked together he made tremendous changes. His dreams had changed in that he takes a much more active role in them.

Mearns and Cooper (2005: 6) talk about therapy as a cauldron. This is not unlike the Jungian concept of therapy as an alchemical vessel within which lead can be turned into gold. In other words, our difficult experiences can be transformed and used by us to become more aware of who we are.

After four years Andrew reports feeling more solid and more in touch with himself. His relationships have improved too. Whereas before he had found it hard to connect with people he now has a circle of friends he sees regularly. He accepts an offer of a job with another company, which involves moving to another part of the country. Two years later he sends me a letter in which he tells me that he has remarried. He encloses a photo of his newly born baby.

New life can only be created when there is true intercourse between people.

For me the birth of this child symbolises the integration that has happened within Andrew, and the new meaning he has created.

WORKING BRIEFLY WITHIN THE RIM

History of Brief Therapies

It was widely believed in the field of psychotherapy up until the 1950s that profound change was only possible through the process of extensive and long-term therapy. Milton Erickson, a well-known psychiatrist at this time, was renowned for successfully working with clients in relatively short time spans. His creative genius inspired many therapists at the time and his ideas and methods had a huge influence on the developing field of brief therapy. Don Jackson, a student of Erickson, a psychiatrist and associate of Gregory Bateson, set up the Massachusetts Research Institute in 1958 and joined by Haley Weakland, Satir, and Watzlawick began to develop what was at the time believed to be a heretical approach. They abandoned the idea that rapid change in therapy is necessarily a superficial flight into health and worked on the premise that significant change did not necessarily take a long time, it could be sudden and profound. Their approach was different from other brief therapeutic work (mostly behavioural approaches), which they found were often seen to be a stop gap or second best option. The MRI group took an interactional view (see chapter 3) focusing on patterns of communication and the definition of relationship between therapist and client. Many aspects of this approach are consistent with the RIM, e.g. the focus on patterns of communication, although the MRI group were less interested in theories of growth, understanding or insight and more interested in how change takes place and what happens in therapeutic conversations.

Nowadays working briefly is generally understood to mean between three and twenty sessions, although one session models of therapy also exist. Long-term brief work favoured by systemic therapists implies relatively few sessions (up to ten) over a period of perhaps a year (as opposed to ten weeks of weekly sessions). Cognitive therapists tend to see clients weekly for between eight and twenty sessions on average.

Cade and O'Hanlon (1993) challenge therapists with the suggestion that we do clients a disservice if we do not attempt to provide therapeutic conditions that bring about change in the shortest possible time. As mentioned previously, clients come to therapy ostensibly looking for change in some aspect of their life and sometimes they want to know why things have happened as they have. This orientation to the past, to search for an answer to the question why, is a search that is not always guaranteed to bring about change. One of the assumptions of brief therapy is that understanding the underlying cause of a problem is not *always* important or useful in helping to solve it. Within the RIM we have an integration of three approaches that are described in our model as overlapping circles (see chapter 2). When working briefly within the RIM our focus will lean towards problem solving and finding solutions and strategies that alleviate symptoms of distress and promote change (see case study below). Therefore it is likely that our orientation will be more towards the cognitive aspects of the RIM (including mindfulness-based strategies), which offer tools and interventions consistent with these goals.

It can be useful to regard problems as being inappropriate attempted solutions to difficulties. An example might be that of using substances to alleviate emotional pain. The substance use then becomes a problem, although originally it was an attempted solution to a difficulty (the emotional pain, grief, etc.). Beck suggests that discussions with a client about concepts within their conscious awareness can bring about change quickly, as clients are able to work collaboratively with the therapist and engage with case conceptualisation, formulations or hypotheses that can be tested and worked with experimentally between sessions (Beck, 1976 in Weishaar, 1993: 85). Beck regards the work between sessions as crucial, whereas other brief therapy models do not subscribe to homework as imperative in quite the same way.

When working briefly whatever the chosen model and certainly within the RIM, it is important early on in the therapy to establish what the client's goals are and then move towards establishing how to achieve them. One important consideration is the idea that motivation is a product of interaction and relationship and does not exist as a personality trait within the client. It is the therapist's job to elicit motivation in the client towards achieving their goals. How the therapist acts can hinder or enhance motivation and induce or reduce resistance to change. Attachment to the status quo and ambivalence to change are part of the context of working towards goals. Client factors constitute the largest contributor to therapy outcome (Cooper, 2009), therefore it is essential to engage the client's participation and involvement early on, in both brief and long-term work. O'Hanlon (1999) also encourages therapists to enlist the client's hopefulness as much as possible and, along with Miller and Rollnick (2002), suggests that evoking a sense of competence in clients will enhance motivation, self-esteem and build an expectation that change is possible.

When working briefly within the RIM the focus is on the meaning attributed to behaviour or symptoms. Therapists need to learn clients' language and utilise this rather than first teaching them their language and then trying to convince them to change. One way of doing this is by using reframing, which according to Watzlawick et al. 'changes the conceptual and or/emotional setting or viewpoint in relation to which a situation is experienced and places it in another frame. This new frame needs to fit the facts of the same concrete situation equally well or even better and thereby changes its entire meaning' (Watzlawick et al., 1974: 95).

Key Principles of a Brief Approach in Therapy

- The therapist is responsible for providing the context for change.
- Align yourself with your own experience of the client's reality: how does this feel, what is the rhythm and the pace, what are the client's metaphors, what are their unique skills and assets?
- Utilise the person's reality and all their responses. Accept that all their responses are adequate and attempts to cooperate with you.
- Open up choice, never take choice away.
- Recognise the client's competence and resourcefulness and orient the client towards their own goals through that competence and resourcefulness.

Skills

Working in collaboration with the client:

1. Clearly define the problem in concrete terms.
2. Ascertain what solutions have been attempted so far.
3. Clearly define concrete change to be achieved.
4. Formulate a plan to produce change.

Tasks may include:

- To check out motivation for change and explore attachment to the status quo and ambivalence about change.
- To work with barriers to change including low self-esteem.
- Double description: the therapist builds on the client's own views introducing new ideas that create new descriptions and news of difference, this includes using reframing and normalising.

Hayes et al. (1999) posit the idea of cognitive fusion that is the relationship that develops between internal experience and its interpretation. This is underpinned by learned associations between experiences[10] (Hayes et al., 2001), habitual ways of responding to a trigger based on the way we process information, which then leads to experiential avoidance; self-harming behaviour falls under this category of experiential avoidance.

ANNE

Anne refers herself to her employee assistance programme following a conversation at work with her manager. Her manager tells her that a client was unhappy with her management of their account. This turn of events has shocked her profoundly and shaken her sense of herself as she has struggled to understand why the client is dissatisfied. She believes that her manager no longer values or respects her work. She is a perfectionist, has always been well liked and prides herself on doing a good job. She now believes that she cannot trust her own judgement while her own mistrust of others has increased. She has had a couple of episodes at work when she felt that she was unable to breathe and has been frequently hyperventilating. The sense of panic she has experienced is new and frightening to her. I wonder why Anne has felt so threatened by this event and also speculate that her symptoms of anxiety are a result of her threat system being activated (Gilbert, 2009b) (see earlier in this chapter).

Initially I explore with Anne how this episode with her manager has affected her in the present. Anne tells me that she takes great pains to hide from others her experience of anxiety and distress, with the consequence that she feels more alone and isolated. This strategy may be a learnt response, i.e. to withdraw in situations of high arousal, conflict or challenge.[11]

She also describes being more tearful since this incident and feeling unable to focus and get on top of things the way she usually does. I ask Anne what she wishes to accomplish in the hour we have together and she says that she would like to feel normal again. As I don't understand quite what she means yet I ask her to describe how she would know that this had happened. Cecchin (1999) suggests that it is useful to 'not understand too quickly'. This avoids the obvious dangers of the therapist jumping to conclusions or 'knowing' the cause or cure of the client's difficulties. She replies that she wants the anxiety to stop and for her self-confidence to return. The goals for therapy have started to become more clearly defined. At this point I can ask her what she has already tried to do to achieve these goals, thus establishing what

---

[10]Hayes et al. (1999) formulated relational frame theory (RFT) in which they suggest that language and cognition are built through a process of networks of associations or relationship (that are derived from learnt associations). This theory underpins acceptance and commitment therapy and a contemplative cognitive approach.

[11]See chapter 2 on neuroscience and attachment.

strategies she has attempted and beginning to gain an understanding of the potential barriers to her accomplishing her goals.

Therapist: Who has noticed these differences in you? (This question serves to broaden out the context and find out a little more about the social and support network but also relational patterns of closeness and distance in Anne's life.)

Anne: Well my boyfriend – he says that I am argumentative and tetchy with him ... which is true.

Therapist: What sort of things have you argued about? (Explorative question tentatively looking for themes and also greater understanding of relational patterns in Anne's life.)

Anne: Well, the other day he was home late from work and I bit his head off.

Therapist: You sound surprised by your reaction. Is this out of character for you?

Anne: Yes! I think I am getting paranoid, I wondered where he was, all sorts of things went through my mind – but I have no reason to think that way and I'm not normally like that.

Therapist: So this is not like you would normally respond if he were late. What are your own thoughts about how your reaction to your boyfriend connects or not to what happened at work?

Anne: I think I have just become more suspicious of other people's motives and less trusting. I think the worst of others.

Mansell suggests that 'the most effective method of engaging with a client and facilitating change is to help them to become aware of their conscious experience of meaning-making' (2008: 19).

Therapist: Was there another time when you remember thinking the worst of others?

Here the therapist explores the territory of the past to see if there are any associations between other episodes or past relationships that may be influencing her responses in the present. Past experience might then furnish us with information about beliefs and interpretations that may be applied in this situation, as well as providing a context for Anne's experience in this situation in her life now.

At this point Anne reveals that she had been bullied at school and had not ever confided in anyone about it. I explore with Anne the feelings and sensations she remembers having had as a child when she was bullied. She remarks how the hyperventilation and some other sensations she experiences now are similar to those she experienced as a child.

Therapist: What did you do to cope with the bullying? (Eliciting news of competence.)

Anne: I kept my head down and tried to keep invisible and avoid being in the firing line of the bullies. It worked some of the time.

As the story of the past unfolds we make connections and associations with Anne's experience in the present. I notice how she had been successful in finding a strategy that worked at least some of the time to ward off the bullies. I am introducing a suggestion of Anne's competence in a story in which she hitherto has felt only a victim. We discuss what the resources were that gave her that ability to remain invisible (it was most important not to reveal any anxiety or distress in front of the bullies because this would only make matters worse). This partially reframes the story of Anne's experience of bullying from one in which she was wholly the victim, to one in which she had managed to survive by developing and utilising some skills to keep the bullies at bay. This then becomes a narrative that tells of her strength, competence and accomplishment in the face of adversity, which we can draw on at other times in the therapy.

What Stories Diminish Us?

There are different views about whether the intention in therapy is to change the story, search for a new story or to co-construct a slightly different take on the old story (White, 1995). What we are not working towards is a 'master narrative'; in other words we do not have the idea that there is a 'better' story or a 'right' story but we are working towards a story that is good enough. A client tells a story of how he had believed for many years that through his mother's abandonment at a young age, he had been deprived of a nurturing maternal love. His difficult relationship with his adoptive mother was built within this frame, one of rejection, and he consequently interpreted his mother's behaviour towards him as hostile rather than caring. When he eventually searched for and met his biological mother as an adult he went through a process of re-evaluating his childhood experience. He had always felt a sense of lack of self-worth, the source of which was his core belief, 'I am not worth anything if my own mother abandons me', and yet when he reflected on his experience with the new lens a different narrative emerged. He engaged in conversations with his adoptive mother, in which they were able to discuss how he had felt and from these conversations could acknowledge that his mother's discipline and behaviours towards him were motivated by caring and love.

At this point I have a choice whether to explore with Anne the episode of the conversation with her manager or the episode of panic and anxiety. I explore with her feelings and thoughts that are associated with the onset of panic. Often for clients (as well as for therapists!) thoughts constitute reality; if they are negative such as those Anne starts to have, then this will have a powerful effect on experience and will feed into the sympathetic and parasympathetic nervous systems or the threat system as conceptualised by Gilbert (2009b).

We explore Anne's thoughts in relation to the episode that she's experienced with her manager.

Anne: I think to myself, 'I must be this incompetent person that they say I am' and 'Where there's smoke there must be fire'. I start to doubt myself and I tell myself that I am useless.

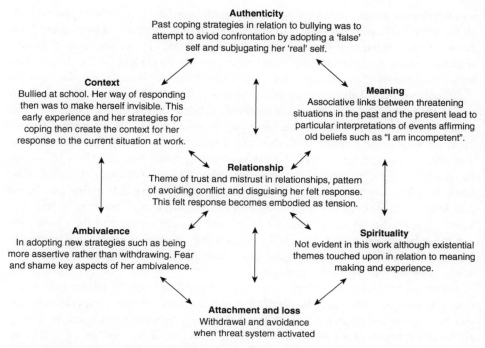

Figure 12   Conceptualisation of case study using Core Concepts

Anne has identified the content of her conversation with her manager as 'fact' and interpreted it as meaning that she is a certain kind of person. This interpretation has undermined her sense of self. It is also connected to a deeply held belief, stemming from her experience of being bullied as a child, that she must be incompetent and useless as the perpetrators said she was. She fears being judged by others who may, in her opinion, believe she really is incompetent, and so she avoids contact with co-workers, thereby also cutting herself off from potential support. It is important for me to create a safe environment so that Anne feels that I can hold the emotional content of what she is bringing. She needs to experience that I am not judgemental of her and I can model acceptance.[12] As Horgan quoted by Baur suggests:

> to be understood deeply and intelligently and to be treasured is a combination that deflects the course of any life. The rest is stuff. (1991: 87)

As she talks about events I see Anne's body posture changing, tightening up and her shoulders hunching. I decide to explore the meaning of this body posture with her, using a modified version of focusing (Gendlin, 1979). Focusing enables the client to tune into their embodied experience in the here and now in order to see what the 'felt sense' may bring in terms of understanding and meaning. In this way we are

---

[12]See chapter 4 on therapeutic relationship.

also developing a meta-perspective, in other words 'promoting active self- observation' (Ryle 1990: 200), which is similar to mindful awareness. I begin by noticing out loud how her posture has changed and asking her if she would be willing to describe the sensations she is experiencing at the moment. I ask her to expand on this description, giving me words that are associated with the sensation. She uses the descriptions tight, knotted, hard ball in the pit of her stomach. I invite her to describe what the ball is expressing and she says fear. I follow this theme of fear through by exploring with her where she thinks the fear is coming from, what it is that she is most frightened of? I ask if she can stay with the sensation and see if she can feel behind it for any other sensation; what does she notice about it now? She describes the edges having become fuzzier, softer; it doesn't feel quite so hard. I wonder if she can take her breath into the area of hardness and fear without judging it, bringing gentleness and kindness to the area. I notice Anne's face relaxing as she breathes in and out. Gently I invite her to expand her focus to the rest of her body and then back into the room before opening her eyes. She reports that the sensation changed when she brought the breath to the area. She is quiet and reflective for a moment and I leave some space for this awareness to settle.

We try and increase the effectiveness of one hour of therapy by setting tasks to do between sessions. These may be observational tasks or behavioural experiments that can be designed to change a pattern that has become entrenched. Crucial in setting such tasks is to construct them collaboratively with the client: they are offered in an invitational way as experiments from which the client may learn or discover something different or new. The therapist sets up the task in such a way that if the client does not do it, it is not framed as a failure or resistance, but rather is a source for exploration and may mean that the therapist has offered the 'wrong' task. I invite Anne to notice when she is tensing her shoulders or body during the coming week and to see if she can experiment with bringing her awareness to the area in her body where she feels the tension most, without judging it or trying to push it away. I also suggest that she may want to try using the breath in the way we have just experimented with. In the second session she reports that this has been helpful, that she has been able to stay with the tension and that it has altered and reduced when she brings the breath to the area. I offer her an exercise to practice called the three-minute breathing space, which she can try as often as she likes during the day. The intention is to take a pause in the business of 'doing' mode of mind to go into what Segal et al. (2002) call 'being' mode of mind. The exercise invites the client to use the breath as an anchor, bringing the focus and attention into the present moment.

We can construct goals or tasks collaboratively by asking the client what they wish to achieve:

> If you were to imagine our conversation in a week's time, what would you like realistically to be saying about what may have changed by then? How feasible do you think this is or how confident do you feel that this will have happened?

Enabling the client to choose and define goals in this hypothetical way makes it more likely that they will feel able to do the task or achieve the goals that have been jointly constructed and agreed upon in the session. A non-judgemental and curious stance about the choices the client is saying they would like to make is important. Anne agrees to try out the breathing space exercise and expresses confidence she can give it a go.

It is important to hear the relevant account. By this we mean checking out that we are discussing the themes that seem most pertinent to the client. When we do this we are bearing witness to and acknowledging the influence of the past. 'How come you are sitting here given what you have told me about your history?' Implicit in this question is the therapist's acknowledgement of the client's resilience. Anne may hear this reflection of herself in my eyes and be able to acknowledge or re-engage with a different aspect of herself hitherto hidden or unacknowledged.

In the third session Anne is more upbeat.

Anne: I felt different after we had spoken – somehow I didn't feel quite so much that I had failed or done something wrong.
Therapist: What did you notice about how this difference in attitude affected you?

I ask Anne to elaborate and to be more specific about how these changes had manifested. In this way we may optimise the possibility for learning and reinforce positive gains or changes.

Anne: I didn't feel so stressed out. And a few times when I did feel anxious or started to get upset I tried the three-minute breathing space and that seemed to help.

Here the client is articulating in more detail what she has done that has made a difference and it is then possible for the therapist to refer back to these successful strategies in other sessions.

In the third and fourth session I help Anne to explore and 'unpack' the conversation that she had with her manager. She remembers feeling an embodied sense of fear and shame the minute her manager talked of the client's complaint. She recognises this as a familiar pattern of responding whenever she feels criticised or judged by others. She immediately made an assumption that she was under threat, but also that there must be some truth in the complaint. As we talk this through we begin to draw a map (or conceptualisation) of how Anne has come to think and feel the way she does and we weave through the map the threads of relationship, beliefs and meanings past and present that have contributed to Anne's current experience. This part of the therapy entails a renegotiation of the possible meanings of the events that have taken place and involves an exploration of the themes of shame and fear, as well as of resilience and use of skilful behaviours in relation to both the present and past. We are exploring the possibilities of other more compelling, persuasive or powerful explanations or descriptions (rather than seeking one true version) that may be more life enhancing and enabling.

In the fifth session Anne reflects and revisits other situations in her adult life where she has withdrawn from confrontation with others in order to protect herself. We spend some time evaluating this strategy and its consequences for her.

Anne: I remember a colleague saying that I had missed a meeting that I was supposed to go to. She hadn't told me about it but I found it hard to say this to her. I felt guilty even though I hadn't known about the meeting.

Therapist: What stopped you from saying you hadn't known?
Anne: I didn't want to challenge her. She would think I was lying.

I have a choice here to explore her fear of not being believed or to explore alternative ways of responding in the future.

First choice response:

Therapist: You were worried that she might not believe you.

O'Hanlon (1999) suggests that we can acknowledge what the client has said while inviting a slightly new perspective by reflecting the client's experience that they have described as truth to one of perception: 'she would think I was lying' changes to 'I would worry that she would think I was lying'. He calls this 'Carl Rogers with a twist'.

Therapist: If she did not believe you, what would that be like for you? (This question starts to deconstruct the episode and the way the client might interpret responses from her colleague.)

Alternative views may emerge about the consequences of not being believed or of the likelihood that her colleague would not believe her. One could explore whether there are any links with occasions in the past when Anne hasn't been believed.

Second choice response:

Therapist: Imagine that I was your colleague and had just said this to you? How would you like to have dealt with it differently? What would you say to me?

Rehearsal, role play and problem solving can be useful techniques to empower the client to respond differently in the future (Sanders and Wills, 2005; Young et al., 2006) to find new coping strategies and methods of acting that are generative rather than diminishing of self-esteem.

Anne tries out a number of more assertive responses in which she is able to express herself more openly, 'I'm sorry that I missed the meeting, it sounds important. Unfortunately I wasn't aware that it was being held. Could you let me know what I missed?' She feels satisfied that this response fits more with how she wishes to be and act, as she is not holding back because of her fears. We explore how confident she is that she could try speaking to her manager again about the client's complaint using a more assertive response.

Alternatively I could have helped Anne to look at the fear of relating openly and genuinely towards others – using imagery to guide through an imaginary conversation a) with her bullies now she is an adult and b) in a replay of a different conversation with her manager.

Anne reports in her final session that she has had another conversation with her manager that has allayed some of her fears. She was able to express her opinion without feeling panicky or being confrontational and felt that the outcome of the meeting was good. She keeps using her mindfulness practices and feels this is helping her to become more even handed in her responses to situations. She has had no further episodes of hyperventilation.

Using the metaphor of a chest of drawers, sometimes it is enough to sort out the drawers that are particularly full, messy or over flowing (Seligman, personal communication). Not all the drawers necessarily need to be sorted at once. Sometimes it is useful for people to come for a short period of therapy to sort some things out, or organise and tweak their thinking. This can have a profound effect and like a stone in a pond the ripples of change can be far reaching. Other times, as described above, longer-term therapy is more appropriate and useful.

SUMMARY

This chapter shows how the techniques and interventions fit within the RIM's approach and method.

The case studies illustrate how the techniques of the RIM can be adapted and applied to working therapeutically with a wide range of difficulties that clients bring. The case examples in the second part of the chapter illustrate the different use of techniques within brief and open-ended therapy. They also show how the pace of therapy will influence our choice of intervention, thus providing both opportunities and constraints. Sometimes brief work can help client and therapist to choose and maintain a focus, making the work challenging but also effective. The pace of long-term work offers a different quality of experience and emphasis. Its open-ended nature makes it possible to explore deeply the client's experience at a relational level. It also offers the possibility for the therapeutic relationship to provide a reparative experience, with the therapist as a new positive attachment figure in the client's life. The possible constraints or risks are those of creating dependence in the client and of the therapy losing power and focus. Which therapy can be offered is largely dictated nowadays by the context in which we work. Agencies with budgets frequently require therapists to work within a time limited framework, whereas those therapists in private practice can choose to work long-term with their clients. The skilful use of appropriate techniques and interventions, however, can influence the effectiveness of the work undertaken, whether with a given class of difficulty or with brief or long-term therapy.

In the final chapter we discuss professional issues and their relevance to practice within the relational integrative model. While professional issues such as supervision cut across modalities, how we think about and practise research, ethics and personal development will be influenced by the approach, method and technique of our particular orientation.

QUESTIONS FOR FURTHER REFLECTION AND DISCUSSION

- What are your own views on brief and open-ended therapy?
- How does this affect your choice of intervention or therapeutic style?

FURTHER READING

Cade, B. and O'Hanlon, W. H. (1993) *A Brief Guide to Brief Therapy.* New York: W. W. Norton.

Cecchin, G. (1992) 'Constructing therapeutic possibilities', in McNamee, S. and Gergen, K. (eds) (1992) *Therapy as Social Construction.* London: Sage. pp. 86–95.

Lewis, G. (2002) *Sunbathing in the Rain.* London: Flamingo.

Rothschild, B. with Rand, M. (2006) *Help for the Helper: Self-care Strategies for Managing Burnout and Stress.* New York: W. W. Norton.

Rothschild, B. (2000) *The Body Remembers: The Psychophysiology of Trauma and Trauma Treatment.* New York: W. W. Norton.

Segal, Z. V., Williams, J. M. G. and Teasdale, J. D. (2002) *Mindfulness-based Cognitive Therapy for Depression: A New Approach to Preventing Relapse.* New York: The Guilford Press.

5

Professional Issues

In this chapter we discuss a number of professional issues that we see as inter-related: ethics, evaluation, the role of research, supervision and personal development.

ETHICS

Definitions

The *Collins English Dictionary* defines ethics as:

1 The philosophical study of the moral value of human conduct and of the rules and principles that ought to govern it.
2 A code of behaviour considered correct, particularly that of a given group, profession or individual.
3 The moral fitness of a course of action.

So ethics is to do with being *moral*, which in turn is defined as:

1 Concerned with or relating to human behaviour, especially the distinction between good and bad.
2 Adhering to conventionally accepted standards of conduct.
3 Principles of behaviour in accordance with standards of right and wrong.

The word 'ought' in the first definition of ethics suggests something fairly rigid or absolute: 'You ought to do such and such', implies that it is the right thing to do and that not to do so would be bad or foolish. The other definitions suggest a more relative view; that what is right or wrong may be a matter of discussion and agreement. This is indeed the case with generally agreed codes or standards of practice, principles or behaviour.

Sometimes the subject of ethics is seen as only relevant when there is a problem. From a relational perspective this is erroneous as everything we do has the potential of impacting on the wellbeing of others. This means that ethical decision making is part and parcel of every therapist's daily working life. Working ethically then implies a commitment to high standards as well as regular reflection, supervision, evaluation and personal and professional development. In order to be ethical practitioners whose practice is congruent with our values, we need to look at the way we work, in the same way that we expect our clients to be open to self-exploration and self-awareness. So this implies regular evaluation and supervision as well as appropriate research and ongoing personal and professional development.

Rule-based Approaches

Historically ethical codes within counselling and psychotherapy were prescriptive, consisting of a list of dos and don'ts. An advantage of such rule-based codes is that it eliminates uncertainty; in case of an ethical dilemma, for example, the practitioner only needs to consult the list to check what action is required. There are, however, a number of disadvantages as set out in the box below:

Disadvantages of Rule-based Ethics

- No matter how many rules are made, it is impossible to cover all eventualities.
- Inflexibility: a 'one size fits all' approach that fails to take into account the context of a situation.
- Developed by professionals rather than clients, therefore tend to 'privilege professional truth' (Coale, 1998: 6) and professional power.
- Rules may appear to protect practitioners rather than clients.
- Tendency to be 'ethnocentric' (Coale, 1998: 8) – based on unexamined cultural, social or theoretical assumptions.
- Codes can become overlong and therefore impractical.
- Having to rely on rules made by others discourages thinking, reflection and responsibility on the part of the individual practitioner.

According to the French philosopher Foucault[1] a collection of rules does not enable the individual to engage in ethical practice as the essential condition for that is the freedom and ability to choose one action over another.

Principle-based Approaches

During the second half of the last century society has become less hierarchical and paternalistic. Also the psychological professions are increasingly seen as professions in their own right, which means that individual practitioners are seen as professional

---

[1]www.michel-foucault.com/concepts/index.html (accessed 9 May 2010).

people, who are accountable for their actions.[2] A rule-based, paternalistic approach to ethics is therefore no longer appropriate, which has prompted several organisations such as the BACP[3] and the British Psychological Society to adopt professional codes based on ethical principles. The UKCP,[4] which presently functions as an umbrella organisation of therapy training and accrediting organisations, also requires its member organisations to publish a principle-based code of ethics.

Ethical Principles

Beneficence:	do good.
Non-maleficence:	do not cause harm.
Justice:	treat everyone equally and fairly.
Autonomy:	honour people's right to make their own decisions.
Fidelity:	professionals honour the trust placed in them.

(Beauchamp and Childress, 2001)

An advantage of principle-based approaches is that it allows individual practitioners to take responsibility for their own ethical decision making. This does, however, go at the expense of certainty. We can no longer say, 'What does the BACP say we should do in this case?' or, 'What is the BPS's stance on this kind of situation?' Principle-based ethics assume that it is possible to start from first principles, which can then be used to make decisions in the particular. Although ethical principles offer guidance to aid our reflections, they do not in themselves provide any answers. Professional codes based on ethical principles require practitioners to develop a reflective attitude, to be able to sit with uncertainty and to tolerate not knowing whether the decision made is 'the right' one, as it is often hard to be sure what 'the right thing' might be. The latter particularly applies to ethical dilemmas where there is a conflict between two or more ethical principles.

Problems that may Arise with a Principle-based Approach

Can Non-maleficence be Guaranteed?
Therapy should clearly not cause harm. And yet, therapy is a risky endeavour; despite our best intentions, we cannot guarantee that someone is not going to be hurt by us. For change to happen we need to help clients 'be with' their experience, which may involve working at the edge of what they are aware of (Mearns and Cooper, 2005).

---

[2]The issue of state or statutory regulation and its possible effects falls outside the remit for this book. It is our hope that practitioners will continue to practise as professionals in their own right, which includes the making of sometimes difficult ethical decisions.

[3]British Association for Counselling and Psychotherapy.

[4]United Kingdom Council for Psychotherapy.

We have no means of knowing what lies beyond that edge, other than our own relational experience with the client to guide us.

Negative Transference or Bad Practice?

Mearns and Cooper (2005) say that during moments of relational depth there is no transference. But can we categorically say that? Given their idea that we are all a multiplicity of selves or self-states, which aspect of self-experience of the client (and the therapist) is doing the relating? Unless we are totally aware in the moment (and other than the enlightened beings among us, most of us do not manage that very often), we experience our world through the vehicle of who we are and that includes all our experiences to date – another way of saying that is 'through transference'. To illustrate this point we offer a personal experience of negative transference one of us had from which she has learnt a great deal.

> During my psychotherapy training I had a lengthy Jungian analysis, one year of which I spent on the couch. Whereas before I had engaged in twice weekly face-to-face therapy, I decided that I would like the experience of the couch. My therapist said, 'Fine, but I only use the couch for people who come three times a week'. So for an entire year I spent three hours a week on the couch, during which time I developed a profound negative transference; only I did not realise it was transference, for me it was real. Whereas before that year we'd had a very good therapeutic alliance and I had felt met by my therapist at relational depth, during that year I felt that she was 'just not getting me'. Curiously though, the negative transference evaporated like mist once we went back to sitting face-to-face; in fact I had trouble remembering exactly what it had been about. All I know is that I felt abandoned and that I experienced my therapist as no longer having any idea as to what was going on for me.

This is only one example of negative transference, but imagine what might have happened if I had decided that the therapist was not working professionally and blamed her for the feelings of abandonment. Would the therapist be held accountable by whichever regulatory body she is accountable to? Would she be seen as having harmed me? In reality the experience provided us with lots of food for thought and reflection. I gained useful insights about myself that I might not have been able to access in any other way. However, I was a therapist in training and therefore deeply committed to understanding my own processes. Leaving the therapy was not an option as that would have been hugely disruptive, might have been frowned upon by the training organisation and would in any case have been a denial of what was really going on inside me. It all provided grist to the mill of my personal development.

   This personal experience shows that clients do not necessarily know when they are in the grip of a negative transference, as the experience feels real! It makes sense in terms of what we now know about early development; it seems that eye contact is crucial. At the same time this was a uniquely personal experience; other people may enjoy lying on the couch. It is therefore impossible to have hard and fast rules regarding how to work! What is good for one client may not be good for another.

What might 'seem' an infringement of the principle of non-maleficence for one person, may be an example of true beneficence for another! For us this example validates the desirability of a relational stance, which includes active exploration by client and therapist of what is happening in the space between them.

Practice is Messy

The psychological professions have moved away from a rule-based ethic, but reflection on principles may not provide the answer either. Principles sound neat and clear, but reality is not clear. As the above example shows, it is often messy, which makes it difficult to know what constitutes 'good' or 'harm' in any given situation.

Conflicting Principles

Another problem arises when two principles are in conflict. Do no harm is generally accepted as the overriding factor – but harm to whom? Most people might say 'the client of course', but would you still say this if this might mean you losing your job and you are the only breadwinner in your household? Say you have a suicidal client who does not want his GP or anyone else to be informed. He says that you are the only person that understands what he is going through and you know that the therapeutic relationship would be irreparably harmed if you betrayed confidentiality. What's more, you feel that in that case he would have lost confidence in the ability of anyone to help him. So one day he is so down that you feel that he is very likely to commit suicide and that unless you do something you may not see him again. You discuss this with your client, but he refuses to go to his GP and does not give you permission to contact the GP or anyone else. You ring your supervisor who is adamant that you must involve the GP, so that she can alert emergency services, and says that if you do not you are going against the principle of non-maleficence. Who is right?

Our aim here is not to give a perfect answer, but to point out the problems involved in a principle-based ethic. Even if we use a tool to help us, such as the framework suggested by Bond (2000), the problems as outlined above still apply. Also, in practice a principle-based ethic may only be used when there is a clear ethical dilemma. However, ethics also involves the nuts and bolts of everyday practice. Yet it is here that practitioners are often guided by many unexamined rules, which may depend on theoretical orientation. Examples include the issue of whether or not it is permissible to touch a client, ask a question, meet a client outside the consulting room, self-disclose, etc., all of which are to do with context. As we will see below, recent approaches to ethics bring a more nuanced approach that takes both the client–therapist relationship and the context into account.

Postmodern Developments

Gender Differences

We have established that both rule-based and principle-based ethical codes have their advantages and disadvantages. Although not perfect, principle-based codes are to be preferred, as they can be used as a basis for reflection in any given situation. However, with the advent of feminism, principle-based codes have come under some criticism. Gilligan's (1982) groundbreaking research demonstrated a fundamental difference in the way men and women discuss ethical issues (bearing in mind of course that we are talking generalities here – men in general and women in general does not include every single man and every single woman). Whereas generally men are able to debate ethical issues abstractly, women (and girls) find this hard to do. Gilligan found that before engaging with a decision making process girls wanted to have more information about the situation. They would say things like, 'I cannot give you the answer to that, I need to have more information, it all depends!' The 'it depends' aspect is crucial and points to the fact that women seem to be more inclined to think relationally.

Here is an example from a course on ethics one of us took many years ago.

My course mates and I were asked to debate the pros and cons of a 'just' war. In other words we were asked to clarify when a war might be justified, which involved deciding under what circumstances it was permissible to have people killed, even if that would mean innocent women and children. A clear gender divide opened up, with most of the men prepared to discuss the circumstances under which they would or would not advocate a war. Most of the women on the other hand, myself included, were adamant that there was no such thing as a 'just' war. Perhaps it was because we were all of a certain age and had children or even grandchildren. For us this kind of discussion inevitably meant trying to imagine ourselves into the position of the men and women who would be involved in the fighting, and the effect this would have on their mothers and fathers. We were thinking not just on the side of the people waging this 'just' war, but also the effect the killings would have on the parents of enemy soldiers. And it just felt wrong. We acknowledged that although it appears to be a fact of life that war is inevitable, in no way can it ever be just! This gender divide made for a very lively debate, the outcome of which was that we agreed to differ, although we respected each other's arguments.

Relational Approaches

Gilligan's research has been influential in the development of a relationship-based approach to ethical decision making according to which decisions regarding the therapist's actions need to be engaged with not only through the practitioner's experience, but also through the experience of the client. Initially this was known as an 'ethic of care' (Benner and Wrubel, 1989; Slote, 2007). It proposes that we start with the phenomenological experience of the client, which must be understood in context and involves really meeting the other at relational depth. An ethic of care implies a way of 'being in the world', not unlike the Rogerian 'way of being' (Rogers, 1980). An ethic of care seems more demanding than a rule- or principle-based ethic (BACP, 2007) for a number of reasons. Firstly, as Taylor (1995: xiv–xx) points out it requires that the therapist 'must have the ability to travel deeply and empathetically with the client into uncharted and often frightening territory'. Secondly, in addition to a willingness to enter the world of the other, it also involves a 'commitment to excellence, expertise and best practice, a furthering of knowledge by research and theoretical development' and a 'striving for excellence' (van Ooijen, 2003: 179). A care-based approach to ethics appears in line with studies of the human brain, on the basis of which scientists are posing the hypothesis that 'compassion, caring, and prosocial behaviour' might be a core state in the 'development of well being' (Gilbert, 2010: xiii). It is also congruent with a postmodernist therapeutic approach that requires 'an ethical response that puts the other first' (Taylor et al., 2006: 95).

Bond (2007: 441) developed the concept of an 'ethic of trust', which focuses on the psychologically intimate nature of therapy. He points out that important factors in a client's decision whether or not to work with us concerns the question, 'Can I see myself in relationship with this person?' and our perceived competence, compassion and respectfulness. However, according to Bond, these factors are not really addressed by the professional literature on ethics, where the emphasis is more on the maintenance of boundaries, confidentiality and privacy. So for Bond an ethic of trust hinges on the relationship we have with our clients. This also implies that our trustworthiness is not something that clients decide on once and for all; it is something that is continuously monitored, albeit often out of conscious awareness.

Tudway (2009: 159), in discussing relational ethics from a cognitive standpoint, recognises how difficult it is to develop a 'set of relational ethics agreed by everyone in all cases'. He states, 'one clear ethical theme that emerges in practice is often associated with clients' expressed wish to have their problems "cured" or thinking process "put right"'. He quotes Dryden (1995) who suggests that to some extent most therapies are a process of persuasion, but feels that this applies particularly to REBT[5] where the therapist actively challenges clients' 'irrational beliefs and inferences'. Cognitive behavioural therapists tend to teach their model to clients, which poses another ethical dilemma as effectively this means 'presenting a theoretical framework that is often in stark contrast to the value and belief system of the client' (Tudway, 2009: 160).

We are committed to work within an ethic of relational trust, and are therefore required to be truthful about our values as well as our model of working. While remaining respectful of the client's needs and wishes, we need to be upfront about any discrepancies between our view and that of clients, so they can make an informed choice about us as a person and about the way we work. However, this needs to be reciprocal, as Tudway (2009: 160) points out, we need to make it clear to clients that for us to work effectively we need them to be 'open and honest'.

Coale (1998: 1) advocates a 'context-based ethics' that sees each client–therapist relationship as unique and 'facilitates ethical decision making as a process'. Coale (1998: 2) defines context as the system of people involved as well as the 'collective meaning in each system'. She sees this as congruent with a constructivist stress on the 'system of meaning', which views context as 'how people talk, think, and believe' about things. In case of a problem the views and beliefs of everyone within the system need to be taken into account, to develop a 'consensual meaning' that can then be used as a basis for a solution (1998: 3). In practice this means that therapists need first to clarify the system of all concerned, so that in case of discrepancies between their

---

[5]Rational emotive behavioural therapy.

system and that of the client, they can build some bridges and develop a consensus about how to go forward. According to Coale (1998: 3) many failures in therapy are due to unexplored mismatches between client and therapist views and expectations.

Principle of Self-care (BACP, 2007)

A relational ethic includes therapists' internal relationship, a reflexive stance and a commitment to continuous personal and professional development. Adequate support and supervision are essential. Sometimes we need someone to say to us, 'Perhaps you should take a break', especially if we are not sufficiently aware of this ourselves, yet feel overwhelmed, burnt out or have recently experienced a trauma.

To conclude, postmodern approaches to ethics take relational factors into account. They honour the fact that we are always in relationship: with ourselves, our personal context and the cultural/societal world.

EVALUATION

Currently there is a tension between being and doing, between neutrality to outcome[6] and a medical approach to therapy that aims to 'cure'. An over focus on outcome seems to ask, 'Did the therapist help to cure the client/patient?' Evaluation tools usually measure 'effectiveness' of pre-set outcomes, many of which sound like a list of symptoms and may not apply to the particular client. From a relational point of view, what happens in therapy is co-created and is therefore a function of the relationship, a large part of which is likely to be played out at an unconscious level. The (unspoken) question that appears to be asked is, 'Have you or have you not managed to make this person less depressed, less anxious, less whatever?' In other words, 'Have you cured them?' So there is a tension between this outcome/cure-based approach and a wish to work with clients at relational depth and provide a space where through being truly met they can explore what is going on inside, whatever the outcome! Pre-determined evaluation tools are in conflict with our model's presupposition of neutrality to outcome, as they set out beforehand what is desirable and expect the therapist to guide the client towards this way of being. Indeed, sometimes it feels as if therapy is seen as nothing more than symptom reduction. It suggests a view of normality that is ethnocentric – based on, often unexamined, rules[7] of what professionals and society see as acceptable.

However, many 'symptoms' are an inevitable consequence of the human condition. We live, we love, and we lose people and things. We have to deal (sometimes kicking and screaming) with the fact that we are finite and that one day we will die. The older we get, the more likely we are to be confronted with illness and death, if not our own than certainly that of friends and family. We may feel profoundly affected by this and go through all kinds of processes. Bland contentment and happiness is

---

[6]See chapter 2.

[7]This point was also made in the section on rule-based ethics.

often the last thing we would, or even should, feel in these situations. To be human is to live and feel what happens and to be tolerant of that. Mindfulness, for example, is not a tool to make us feel happy, but to allow ourselves to 'be' and 'be with' whatever is going on inside. It is not something that helps to avoid, deny or suppress feelings and emotions; to the contrary, it can allow us to be with ourselves, to allow a process (such as mourning) to happen, however difficult and painful this may be. As relational beings, however, it is hard not to get influenced by the 'cure' expectation as it is within our context and part of the world in which we live.

Leader (2008) notes that fifty years ago there was barely any evidence of depression in therapeutic literature, yet now it appears to be a global epidemic. He sees this as partly due to the advent and enormous growth in the use of anti-depressants. He makes the point that basically depression appears to be something that is affected by anti-depressants – which makes the 'evidence' on effectiveness rather circular. There is an often unexamined assumption underlying the current emphasis on cure and the corresponding increase in the use of anti-depressants, that not to feel content and happy at all times is bad. There seems to be an intolerance of the human condition that gets dangerously close to Aldous Huxley's Brave New World where everyone is 'happy' all the time because they take 'soma'. A client stopped taking anti-depressants because she could not stand the feeling of 'bland happiness' and preferred not feeling good to being out of touch with herself. Rather than a cure, relational therapy provides a space where people can reflect on what is going on for them. We see therapy as a place where people can allow themselves to be in touch with the human condition.

Another issue is that 'therapy and its promised results have been oversold' as its actual effects appear quite small when compared with many other factors in clients' lives (Coale, 1998: 9).

Yet it does not seem unreasonable to monitor and evaluate what is happening in therapy, indeed it may be seen as an ethical requirement. We suggest that rather than using pre-set tools based on symptoms and outcomes, evaluation can be made part of the process and involve clients overtly so that it becomes part of the therapy. We suggest that the manner of evaluation is developed in collaboration with clients. For example as part of the assessment process clients might be asked:

- What are the kind of things you would like to change?
- How will you help this process?
- What might you do to sabotage this?

These questions might be pondered on from time to time to help clients reflect on how they are participating with their process. Other questions that might be asked are along the lines of:

- How well do I 'get' you?
- What happens when I do not?
- What can we do about this?
- What has changed for you?
- What has made that possible?

- What has not yet happened that you would like to happen?
- What might help bring that about?
- What would you need?

So evaluation can become a conversation. A rating scale might be agreed upon, which would allow us to track the process. The client could be given a copy of what was discussed in each evaluation. This idea is in an early stage of development, but we feel that it has the potential to make more concrete what many of us already do as part of the therapy. It may allow us to inquire into the process (and the outcome) of therapy in a relational way that is therapeutic for the client. Ultimately it is hoped that it will help both clients and therapists.

RESEARCH

According to Wharton (2005) authentic psychotherapeutic research is an ethical imperative, as its ultimate aim is to improve our practice and benefit clients. This appears to suggest that all practitioners should in some way be involved in research. According to McLeod (1999; 2002), however, there is a relative lack of practitioner research, a phenomenon he calls the 'research-practice gap'. Perhaps this is partly due to an ongoing tension between positivist research, where the researcher objectively looks at 'subjects', and a phenomenological kind of inquiry (Heron, 1996). For example, the American philosopher Erwin states:

> there is no need, and … no good reason at all, to accept the postmodern epistemologies currently popular in the field, epistemologies that devalue experimental research and which are likely to inhibit the development of a genuine science of psychotherapy. (1996: 160).

The current reliance on outcome studies to provide proof of effectiveness, on the other hand, has been criticised as flawed. As Fonagy states, 'the reductionist assumption that there is a linear logical correlation between process variables and outcomes' is unwarranted, as 'the outcome of psychotherapy is what outcome measures happen to measure' (1995: 174).

This is reminiscent of the last century's use of intelligence tests, the validity of which is now regarded as questionable. Also, research about people is socially constructed, and can never be objective or value-free (West, 2001).

A Postmodern View of Research

Research influenced by a modernist paradigm tends to imply a positivistic epistemology and the use of experimental and quantitative methods (Mason, 2002). According to Tyson (1995: xxii) the tendency to equate quantitative research with a positivistic paradigm, and a qualitative approach with a post-positivist framework, is a conceptual error that confuses data analysis issues with those pertaining to the gathering of data. Quantitative methods, such as the randomised clinical trial, cannot do justice to therapy's rich experience (Elton Wilson and Barkham, 1994) and a postmodernist stance is becoming increasingly acceptable (Henwood, 1996).

A Heuristic Paradigm

Rather than an adversarial either/or quantitative vs qualitative stance, we observe a move towards a 'heuristic paradigm' (Tyson, 1995) where both are regarded as valuable, indeed complementary. Heineman Pieper defines a heuristic paradigm as 'any problem solving strategy that appears likely to lead to relevant, reliable, and useful information' (1989: 207). Within a heuristic paradigm research and knowledge development are not tied to a specific methodology, but can include quantitative methods as well as other methods geared to the 'observer-practitioner who is close to the data' (Tyson, 1995: xviii). The flexibility of the heuristic paradigm means that the method to be used depends on the kind of information one is interested in. Whereas quantitative research is useful for the testing of hypotheses and measurement, qualitative methods are more appropriate for inquiring into people's subjective experience, meanings and interpretations (Al Rubaie, 2006; Henwood, 1996). Qualitative methods such as ethnography, phenomenology, grounded theory, conversation analysis, narrative inquiry, discourse analysis or cooperative analysis (Barber, 2006), to name but a few, can help develop knowledge that is 'experience-near' (Tyson, 1995: xviii). A heuristic paradigm offers a pragmatic solution, as it avoids an adversarial qualitative/quantitative dichotomy (Olsen, 2003; Tyson, 1995). Heineman Pieper's position appears similar to a stance of methodological pluralism (Kvale, 1996a), which embraces both positivist and relativist approaches, depending on the needs of the study.

A methodological pluralist stance has been criticised as 'not grasping the nettle' (Kopala and Suzuki, 1999: 4) or implying that 'anything goes' (Olsen, 2003). However, such criticism is erroneous, as working within a heuristic paradigm, or holding a stance of methodological pluralism, necessitates a stance of reflexivity on the part of the researcher (Olsen, 2003), which is not an easy option. Researchers using a quantitative methodology may wish to pay attention to context and reflexivity, and those favouring a qualitative approach may look into matters of validity and generalisability in their findings (Aveline, 2006: 21).

> To be reflexive we need to be aware of our personal responses and to be able to make choices about how to use them. We also need to be aware of the personal, social and cultural contexts in which we live and work and to understand how these impact on the ways we interpret our world. (Etherington, 2004: 19)

Etherington's quote is congruent with a relational therapeutic stance. As Socrates said, 'the unexamined life is not worth living' (Socrates in Plato, *Apology*: 38a). In the same way that we help clients reflect on their lives, as therapists we perhaps need to reflect on and examine our practice, both by regular evaluation and by research.

SUPERVISION

In this section we share a few thoughts about supervision as they apply to the RIM. Therapy practitioners observe, decide what to do and then review what happened in a continuous cycle, guided by their personal and professional experience, as well as that of others such as their supervisors. From this perspective supervision is a kind of 'relational research' with the intention of continuously improving practice (Rose and Loewenthal, 2006: 138).

Relational integrative supervision focuses on relationship and integration. Clients' participation in the therapeutic relationship can provide information about their internal integration, as well as relationships outside the consulting room. It is useful to focus on what is created between client and therapist, or between supervisee and supervisor. Because of the intersubjective nature of human beings, we use ourselves as a therapeutic tool, both in therapy and in supervision. A contemplative stance helps us to be aware and notice what is going on from moment to moment. So experiences by the therapist (countertransference), or by the supervisor (supervisor's countertransference), provide information regarding what may be going on internally for the client.

While a prospective client relates a catalogue of losses I sense profound pain and sadness.

Therapist: That is a lot of loss.
Client: Yes, I don't want any more, that's enough now … (silence, stares into the distance, then continues) Actually, I've met someone, but don't know whether I can let myself get involved.
Therapist: I wonder whether there might be a need to grieve, to give yourself space to process all these losses?
Client: No, I've done that, after x died I had some therapy.
Therapist: How was that?
Client: Well, it was useful I suppose, but it did not change anything, he was still dead and I got fed up and left.
Therapist: You left the therapy?
Client: Yes, I did not think it was going anywhere, every week I'd go there, she'd listen, I'd cry and that was that. I just felt that I needed to move on.
Therapist: Yet here you are.
Client: (slightly irritably) Yes … so, do you think that you can help me?
Therapist: Mmm, well … we don't know a lot about each other yet … but I'm still sitting with the impact of all these losses.
Client: I do not want to talk about those any more, that is not what I need.
Therapist: You sound angry.
Client: Yes, I get angry when …

The therapist tells her supervisor that throughout the session she sensed pain, sadness and enormous anger, which felt directed straight at her. Her attempts at empathy, immediacy and connection did not go anywhere. She says that she feels useless and wonders whether she is up to working with the client, particularly as after the session it felt as if she had been pulled 'through a hedge backwards' and does not remember having had quite such a strong reaction for a long time.

The supervisor wonders whether this strong countertransference indicates that the client's defences are very rigid and perhaps dangerous to dismantle; there seems to be a split between the client's everyday life as a successful professional and her internal world. She wonders how anyone can bear so much loss and feels that by mentioning the loss the therapist drew the anger to her. Although difficult for the therapist it offered the client a sense of what might be involved in therapy, which might help her decide whether or not therapy is right for her at the moment. If she does decide that the time is right, there is a need to work carefully and be guided by the co-transference that arises.

Good supervision that helps us to feel firmly 'held' and supported is essential for the kind of therapy where we use ourselves as an instrument and meet the other at relational depth. Therapeutic relationships where we aim to truly meet the other are not always easy and co-transference experiences can be difficult. A good working relationship is therefore essential in supervision. In order to be supportive, supervisors need to be authentic, compassionate and validating. Gilbert (2010) advocates asking questions such as, 'Tell me what you did well since we last met. What are you proud of?' If supervisees are upset about something that has not gone well, it can be helpful to suggest that they write a compassionate letter to themselves that can be read out either by them or the supervisor. A compassionate supervisory stance helps supervisees to develop a compassionate internal supervisor (Gilbert, 2010). As practitioners we need to accept our limitations and that despite our best efforts, some clients may not feel helped by us.

Supervisors may ask a practitioner, 'What do you feel in your body as you are talking about this?' If there is a sense of fear, shame or other difficult emotion, it is useful to ask, 'Whose stuff is that, is it yours, your clients, or perhaps both?' This kind of mindful supervision involves a slowing down, a creation of space. 'What do you need?' 'What would be helpful to you and your client?' Supervisors' non-judging attitude of curiosity and equanimity helps supervisees develop the same attitude towards themselves and their clients. A mindful, compassionate stance can help practitioners to be in touch with their felt sense.

When we are having difficulties, shame may prevent us from reaching out; we may assume that everyone else is problem free (Gilbert and Evans, 2000). Supervisors are in a good place to know that no one is perfect and that we all make mistakes. A compassionate stance will help supervisees to be able to share any difficulties they may have. Gilbert (2010) suggests that it is useful for all of us (therapists and supervisors alike) to open our hearts to difficulties.

Sit quietly for a few minutes. Breathe gently and let yourself slowly become aware of your body. Scan your body and notice any tension. Breathe into that tension and allow it to dissolve. Now focus on your heart. Imagine that it opens like a flower … it is spacious … allow any difficulties or problems to come into that space … and be received with compassion. As you breathe in and out know that you are at one with the world … with every breath allow yourself both to receive and to give compassion.

This brief mindfulness practice can help us be with clients (or supervisees) and 'bear' their feelings of stuckness. Rather than seeing stuckness as a problem, or as something to break through, there may be value in the stuckness; it may have a lesson to teach us. Our compassionate mind knows that life is tough, but we have to live it (Gilbert, 2010). Working compassionately with supervisees and with clients means giving space to and feeding our own compassionate self.

PERSONAL AND PROFESSIONAL DEVELOPMENT

From First Order to Second Order

The creation and organisation of socially constructed realities and meanings are dependent on context. A major shift from general systems theory and cybernetics involved the move from a first-order to a second-order perspective. A first-order perspective contains the idea that there is an objective reality that can be perceived by an observer of a system. Second-order cybernetics perspectives maintain that any system is not merely observed but contains and is influenced by the observer. This postmodern perspective therefore requires the observer (in our case the therapist) to adopt a self-reflexive stance and to engage with co-existing multiple realities when working with people (Anderson and Goolishian, 1988; Gergen and Kaye, 1992).

Ethics of Professional and Personal Development

Jenkins (2008), describing his work with violent men, invites therapists to consider the ethics of our practice when faced with dilemmas that may elicit strong responses in us: how, he asks, can we engage in respectful practice in which we are aware and cognisant of our own prejudices, our expectations of ourselves and our clients and the possibility of feeling tempted by our beliefs and expectations to engage in 'coercive practices of power' (Jenkins, 2008). These are crucial questions for practitioners engaged in extra-ordinary conversations where the therapist has, by the very nature of the enterprise, considerable power and influence.[8] If we engage in these dialogues without sufficient awareness of ourselves, the impact of our participation and our observation, we may unwittingly try to coerce clients to act in ways that we judge 'correct'. Given our presuppositions of the intersubjective nature of the therapeutic endeavour, we need to consider how we position ourselves, or what may be playing out within the encounter with the client, so that these aspects do not remain hidden from awareness. Continuing professional training and personal development are ethical priorities endorsed by the main therapy professional bodies, because they are considered essential requirements in order to be able to maintain a self-reflexive and constructively self-critical stance in our practice. Exercises in which we consider aspects of our social identities (Roberts, 2005) can help us to be more careful about how these identities may impose themselves in the therapeutic domain.

---

[8]See chapters 1 and 2.

Therapy as Cross-cultural Encounter

It could be argued that all therapy constitutes a cross-cultural encounter, one in which all participants, including the therapist, bring with them differences in cultural background.

The idea of plural selves arises over and over again in the therapeutic literature (Assagioli 1965; Rowan and Cooper 1999; Young et al., 2006). Janine Roberts (2005) refers to social identities that are constructed from several aspects of self such as gender, sexuality, ethnicity, race and class. It could be said that 'culture' is the term that provides an overarching frame for all these 'micro-cultures' or aspects of self and that therapists are always working cross-culturally (Wittstock et al., 1992). Burnham (1993) identifies the social GRRAACCEES as an acronym for aspects of identity that therapists need to pay attention to when working towards anti-discriminatory, anti-oppressive and ethical practice that also promotes social inclusion. These are Gender, Race, Religion, Age, Appearance, Class, Culture, Ethnicity, Education, Sexuality.

Cultural competence defined in this broad sense, seems to be achieved by a number of factors. One of these factors is the therapist's awareness of their own culturally informed beliefs and values and attention to the dominant discourses that might inadvertently influence the therapeutic domain. Several authors (Burnham and Harris, 1996; Krause, 1998; Ryde, 2009; Woodcock, 1997) discuss the importance of the therapist's awareness of their own cultural mores and values. Culturally informed assumptions and beliefs inevitably influence the self of the therapist and will form the basis of the interventions that they choose.[9] When therapists are not attuned to their own cultural identity, they may be less able to act in ways that facilitate a dialogue that generates an understanding of the values and beliefs of individuals and families who come from different cultural and ethnic backgrounds.

Several authors provide examples of how therapists may develop this lens. Woodcock (1997) describes how he and colleagues pro-actively discussed with each other their gendered assumptions about working together in the context of a refugee therapy group. They then went on to explore with each other how their identities as white Europeans might be utilised in this setting. Such explorations serve to make explicit the possible constraints as well as opportunities that the cultural identity of the therapist may have in the therapeutic context. It seems important to ensure that there are processes available for us to reflect on issues of difference, privilege, marginalisation and how we personally experience these. Cultural genograms help to develop this awareness and understanding, where therapists explore their own culture across three or more generations within their family of origin and examine themes of pride and shame within this context (Hardy and Laszloffy, 1995).

---

[9]We might want to ask ourselves whether Eurocentric assumptions and dominant discourses underpinning Western psychotherapy that privilege individualism, autonomy and independence, fit with people from cultures with different values and beliefs. Are the rituals and artefacts of Western psychotherapies able to respond sensitively and usefully to the complex multilayered contexts of peoples from very different cultural backgrounds from those of the therapist, such as refugees and asylum seekers, or are there other models that might be more appropriate?

A second theme in the establishment of cultural competence is the importance of attending to and developing an understanding of the beliefs, values, traditions, socio-political history and contexts of the people therapists work with. A stance that actively seeks to explore and be curious about the cultural identities of clients (whether the client comes from an obviously different cultural and ethnic background from that of the therapist or not) can greatly improve understanding and facilitate a sensitive and appropriate collaboration (Chen, 1995; Krause, 1998; McGoldrick 1998). The exploration of the cultural self and social identities of the therapist is part of the work of personal and professional development.

> Personal development is a purposeful process, within the overall aim of professional development in the service of client and within the ethics and practice of counselling. (Johns, 1996: 3)

The general agreement across all modalities of the importance of the therapeutic relationship requires that attention be paid to all participants, both the client and the therapist (Johns, 1996; Padesky, 1996).

Continuing professional development and personal development in therapy training are also part of self-care. Therapists are subject to secondary or vicarious traumatisation and therefore need to be mindful of signs of burnout and stress that may be related to practice. The intersubjective perspective on the therapeutic relationship also points to the mutual influencing between client and therapist. Rothschild (2006: 11) suggests that compassion fatigue, or difficulties resulting from therapy practice, are often a result of unconscious empathy (an empathic feeling that persists beyond the session), processes of empathic engagement that the therapist is not aware of as opposed to empathic feeling that is conscious. This can manifest in experiencing sadness after a session with a bereaved client, or feeling tired and low in mood after working with a depressed client. Being able to make the distinction between one's own feelings and those of the client therefore is an important skill in therapy and one that needs to be cultivated. Rothschild suggests a number of exercises that help to develop the ability to tune into and align with one's own natural state (mind and body) and make this distinction; they include conscious mirroring and un-mirroring exercises in which therapists work with each other to deliberately mirror the other's posture and then make their own posture different from those of their partner.

The Context of Professional and Personal Development

The Reflexive Practitioner

The big question that therapists continue to address throughout their work is: how do I maintain a practice in which I am accountable, responsible, self-aware, ethical, non-oppressive and inclusive? Traditional approaches to personal development within training have included personal therapy.

Personal therapy has been a mandatory requirement in many therapy trainings, most notably psychodynamic training. The benefits have been discussed in chapter 1; however, mandatory therapy for trainees holds the same difficulties as mandated therapy for clients and one cannot assume that trainees will engage fully with the process. There is no research evidence that suggests therapists who have had personal therapy have better client outcomes (Beutler et al., 2004; Ronnestadt and Ladany 2006). In our experience trainees are often reluctant initially to start personal therapy; however, many students report that they have found it invaluable once they have engaged with the process. Therapists who have undertaken personal therapy report it as one of the most valuable aspects of personal development (Norcross, 2005) as it facilitates the ability to identify one's own from the client's feelings and emotional responses, to hold uncertainty, to take care of the self and possibly to identify one's tendencies in relation to beliefs, values, judgements, expectations and assumptions.

Personal development training on therapy courses has often relied heavily on the unstructured process-based group. However, previous research (Irving and Williams, 1996) indicates that although some students find this an intensely formative experience, others found it unhelpful or indeed a negative experience. Other work that assesses a range of approaches to personal development (e.g. structured vs unstructured; facilitated vs unfacilitated; individual vs group) suggests that there are considerable differences in the responses of individual students to different approaches to personal development (Spencer, 2006).

Alternative Approaches: Action Research Using World Café Design – A Case Example

In response to the mixed feedback on existing processes for personal development learning and in order to maximise trainee engagement and learning opportunities, an action research/cooperative enquiry style was introduced to some of the cohorts that we have taught (Faris and James, 2009). A world cafe design (Brown with Isaacs, 2005) was utilised in order to generate 'conversations that matter' about personal development, individual learning needs and attitudes to the cultivation of self-awareness among the trainee groups. The café style discussion operates on feedback loops, so that small groups of up to five participants spend a limited amount of time discussing a particular question, for example, 'How can we maximise our learning and personal development?' The groups then swap around and change, leaving a host at each table who can synthesise and explain the previous group's ideas for the new group. In this way collective knowledge, information and ideas can be built upon and co-constructed. These conversations then resulted in trainee led designs for personal development learning in the academic year to come. Those with the least experience of personal development training in this context designed the most radical plan with mixed results, particularly as the choice included unfacilitated, rotating small group discussions. It may be that at this early stage of training this design contained too much uncertainty and lack of safety, whereas for students further on in their training such a design may have been more fruitful. Interestingly all groups chose to incorporate further cafés as part of an ongoing review of the success of their designs.

Some difficulties arose where trainees had insufficient prior knowledge about the concept of personal development within the context of therapy/counselling training. Trainees often need help to understand both what is meant by personal development (as it can be hard to define) and why it is an essential component of therapy training. Cooperative enquiry as a methodology in the cultivation of personal development needs further exploration, but we believe it has a great deal of potential to generate useful processes to optimise reflexivity and self-awareness.

Relational Responsibility and Personal Development

In learning communities the context of assessment can often hinder student participation. Anderson suggests that the authority bestowed on teachers/lecturers/supervisors in such learning environments places them inevitably in positions of power and privilege (1999: 66). When teachers choose to work collaboratively and respectfully within such a context, this can reduce the constraints of such differences on student learning. McNamee and Gergen (1999) invite us to adopt a position of relational responsibility, not only to our clients but also in our roles as trainers and trainees. The isomorphic nature of personal development training in therapy training courses and therapy itself enables us to transfer knowledge and understanding gained in one to use in the other. Questions about the students' learning agendas and expectations of course tutors and the course itself help to invite students to take responsibility for their learning. Remaining in respectful, curious and interested dialogue with each other constitutes fertile ground for students to continue to take risks and for trainers to reflect on their own teaching and the interpersonal dynamics that enhance or hinder learning processes.

Evaluation and Practice-based Research as Personal Development – A Case Study

Seligman (2002) offers a potential template for therapists' own research and evaluation of their practice. She undertook a small scale, qualitative study that sought to elicit the views of her clients on their experience of therapy and whether they found it helpful or unhelpful. The purpose of this practice-based research was to: investigate clients' perceptions and experience of therapy, to evaluate practice as personal development and as part of an ethical and professional obligation to monitor clients' views, to engage in professional enquiry and contribute to research in the field. The research was based on a semi-structured questionnaire, which allowed clients to expand on any answers they gave.

In answer to the question about factors that contributed to them continuing therapy after the first session, the majority of clients included the importance of the relationship with the therapist and within that as many people cited the importance of being challenged as well as being supported. These findings give further credence to other research in the field suggesting empathy and the therapeutic relationship are highly significant, but that challenge (which might suggest being taken out of a comfort zone or invited to entertain different views or perspectives) within the context of a good therapeutic alliance is also important. The outcomes most cited by clients were: gaining better coping strategies, clarification of issues and greater self-awareness. This research enabled the researcher/therapist to gain a meta-perspective on clients' views of what their experience had been, a view or lens that is rarely available to us from within the therapy itself. While in this particular case the information provided gave no indication of a need for change in the therapist's practice, it was enlightening and helped her to reflect more deeply on her work. Seligman encourages us to consider the ethical obligation to survey our clients' views. This also fits with a self-reflexive stance and the idea of relational responsibility. If we regard a collaborative process in therapy as important, then why not include feedback about the therapy and therapist in this. This is similar to action research where the research findings feed back into the continuing development of the research design in reflexive feedback loops.

Personal Development Exercises

Within the context of therapy training we see it as vital that the training process includes aspects of processes and practices that we integrate into our approach with clients. We therefore included mindfulness practice as part of the course teaching day and as Segal et al. (2002) found, believe that developing a personal mindfulness-based practice is not only essential if we wish to work with mindfulness with clients, but also an invaluable tool for cultivating self-awareness and attention. We recommend that students and therapists try to maintain a daily sitting practice as both a method of self-enquiry and self-care. Guided imagery and focusing exercises also form part of our methods for self-enquiry and development. An exercise students have found very enlightening has been a guided imagery that invites the participant to explore and have an internal dialogue with aspects of self, the intention being to contact and explore different parts of ourselves with the purpose of gaining insight and integration.

The Bus

You are walking across a meadow. It is a beautiful day, quiet and sunny. At some point you notice a road ahead in the distance, and become aware that there is a bus coming along the road. You see it stopping as you approach and notice several people in the bus. All of these people are aspects of yourself. One by one they start to get off and your attention is drawn to two or three of the characters. What do you notice about them, what are they doing? You might find yourself drawn to one. You have a conversation with this aspect of yourself. What does it want from you, what are its strengths, qualities, when does it appear in your life, is it dominant or not? Maybe you want to ask a question of this aspect of yourself.

And now it is time to take your leave. The people start to get back on the bus. As the bus draws away and starts to leave, notice who it is that is driving the bus.

We might ask students to first write their experience down and then to share their experiences in pairs. This guided imagery exercise can be a very useful exercise for clients as well as trainees. It can bring forth themes, hidden aspects of self, or facilitate the beginnings of a new relationship between certain aspects of self within us.

Reflecting Team

As part of our interest in developing a self-reflexive stance, reflexive processes are generally very useful. Students or therapists in group supervision, for example, may interview each other in pairs about an aspect of practice or development. The pair then listens, as a reflecting discussion takes place between their peers on the interview that has just taken place. Reflecting team processes offer multiple perspectives and can generate rich and useful information for the enquirer, be they client or therapist, in a personal development exercise. Writing process notes, reflective journals and eliciting the views of colleagues and trainers all contribute to a process of ongoing 'self-in-practice' enquiry.

Questions We May Ask Ourselves Include:

Who am I? What are my social identities: gender, class, ethnicity, race, sexuality, etc.? How might these identities along with my relational experiences contribute to the ecology of beliefs, assumptions, values, aspirations, expectations that form the self that I bring into the therapy room? What are my interpersonal and relational patterns, prejudices, preferences and blind spots? How do the socially constructed, cultural/political/historical/social discourses influence how I might work as a therapist?

SUMMARY

In this chapter we show how working relationally informs all aspects of practice; it is not just a technique that can be applied in some circumstances. In other words, a relational ethic lies at the heart of practice together with ethics, evaluation, research and supervision. Furthermore, continuous personal and professional development are vital to support practitioners' ability to maintain a relational stance in everything they do.

QUESTIONS FOR FURTHER REFLECTION AND DISCUSSION

- How has reading this chapter affected how you think and feel about the topics discussed?
- What do you think about our assertion that working relationally involves the integration of a relational ethic in everything we do?
- Do you agree or disagree with the ideas discussed here? Can you give reasons for your opinion?

FURTHER READING

Barber, P. (2006) *Becoming a Practitioner Researcher: A Gestalt Approach to Holistic Inquiry.* London: Middlesex University Press.

Burnham, J. (1993) 'Systemic supervision: the evolution of reflexivity in the context of the supervisory relationship', *Human Systems*, 4: 349–81.

Gabriel, L. and Casemore, R. (2009) *Relational Ethics in Practice: Narratives from Counselling and Psychotherapy.* Hove, East Sussex: Routledge.

Johns, H. (1996) *Personal Development in Counsellor Training.* London: Cassell.

Pretorius, W. M. (2006) 'Cognitive behavioural therapy supervision: recommended practice', *Behavioural and Cognitive Psychotherapy*, 34: 413–20.

Van Ooijen, E. (2003) *Clinical Supervision Made Easy.* Edinburgh: Churchill Livingstone/ Elsevier.

Conclusion

if lofty be your thoughts, if rare emotion
touches your spirit and your body.
The Laestrygonians and the Cyclopes,
the fierce Poseidon you'll not encounter,
unless you carry them along with your soul,
unless your soul raises them before you.

(Cavafy, [1911] 2007: 37)

We bring forth a 'truth' or 'reality' based on our perception and interpretation of events; what is seen is in the eye of the beholder. What we hope to have illustrated is something of our process of integrating and the means whereby we have come to select aspects of approach, built a particular method that is consistent with that approach and then selected techniques of ways of intervening and being with clients in order to make a coherent and yet evolving 'live' integrating framework. The relational and contemplative perspectives provided us with a starting place: they act as a central ground from which to explore theoretical perspectives. Sometimes it is in the midst of crisis that we find a solution, a way forward, a new possibility, a creative catharsis. The intensity of the debates in the UK regarding statutory regulation and the Increasing Access to Psychological Therapies (IAPT) strategy form the backdrop that gave the work an energy and inspired us to try and find an ecological framework that can encompass complementary but perhaps different perspectives. The CBT debate in particular illustrates the passion with which ideas can be held, privileged, fought for and against.

According to research into therapeutic effectiveness, theoretical orientation and therapeutic model account for only 8 per cent of the variation; this is known as the 'dodo effect' (Wampold, 2001). Differences in effectiveness *between* therapists are larger than differences between therapy modalities (Elkin et al., 1999; Huppert et al., 2001). Hemmings (2008: 43) makes the point that it is not possible to separate out the techniques used from the person using them, yet the current trend towards privileging empirically supported treatment would suggest that this *can* be done.

We wonder whether it is therapists' confidence in their chosen model that affects the work's effectiveness. A doctor's belief in a particular type of medication, for example, tends to increase its effectiveness, whether or not the patient actually knows the doctor's opinion about the medication or not (Gracely et al., 1979). Mansell (2008) encourages a constructive dialogue between modalities; in our opinion this can be of great benefit to the field of therapy and ultimately to the client. Rigorous debate is always useful and helps the field of therapy to continue to evolve. This kind of debate is illustrated well in a recent publication that contains a dialogue between cognitive behavioural therapists and those from other modalities (House and Loewenthal, 2008). Here some authors criticise CBT for its seeming lack of acknowledgement of unconscious and interpersonal processes or the role of social contexts and discourses, while others offer an analysis that counters these critiques. Drawing on the work of Gilbert (2009a) and Strong et al. (2008) Mansell (2008) argues that there is an acknowledgement of the influence of interpersonal processes on intra-psychic processes within CBT. He counters the critique of CBT as a pathologising model by referring to its originator Beck who suggests that distress falls along a continuum.

Within the field of CBT itself there are those who privilege technique and others who privilege formulation. Loewenthal argues that CBT is a product of this 'age of happiness' (2008: 147) and wellbeing and that its adoption as a treatment of choice underpins the dominant belief that we will be better off the less we think about our problems. Strong et al.'s (2008) dialogical and social constructionist perspective of CBT characterises it as a dialogic practice where conversation and language provide the focus and context for change. However, if practised monologically (instrumentally) they argue that it can be seen as prescribing, thus imposing a particular truth and version of reality on others.

The examples given here of this particular debate serve to illustrate the importance of constructive conversations between and within therapeutic modalities; we hope such dialogue may continue to influence the field towards greater integration in a creative and energetic process that unifies rather than separates. Interestingly the recent development of mindfulness-based applications appears to provide a contribution that has great potential for bridging therapeutic approaches (Mace, 2008). Indeed Martin (1997: 292) suggests that 'the processes of mindfulness have been tacitly contained in western psychotherapies all along'. Mindfulness practice within therapy appears to contain a number of paradoxes; it comes from a tradition that suggests that there is no actual individual 'I' or self upon which to reflect, yet seems to focus on inward reflection, while at the same time constituting a relational approach that focuses on internal and external patterns of relating. Also, while psychotherapy has adopted mindfulness-based approaches in order to alleviate symptoms of depression and anxiety, the goal in the practice of mindfulness as far as there is one is the cultivation of awareness and being fully present in the here and now.

So the invitation we have offered to you, the reader, is to engage with, disagree, fight with, like and/or be inspired by what we have put together. As well as the perspectives that we have privileged in this RIM you will have your own preferred lens and prejudices. We hope that by reading this book you have been able to enter into a dialogue with us and with the theoretical ideas of the many authors, psychotherapists and thinkers who have contributed to the ecology of ideas represented here.

Bibliography

Ainsworth, M., Blehar, M., Waters, E. and Wall, S. (1978) *Patterns of Attachment: Assessed in Strange Situations and at Home.* New York: Erdbaum.

Ainsworth, M. and Bowlby, J. (1991) 'An ethological approach to personality development', *American Psychologist*, 46: 331–41.

Alexander, F. and French, T. (1946) *Psychoanalytic Therapy: Principles and Application.* New York: Ronald Press.

Al Rubaie, T. (2006) 'Case study revisited', in Loewenthal, D. and Winter, D. (eds), *What Is Psychotherapeutic Research?* London: Karnac. Chapter 2.

Anderson, H. (1999) 'Collaborative Learning Communities', in McNamee, S. and Gergen, K. *Relational Responsibility: Resources for Sustainable Dialogue.* Thousand Oaks, CA: Sage.

Anderson, H. and Goolishian, H. (1992) 'The client is the expert: a not knowing approach to therapy', in McNamee, S. and Gergen, K. J. (eds), *Therapy as Social Construction.* London: Sage. pp. 25–39.

Anderson, H. and Goolishian, H. A. (1988) 'Human systems as linguistic systems: preliminary and evolving ideas about the implications for clinical theory', *Family Process*, 26: 415–28.

Andrews, J. D. (1991) 'Integrative psychotherapy of depression: a self-confirmation approach', *Psychotherapy: Theory, Research, Practice, Training*, 28 (2): 232–50.

Assagioli, R. (1965) *Psychosynthesis.* New York: Esalen Books.

Atwood, G. and Stolorow, R. D. (1993) *Structures of Subjectivity: Explorations in Psychoanalytic Phenomenology.* Hillsdale, London: The Analytic Press.

Avants, S. K., and Margolin, A. (2004) 'Development of spiritual self-schema therapy for the treatment of addictive and HIV risk behavior: a convergence of cognitive and Buddhist psychology', *Journal of Psychotherapy Integration*, 14 (3): 253–89.

Aveline, M. (2006) 'Psychotherapy research: nature, quality, and relationship to clinical practice', in Loewenthal, D. and Winter, D. (eds), *What Is Psychotherapeutic Research?* London: Karnac. Chapter 1.

BACP (2007) *Ethical Framework for Good Practice in Counselling and Psychotherapy.* British Association for Counselling and Psychotherapy. First published 2002, revised edition published 1 April 2007.

Barber, P. (2006) *Becoming a Practitioner Researcher: A Gestalt Approach to Holistic Inquiry.* London: Middlesex University Press.

Bateson, G. (1972) *Steps to an Ecology of Mind.* London: Paladin.

Bateson, G. (1980) *Mind and Nature – a Necessary Unity.* Glasgow: Fontana/Collins.

Baur, S. (1991) *The Dinosaur Man.* New York: Harper Collins.

Beauchamp, T. L. and Childress, J. F. (2001) *Principles of Biomedical Ethics* (5th edn). Oxford: Oxford University Press.

Beck, A. T. (1976) *Cognitive Therapy and the Emotional Disorders*. New York: International Universities Press.

Becker, E. ([1973] 1997) *The Denial of Death*. New York: Simon and Schuster.

Benner, P. and Wrubel, J. (1989) *The Primacy of Caring: Stress and Coping in Health and Illness*. New York: Addison-Wesley.

Bertrando, P. (2006) 'Understanding and influencing: Two pathways for systemic therapy'. Keynote speech at AFT Annual Conference, Bristol.

Beutler, L. E., Malik, M., Alimohamed, S., Harwood, M., Talebi, K. H. and Noble, S. (2004) 'Therapist Variables', in M. J. Lambert (ed.), *Bergin and Garfield's Handbook of Psychotherapy and Behaviour Change* (5th edn). Chicago: John Wiley, pp. 227–306.

Bion, W. ([1962] 1984) *Learning from Experience*. London: Karnac.

Bion, W. R. (1967) 'Notes on memory and desire', *Psycho-analytic Forum*, 2 (3): 271–80.

Bion, W. R. (1970) *Attention and Interpretation*. London: Tavistock.

Bollas, C. (1995) *Cracking Up: The Work of Unconscious Experience*. London: Routledge.

Bollas, C. (2007) *The Freudian Moment*. London: Karnac.

Bond, T. (2000) *Standards and Ethics for Counselling in Action* (2nd edn). London: Sage.

Bond, T. (2007) 'Ethics and psychotherapy: an issue of trust', in Ashcroft, R. E., Dawson, A., Draper, H. and McMillan, J. R. (eds), *Principle of Health Care Ethics* (2nd edn). London: John Wiley.

Boscolo, L. and Bertrando, P. (1992) 'The reflexive loop of past, present and future in systemic therapy and consultation', *Family Process*, 31 (2): 119–30.

Bowlby, J. (1951). 'Maternal care and mental health', *World Health Organization Monograph* (Serial No. 2).

Bowlby, J. (1969) *Attachment*. New York: Basic Books Inc.

Bowlby, J. (1980) *Loss*. New York: Basic Books Inc.

Bowlby, J. (1988) A *Secure Base: Clinical Applications of Attachment Theory*. London: Routledge.

Bradshaw, J. (1999) *Home Coming: Reclaiming and Championing Your Inner Child*. London: Judy Piatkus (Publishers) Ltd.

Briggs Myers, J. (1962) *The Myers-Briggs Type Indicator*. Michigan: University of Michigan.

Brown, J. with Isaacs, D. (2005) *The World Café: Shaping Our Futures Through Conversations that Matter*. San Francisco: Berrett-Koehler.

Buber, M. ([1923] 1958) *I and Thou*. Edinburgh: T & T Clark. First edition published 1937, T & T Clark Ltd. Authorised English Translation of *Ich und Du*, copyright © Shocken Verlag, Berlin.

Burnham, J. (1992) 'Approach – Method – Technique: making distinctions and creating connections', *Human Systems*, 3 (1): 3–26.

Burnham, J. (1993) 'Systemic supervision: the evolution of reflexivity in the context of the supervisory relationship', *Human Systems*, 4: 349–81.

Burnham, J. (2005) 'Relational reflexivity: a tool for socially constructing therapeutic relationships', in Flaskas, C., Mason, B. and Perlesz, A. (eds), *The Space Between: Experience, Context, and Process in the Therapeutic Relationship*. London: Karnac.

Burnham, J. and Harris, Q. (1996) 'Emerging ethnicity: a tale of three cultures', in Dwivedi, K. and Varma, V. (eds), *Meeting the Needs of Ethic Minority Children*. London: Jessica Kingsley.

Byng Hall, J. (2005) 'Foreword', in Flaskas, C., Mason, B. and Perlesz, A. (eds), *The Space Between: Experience, Context, and Process in the Therapeutic Relationship*. London: Karnac.

Cade, B. and O'Hanlon, W. H. (1993) *A Brief Guide to Brief Therapy*. New York: W. W. Norton.

Campbell, J. (1949) *The Hero with a Thousand Faces*. New York: Bollingen Foundation/Pantheon Press.

Capra. F. (1996) *The Tao of Physics*. New York: Fontana.

Capra, F. (1997) *The Web of Life*. New York: Random House.

Carlson, R. (1989) 'Malcolm Knowles: apostle of Andragogy', *Vitae Scholastica*, 8 (1), 217–34.

Carroll, L. (1872) *Through the Looking-Glass*. Raleigh, NC: Hayes Barton Press.

Carroll, L. (1962 [1865]) *Alice's Adventures in Wonderland*. Harmondsworth, Middlesex: Penguin.

Cavafy, C. P. ([1911] 2007) *Collected Poems*, trans. Evangelos Sachperoglou. Oxford: Oxford University Press.

Cecchin, G. (1992) 'Constructing therapeutic possibilities', in McNamee, S. and Gergen, K. (eds), *Therapy as Social Construction*. London: Sage.

Cecchin, G. (1999) Workshop for *The Family Institute*, Cardiff.

Cecchin, G., Lane, G. and Ray, W. A. (1992) *Irreverence: A Strategy for Therapists' Survival*. London: Karnac.

Chambers, J. C. and Maris, J. A. (2010) 'Integrating mindfulness as self-care into counselling and psychotherapy training', *Counselling and Psychotherapy Research*, 10 (2): 114–25.

Chen, C. (1995) 'Group counseling in a different cultural context: several primary issues in dealing with Chinese clients', *Group*, 19 (1): 45–55.

Cioran, E. M. (1992) *On the Heights of Despair*. Chicago: The University of Chicago Press.

Clarkson, P. (2003) *The Therapeutic Relationship* (2nd edn). London: Whurr.

Coale, H. W. (1998) *The Vulnerable Therapist: Practicing Psychotherapy in an Age of Anxiety*. Binghamton, NY: The Haworth Press, Inc.

Collins English Dictionary and Thesaurus (2000) (2nd edn). Glasgow: Harper Collins Publishers.

Cooper, M. (2007) 'Person-centred therapy: the growing edge', *Therapy Today*, July: 33–6.

Cooper, M. (2009) *Essential Research Findings in Counselling and Psychotherapy*. London: Sage.

Cooper, M. and McLeod, J. (2007) 'A pluralistic framework for counselling and psychotherapy: implications for research', *Counselling and Psychotherapy Research*, 7 (3): 135–43.

Crittenden P. M. and Claussen, A. H. (eds) (2000) *The Organization of Attachment Relationships: Maturation Culture and Context*. Cambridge: Cambridge University Press.

Cronen, V. E., Johnson, K. M. and Lannamann, J. W. (1982) 'Paradoxes, double binds, and reflexive loops: an alternative theoretical perspective', *Family Process*, 20: 9–112.

Cronen, V. E. and Pearce W. B. (1985) 'Towards an explanation of how the Milan method works: an invitation to a systemic epistemology and the evolution of family systems', in Campbell, D. and Draper, R. (eds) *Applications of Systemic Family Therapy: The Milan Approach*. London: Grune and Stratton. pp. 69–86.

Dass, R. (2000) *Still Here: Embracing Aging, Changing and Dying*. London: Hodder and Stoughton.

De Young, P. A. (2003) *Relational Psychotherapy, a Primer*. London: Brunner-Routledge.

De Waal, F. (2009) *The Age of Empathy: Nature's Lessons for a Kinder Society*. New York: Harmony Books.

Doka, K. J. (ed.) (2001) *Disenfranchised Grief* (3rd edn). New York: Lexington.

Dolan, Y. M. (1991) *Resolving Sexual Abuse: Solution-Focused Therapy and Ericksonian Hypnosis for Adult Survivors*. London: W. W. Norton.

Dryden, W. (1984) 'Issues in the eclectic practice of individual therapy', in Dryden, W. (ed.), *Individual Therapy in Britain*. London: Harper and Row.

Dryden, W. (ed.) (1995) *Rational Emotive Behaviour Therapy: A Reader*. London: Sage.

Duncan, B. L., Parks, M. and Rusk, G. S. (1990) 'Eclectic strategic practice: a process constructive perspective', *Journal of Marital and Family Therapy*, 16: 165–78.

Egan, G. ([1975] 1994) *The Skilled Helper: A Systematic Approach to Effective Helping* (5th edn). Belmont: CA: Brooks/Cole.

Eisler, I. (2005) 'The empirical and theoretical base of family therapy and multiple family day therapy for adolescent anorexia nervosa', *Journal of Family Therapy*, 27 (2): 104–31.

Eisler, R. (1987) *The Chalice and the Blade*. San Francisco, CA: Harper & Row.

Elkin, I., Yamaguchi, J. L., Arnkoff, D. B., Glass, C. R., Sotsky, S. M. and Krupnick, J. L. (1999) 'Patient–treatment fit and early engagement in therapy', *Psychotherapy Research*, 4: 437–51.

Elton Wilson, J. and Barkham, M. (1994) 'A practitioner-scientist approach to psycho-therapy process and outcome research', in Clarkson, P. and Pokorny, M. (eds), *The Handbook of Psychotherapy*. London: Routledge.

Engle, D. E. and Arkowitz, H. (2006) *Ambivalence in Psychotherapy: Facilitating Readiness to Change*. New York: The Guilford Press.

Epstein, M. (1999) *Going to Pieces Without Falling Apart: A Buddhist Perspective on Wholeness*. London: Thorsons.

Erwin, E. (1996) *Philosophy and Psychotherapy*. London: Sage.

Estes, C. P. (1997) *Women Who Run with the Wolves*. London: Rider.

Etherington, K. (2004) *Becoming a Reflexive Researcher: Using Our Selves in Research*. London: Jessica Kingsley.

Evans, K. R. and Gilbert, M. C. (2005) *An Introduction to Integrative Psychotherapy*. Basingstoke, Hampshire: Palgrave Macmillan.

Fairbairn, R. D. (1958) 'On the nature and aims of psycho-analytic treatment'. *International Journal of Psychoanalysis*, 39: 374–85.

Faris, J. D. (2010) Personal communication, Cardiff.

Faris, A. and James, N. (2009) 'Innovations in cultivating personal development and self awareness', *Nexus Conference*, University of Wales, Newport.

Faris, A. and van Ooijen, E. (2009) 'Integrating approaches', *Therapy Today*, 20 (5): 24–7.

Fennell, M. (1989) 'Depression', in Salkovskis, P., Kirk, J. and Clark, D. (eds), *Cognitive Behaviour Therapy for Psychiatric Problems: A Practical Guide*. Oxford: Oxford University Press, pp. 169–234.

Festinger, L., Riecken, H. and Schachter, S. (1956) *When Prophecy Fails: A Social and Psychological Study of a Modern Group that Predicted the Destruction of the World*. New York: Harper-Torchbooks.

Flaskas, C. and Perlesz, A. (1996) *The Therapeutic Relationship in Systemic Therapy*. London: Karnac.

Flaskas, C. (2007) 'Holding hope and hopelessness: therapeutic engagements with the balance of hope', *Journal of Family Therapy*, 29 (3): 186–203.

Fonagy, P. (1995) 'Is there an answer to the outcome research question? – "Waiting for Godot"', *Changes*, 13 (3): 168–77.

Fordham, M. (1976) *The Self and Autism*. London: William Heinemann Medical Books.

Forster, E. M. (1992) *Howards End*. London: Hodder and Stoughton/Edward Arnold.

Foucault, M. ([1969] 2002) *The Archeology of Knowledge*. Trans. A. M. Sheridan Smith. London and New York: Routledge.

Foucault, M., Faubion, J., Ruas, C. and Ashberr, J. (1986) *Death and the Labyrinth: The World of Raymond Roussel. Part 4*. London: Doubleday and Co. Inc.

Foulkes, S. H. (1964) *Therapeutic Group Analysis*. New York: International Universities.

Frank, J. D. and Frank, J. B. ([1961] 1993) *Persuasion and Healing. A Comparative Study of Psychotherapy* (3rd edn). Baltimore, Maryland: The John Hopkins University Press.

Frankl, F. (1972) www.ted.com/talks/viktor_frankl_youth_in_search_of_meaning.html (accessed 25 April 2011).

Frankl, F. (1987) *Man's Search for Meaning: An Introduction to Logotherapy*. London: Hodder and Stoughton.

Frankl, V. E. ([1946] 2004) *Man's Search for Meaning*. London: Rider.

French, T. M. (1933) 'Interrelations between psychoanalysis and the experimental work of Pavlov', *American Journal of Psychiatry*, 89: 1165–203.

Freud, S. ([1917] 1955a) *Mourning and Melancholia*, XVII (2nd edn). London: Hogarth Press.

Freud, S. ([1923] 1955b) Two encyclopaedia articles, in J. Strachey (ed. and trans.), *The Standard Edition of the Complete Works of Sigmund Freud* (vol. 18). London: Hogarth, pp. 235–59.

Fruggeri, L. (1992) 'Therapeutic process as the social construction of change', in McNamee, S. and Gergen, K. (eds), *Therapy as Social Construction*. London: Sage, pp. 40–53.

Fruggeri, L. (2010) 'The construction of the therapeutic relationship', Paper presented at the AFT Eileen Jamieson Memorial lecture , Cardiff, South Wales.

Gabriel, L. and Casemore, R. (2009) *Relational Ethics in Practice: Narratives from Counselling and Psychotherapy*. Hove, East Sussex: Routledge.

Gadamer, H. (1975) *Truth and Method*. New York: Seabury Press.

Gendlin, E. T. (1979) *Focusing*. New York: Bantam Books.

Gendlin, E. T. (1996) *Focusing-Oriented Psychotherapy: A Manual of the Experiential Method*. New York, London: The Guilford Press.

Gergen, K. and Kaye, J. (1992) 'Beyond narrative in the negotiation of therapeutic meaning', in McNamee, S. and Gergen, K.(eds), *Therapy as Social Construction*. London: Sage, pp. 166–85.

Gerhardt, S. (2004) *Why Love Matters: How Affection Shapes a Baby's Brain*. London: Routledge.

Germer, C. K., Siegel, R. D. and Fulton, P. R. (eds) (1995) *Mindfulness and Psychotherapy*. London: The Guilford Press.

Gilbert, M. and Evans, K. (2000) *Psychotherapy Supervision: An Integrative Relational Approach*. Buckingham: Open University Press.

Gilbert, P. (2005) *Compassion: Conceptualizations, Research and Use in Psychotherapy*. London: Routledge.

Gilbert P. (2009a) *The Compassionate Mind: A New Approach to Life's Challenges*. London: Constable and Robinson Ltd.

Gilbert, P. (2009b) 'Introducing compassion-focussed therapy', *Advances in Psychiatric Treatment*, 15: 199–208.

Gilbert, P. (2009c) Keynote speech, Mindfulness and Beyond Conference, London.

Gilbert, P. (2010) *Compassion Focused Therapy*. London: Routledge.

Gilligan, C. (1982) *In a Different Voice. Psychological Theory and Women's Development*. Cambridge, MA: Harvard University Press.

Gold, J. R. (1996) *Concepts in Psychotherapeutic Integration*. New York: Plenum Press.

Goldfried, M. R., Panchankis, J. E. and Bell, A. C. (2005) 'A history of psychotherapy integration', in Norcross, J. C. and Goldfried, M. R. (eds), *Handbook of Psychotherapy Integration* (2nd edn). Oxford: Oxford University Press.

Gomperts, W. (2009) 'Van doodsbange kinderen tot levensgevaarlijke volwassenen. ('From terrified children to dangerous adults'). http://nopapers.nl/azfeastforpeace/gomperts.html (accessed 2 June 2010).

Gotfried, M. R. (1995) 'Toward a common language for case formulation', *Journal for Psychotherapy Integration*, 5 (3): 221–4.

Gracely, R. H., Dubner, R. and McGrath, P. A. (1979) 'Narcotic analgesia: fentanyl reduces the intensity but not the unpleasantness of painful tooth pulp sensations', *Science*, 203 (4386): 1261–3.

Gray, A. (1994) *An Introduction to the Therapeutic Frame*. London: Routledge.

Hardy, V. K. and Laszloffy, T. A. (1995) 'The Cultural genogram: key to training culturally competent family therapists', *Journal of Marital and Family Therapy*, 21 (3): 227–37.

Hayes, S. C., Barnes-Holmes, D. and Rosche, B. (2001) *Relational Frame Theory: A Post-Skinnerian Account of Human Language and Cognition*. New York: Skinner.

Hayes, S. C., Strosahl, K. D. and Wilson, K. (1999) *Acceptance and Commitment Therapy: An Experiential Approach to Behavior Change*. New York: The Guilford Press.

Hayley, J. (1963) *Strategies of Psychotherapy*. New York: Grune and Stratton.

Hayley, J. (1981) *Reflections on Therapy and Other Essays*. Washington DC: The Family Therapy Institute.

Hedges, F. (2005) *An Introduction to Systemic Therapy with Individuals: A Social Constructionist Approach*. London: Palgrave Macmillan.

Heineman Pieper, M. (1989) 'The heuristic paradigm: a unifying and comprehensive approach to social work research', in Tyson, K. (1995) *New Foundations for Scientific Social and Behavioral Research. The Heuristic Paradigm*. Needham Heights, MA: Allyn and Bacon.

Hemmings, A. (2008) 'A response to the chapters in *Against and For CBT*', in House, R. and Loewenthal, D. (eds), *Against and For CBT: Towards a Constructive Dialogue?* Ross-on-Wye: PCCS Books.

Henwood, K. (1996) 'Qualitative inquiry: perspectives, methods and psychology', in Richardson, J. T. R., *Handbook of Qualitative Research Methods for Psychology and the Social Sciences*. Leicester: BPS Books (The British Psychological Society).

Heron, J. (1996) *Co-operative Inquiry: Research into the Human Condition*. London: Sage.

Hillesum, E. (1981) *An Interrupted Life: The Diaries of Etty Hillesum 1941–43*. New York: Washington Square Press.

Hoffding, H. and Lowndes, M. E. ([1881] 2004) 'The conscious and the unconscious: From *Outlines of Psychology* (1881)', *American Imago*, 61 (3): 397–5.

Hollis, J. (1998) *The Eden Project: In Search of the Magical Other*. Toronto: Inner City Books.

Hollis, J. (2005) *Finding Meaning in the Second Half of Life: How to Finally Really Grow Up*. New York: Gotham Books.

House, R. (2003) *Therapy Beyond Modernity: Deconstructing and Transcending Profession-centred Therapy*. London: Karnac.

House, R. and Loewenthal, D. (eds) (2008) *Against and For CBT: Towards a Constructive Dialogue?* Ross-on-Wye: PCCS Books.

Hudson Allez, G. (2008) *Infant Losses, Adult Searches: A Neural and Developmental Perspective on Psychopathology and Sexual Offending*. London: Karnac.

Huppert, J. D., Bufka, L. F., Barlow, D. H., Gorman, J. M., Shear, M. K. and Woods, S. W. (2001) 'Therapists, therapist variables, and cognitive-behavioural therapy outcome in a multi-center trial for panic disorder', *Journal of Consulting and Clinical Psychology*, 75 (1): 194–8.

Hycner R. and Jacobs, L. (1995) *The Healing Relationship in Gestalt Therapy: A Dialogic/Self Psychology Approach*. Highland, NJ: The Gestalt Journal Press, Inc. In Loewenthal, D. and Winter, D. (eds) *What Is Psychotherapeutic Research?* London: Karnac. Chapter 14.

Irving, J. and Williams, D. T. (1996) 'The role of group work in counsellor training'. *Counselling: Journal of the British Association for Counselling*, 7 (2): 137–9.

Jacobs, M. (1998) *The Presenting Past. The Core of Psychodynamic Counselling and Therapy* (2nd edn). Maidenhead, Berkshire: Open University Press.

Jenkins, A. (2008) 'Ethics of restorative practice: an invitational approach for respectful and accountable intervention with men who have engaged in violence and abusive behaviour'. Workshop notes. Cardiff, South Wales: Family Institute.

Johansen, A., Sundet, R. and Torsteinsson, V. W. (2004) *Self in Relationships: Perspectives on Family Therapy from Developmental Psychology*. London: Karnac.

Johns, H. (1996) *Personal Development in Counsellor Training*. London: Cassell.

Johnson, D. (2010) *Love: Bondage or Liberation. A Psychological Exploration of the Meaning, Values, and Dangers of Falling in Love*. London: Karnac.

Johnson, R. A. (1991) *Owning Your Own Shadow. Understanding the Dark Side of the Psyche*. San Francisco: Harper.

Johnson, S. M. (1994) *Character Styles*. New York and London: W. W. Norton.

Jones, E. (1993) *Family Systems Therapy: Developments in the Milan-systemic Therapies.* London: John Wiley.

Jones, E. (2003) 'Working with the "self" of the therapist in consultation', *Human Systems*, 14 (1): 7–16.

Jones, E., and Asen, E. (2000) *Systemic Couple Therapy and Depression.* London: Karnac.

Jung, C. (1912) 'On the psychology of the unconscious', in *Collected Works 7: Two Essays on Analytical Psychology*, ed. H. Read, M. Fordham and G. Adler. London: Routledge & Kegan Paul. p. 35.

Kabat-Zinn, J. (1990) *Full Catastrophe Living.* New York: Delta.

Keeney, B. P. (1983) *Aesthetics of Change.* London: The Guilford Press.

Kelly, G. (1955) *The Psychology of Personal Constructs* (vols 1 and 2). New York: W. W. Norton.

Kennedy, D. (2006) 'The importance of being authentic', paper presented at the annual *Marianne Fry Memorial Lecture*, July, Bristol.

Khalsa, S. P. K. (1996) *Kundalini Yoga: A Simple Guide to the Yoga of Awareness. As Taught by Yogi Bhajan.* Berkeley: Perigree Book, Berkeley Publishing Group.

Klass D., Silverman P. R. and Nickman S. L. (eds) (1996) *Continuing Bonds: New Understandings of Grief.* Washington: Taylor and Francis.

Knox, J. (2003) *Archetype, Attachment, Analysis: Jungian Psychology and the Emerging Mind.* Hove, East Sussex: Brunner-Routledge.

Kohut, H. (1971) *The Analysis of the Self.* New York: International Universities Press.

Kohut, H. (1977) *The Restoration of the Self.* New York: International Universities Press.

Kopala, M. and Suzuki, L. A. (eds) (1999) *Using Qualitative Methods in Psychology.* London: Sage.

Kramer, G. (2007) *Insight Dialogue: The Interpersonal Path to Freedom.* Boston and London: Shambhala Publications, Inc.

Krause, I. B. (1998) *Therapy Across Culture.* London: Sage.

Kubler Ross, E. (1970) *On Death and Dying.* London: Tavistock.

Kubler Ross, E. (2009) *On Death and Dying: What the Dying Have to Teach Doctors, Nurses, Clergy and their own Families.* 40th anniversary edition. London: Routledge.

Kuhn, T. (1962) *The Structure of Scientific Revolutions.* Chicago: University of Chicago Press.

Kuhn, T. (1977). *The Essential Tension: Selected Studies in Scientific Tradition and Change.* Chicago: University of Chicago Press.

Kurtz, Z. E. (1979) *Not-God: A History of Alcoholics Anonymous.* Center City, Mn 55012: Hazelden Books.

Kuyken, W., Padesky, C. A. and Dudley R. (2009) *Collaborative Case Conceptualisation.* New York: The Guilford Press.

Kvale, S. (1996a) *InterViews: An Introduction to Qualitative Research Interviewing.* Thousand Oaks, CA: Sage.

Kvale, S. (ed.) (1996b) *Psychology and Postmodernism.* London: Sage.

Lakoff, G. and Johnson, M. (1980) *Metaphors We Live By.* London: University of Chicago Press.

Langs, R. J. (1980) *Interaction: The Realm of Transference and Countertransference.* New York: Jason Aronson.

Lapworth, P., Sills, C. and Fish, S. (2001) *Integration in Counselling and Psychotherapy: Developing a Personal Approach.* London: Sage.

Laurence, T. (2004) *The Hoffman Process.* New York: Bantam Dell, Random House Inc.

Lazarus, A. A. (1981) *The Practice of Multimodal Therapy.* New York: McGraw-Hill.

Leader, D. (2002) *Stealing the Mona Lisa: What Art Stops Us from Seeing.* New York: Counterpoint.

Leader, D. (2008) *The New Black: Mourning, Melancholia and Depression.* London: Hamish Hamilton.

Lee, L. and Littlejohns, S. (2007) 'Deconstructing Agnes – externalization in systemic supervision', *Journal of Family Therapy*, 29 (3): 222–38.

Levine, P. (1997) *Waking the Tiger: Healing Trauma*. Berkeley, CA: North Atlantic Books.

Lewis, C. S. (1961) *A Grief Observed*. London: Faber and Faber.

Lewis, G. (2002) *Sunbathing in the Rain*. London: Flamingo.

Linehan, M. M. (1987) 'Dialectical behaviour therapy for borderline personality disorder: theory and method', *Bulletin of the Menninger Clinic*, 51: 261–76.

Linehan, M. (1993) *Cognitive Behavioral Treatment of Borderline Personality Disorder*. New York: The Guilford Press.

Loewenthal, D. (2008) 'Post-existentialism as a reaction to CBT?', in House, R. and Loewenthal, D. (eds) *Against and For CBT: Towards a Constructive Dialogue?* Ross-on-Wye: PCCS Books.

Luecken, L. J. (1998) 'Childhood attachment and loss experiences affect adult cardiovascular and cortisol function', *Psychosomatic Medicine*, 60 (6): 765–72.

Mace, C. (2008) *Mindfulness and Mental Health: Therapy, Theory and Science*. London: Routledge.

MacKenna, C. (2008) 'Childe Roland and the mystic's quest: analytic faith in a world of lost meanings, *British Journal of Psychotherapy*, 24 (4): 472–87.

Macy, K. and Brown, M. J. (1998) *Coming Back to Life: Practices to Reconnect Our Lives, Our World*. Gabriola Island: New Society Publishers.

Mahrer, A. (1989) *The Integration of Psychotherapies: A Guide for Practicing Therapists*. New York: Human Sciences Press.

Mair, M. (2006) 'Imaginative writing as psychological inquiry'. Specialist Doctorate in Psychotherapy Seminar, 30 June. London: The Metanoia Institute.

Mansell, W. (2008) 'What is CBT really and how can we enhance the impact of effective psychotherapies such as CBT', in House, R. and Loewenthal, D. (eds) *Against and For CBT: Towards a Constructive Dialogue?* Ross-on-Wye: PCCS Books.

Martin, J. (1997) 'Mindfulness: a proposed common factor', *Journal of Psychotherapy Integration*, 291–312.

Maselko, J. (2010) 'Mother's affection at 8 months predicts emotional distress in adulthood', *Journal of Epidemiology and Community Health*. http://jech.bmj.com/content/early2010/07/07jech.2009.0978 (accessed 1 August 2010).

Mason, B. (1993) 'Towards positions of safe uncertainty', *Human Systems: The Journal of Systemic Consultation and Management* (special issue), 4 (3–4): 189–200.

Mason, J. (2002) *Researching Your Own Practice: The Discipline of Noticing*. London: Routledge Falmer.

Maturana, H. R. and Varela, F. (1998) *The Tree of Knowledge: The Biological Roots of Human Understanding*. Boston, MA: Shambala.

McGoldrick, M. (ed.) (1998) *Re-visioning Family Therapy: Race, Culture and Gender in Clinical Practice*. London: The Guilford Press.

McLeod, J. (1998) *Introduction to Counselling* (2nd edn). Oxford: Open University Press.

McLeod, J. (1999) *Practitioner Research in Counselling*. London: Sage.

McLeod, J. (2002) 'Case studies and practitioner research: building knowledge through systematic inquiry into individual cases', *Counselling and Psychotherapy Research*, 2 (4): 265–8.

McLeod, J. (2003a) *Doing Counselling Research* (2nd edn). London: Sage.

McLeod, J. (2003b) *An Introduction to Counselling* (3rd edn). Maidenhead: Open University Press.

McNamee, S. (1997) 'The pain of politics and the politics of pain', *Human Systems*, 8 (3–4): 311–27.

McNamee, S. and Gergen, K. (1992) *Therapy as Social Construction*. London: Sage.

McNamee, S. and Gergen, K. (1999) *Relational Responsibility: Resources for Sustainable Dialogue*. London: Sage.

Mearns, D. and Cooper, M. (2005) *Working at Relational Depth in Counselling and Psychotherapy*. London: Sage.

Mearns, D. and Thorne, B. (2007) 'Recent developments in person-centred theory', in *Person-centred Counselling in Action* (3rd edn). London: Sage.

Mehr, K. E., Ladany, N. and Caskie, G. I. L. (2010) 'Trainee nondisclosure in supervision: what are they not telling you?', *Counselling & Psychotherapy Research*, 10 (2): 103–13.

Meng, H. and Freud, S. (eds) (1963) *Psychoanalysis and Faith: The Letters of Sigmund Freud and Oskar Pfister*. Trans. E. Mosbacher. London and New York: Hogarth and the Institute of Psychoanalysis.

Menninger, K. (1958) *Theory of Psychoanalytic Technique*. New York: Basic Books.

Merleau-Ponty, M. (1962) *Phenomenology of Perception: An Introduction*. Trans. Colin Smith. London: Routledge and Kegan Paul.

Miller, J. C. (2004) *The Transcendent Function: Jung's Model of Psychological Growth*. Albany: State University of New York.

Miller, W. R. and Brown, J. M. (1991) 'Self regulation as a conceptual basis for the prevention and treatment of addictive behaviours', in Heather, N., Miller, W. R. and Greeley, J. (eds), *Self Control and the Addictive Behaviours*. Sydney: Maxwell Macmillan Publishing Australia, pp. 3–79.

Miller, W. R. and Rollnick, S. (2002) *Motivational Interviewing: Preparing People for Change*. New York: The Guilford Press.

Mitchell. S. (1997) *Influence and Autonomy*. Hillsdale, NJ: The Analytic Press.

Mitchell, S. A. (2000) *Relationality: From Attachment to Intersubjectivity*. Hillsdale, NJ: The Analytic Press.

Mitchell, S. A. and Aron, L. (eds) (1999) *Relational Psychoanalysis. The Emergence of a Tradition*. Hillsdale, NJ: The Analytic Press.

Moore, T. (1992) *Care of the Soul*. New York: Harper Collins.

Murdin, L. (2008) 'Introduction: why spirituality', *British Journal of Psychotherapy*, 24 (4): 469–71.

Natterson J. M. and Friedman R. J. (1995) *A Primer of Clinical Intersubjectivity*. London: Jason Aronson.

Neimeyer, R. A. (ed.) (2001) *Meaning Reconstruction and the Experience of Loss*. Washington, DC: American Psychological Association.

Nijenhuis, E. R. S., Van der Hart, O. and Steele, K. (2004) 'Trauma-related structural dissociation of the personality', *Trauma Information Pages*, January. www.trauma-pages.com/a/nijenhuis-2004.php (accessed 28 June 2010).

Norcross, J. C. (2005) 'The psychotherapist's own psychotherapy: educating and developing psychologists', *American Psychologist*, 60 (8): 840–50.

Norcross, J. C. and Goldfried, M. R. (eds) (2005) *Handbook of Psychotherapy Integration* (2nd edn). Oxford: Oxford University Press.

Norcross, J. C., Levant, R. and Beutler, L. (2005) *Evidence-based Practices in Mental Health: Debate and Dialogue on the Fundamental Questions*. Washington, DC: American Psychological Association Press.

Oakes, L. (2002) 'The body remembers: an interview with Babette Rothschild', *Psychotherapy in Australia*, February, 8 (2). www.psychotherapy.com.au/pages/journal/abstract_detail.asp?id=30 (accessed 14 April 2011).

O'Brien, M. and Houston, G. (2007) *Integrative Therapy. A Practitioner's Guide* (2nd edn). London: Sage.

O'Hanlon, W. H. (1999) *A Guide to Possibility Land*. New York: W. W. Norton.

Olsen, W. (2003) 'Pluralism, tenancy and poverty. Cultivating open-mindedness in poverty studies'. Paper presented to the Development Studies Association, Glasgow, 11 September.

Orange, D. (1995) *Emotional Understanding: Studies in Psychoanalytic Epistemology.* New York and London: The Guilford Press.

Orange, D. (2003) 'Antidotes and alternatives: Perspectival realism and the new reductionisms', *Psychoanalytic Psychology,* 20 (3): 472–86.

Orange, D. M., Atwood, G. E., Stolorow, R. D. (1997) *Working Intersubjectively: Contextualism in Psychoanalytic Practice.* London: The Analytic Press.

Padesky, C. A. (1993) 'Socratic questioning: changing minds or guiding discovery'. Keynote speech at European Congress of Behavioural and Cognitive Therapies, London.

Padesky, C. A. (1996) 'Developing cognitive therapist competency: teaching and supervision models', in P. M. Salkovskis (ed.), *Frontiers of Cognitive Therapy.* New York: The Guilford Press.

Panksepp, J. (2004) *Affective Neuroscience: The Foundations of Human and Animal Emotions.* New York: Oxford University Press.

Perls, F., Hefferline, R. F. and Goodman, P. (1951) *Gestalt Therapy: Excitement and Growth in the Human Personality.* London: Souvenir Press.

Pert, C. B. (1999) *Molecules of Emotion: Why You Feel the Way You Feel.* London: Pocket Books.

Phillips, A. (1988) *Winnicott.* London: Fontana Press.

Piontelli, A. (1992) *From Fetus to Child: An Observational and Psychoanalytic Study.* London and New York: Tavistock/Routledge.

Popper, K. (2002) *All Life Is Problem Solving.* London: Routledge.

Pretorius, W. M. (2006) 'Cognitive behavioural therapy supervision: recommended practice', *Behavioural and Cognitive Psychotherapy,* 34: 413–20.

Principe, J. M., March, C. D., Glick, D. M. and Ablon, J. S. (2006) 'The relationship among patient contemplation, early alliance, and continuation in psychotherapy', *Psychotherapy: Theory, Research, Practice, Training,* 43 (2): 238–43.

Prochaska, J. O. and Diclemente, C. C. (1982) 'Transtheoretical therapy: toward a more integrative model of change', *Psychotherapy: Theory, Research, and Practice,* 19: 276–288.

Prochaska, J., Velicer, W., Redding, C., Rossi, J., Goldstein, M., DePue, J., Greene, G., Rossi, S., Sun, X., Fava, J., Laforge, R., Rakowski, W. and Plummer, B. (2005) 'Stage-based expert systems to guide a population of primary care patients to quit smoking, eat healthier, prevent skin cancer, and receive regular mammograms', *Preventive Medicine,* 41: 406–16.

Purkiss, J. (2010) 'Working with loss and separation: postmodern perspectives', *The British Journal of Psychotherapy Integration,* 7 (1): 33–41.

Rake, C. and Paley, G. (2009) 'Personal therapy for psychotherapists: the impact on therapeutic practice. A qualitative study using interpretative phenomenological analysis', *Psychodynamic Practice: Individuals, Groups and Organisations,* 15 (3): 275–94.

Raval, H. and Maltby, M. (2005) 'Not getting lost in translation: establishing a working alliance with co-workers and interpreter', in Flaskas, C., Mason, B. and Perlesz, A. *The Space Between: Experience, Context, and Process in the Therapeutic Relationship.* London: Karnac.

Redei, E., Hildebrand, H. and Aird, F. (1995) 'Corticotropin release-inhibiting factor is preprothyrotropin-releasing hormone (178-199)', *Endocrinology,* 136 (8): 3557–63.

Reich, W. (1983) *The Function of the Orgasm.* London: Souvenir Press.

Reynolds, R. (2007) 'How does therapy cure? The relational turn in psychotherapy, *Counselling, Psychotherapy, and Health,* 3 (2): 127–50.

Richo, D. (2008) *Building Self-respect and Loving Kindness: Practical Steps to Self-respect and Compassionate Relationships.* Berkeley, California: Human Development Books.

Rizzolatti, G. and Arbib, M. A. (1998) 'Language within my grasp', *Trends in Neuroscience*, 21: 188–94.

Roberts, J. (1994) *Tales of Transformation: Stories in Families and Family Therapy*. New York: W. W. Norton.

Roberts, J. (2005) 'Transparency and self-disclosure in family therapy: dangers and possibilities', *Family Process*, 44 (1): 45–63.

Rogers, C. (1951) *Client-centered Therapy*. Boston: Houghton Mifflin.

Rogers, C. (1957) 'The necessary and sufficient conditions of therapeutic personality change', *Journal of Consulting Psychology*, 21: 95–103.

Rogers, C. (1959) 'A theory of therapy, personality and interpersonal relationships, as developed in the client-centered framework', in S. Koch (ed.), *Psychology: A Study of Science*. New York: McGraw Hill. pp. 184–256.

Rogers, C. (1961) *On Becoming a Person*. Boston: Houghton Mifflin.

Rogers, C. (1963) 'Psychotherapy today: or, where do we go from here?', *American Journal of Psychotherapy*, 17 (1): 5–16.

Rogers, C. (1980) *A Way of Being*. Boston: Houghton Mifflin.

Rolf, I. P. (1989) *Rolfing: Re-establishing the Natural Alignment and Structural Integration of the Human Body for Vitality and Well-being*. Rochester, Vermont: Healing Arts Press.

Romanyshyn, R. D. (2007) *The Wounded Researcher: Research with Soul in Mind*. New Orleans: Spring Journal Books.

Ronnestadt, M. H. and Ladany, N. (2006) 'The impact of psychotherapy training: introduction to the special section', *Psychotherapy Research*, 16 (3): 261–7, in Cooper, M. (2009) *Essential Research Findings in Counselling and Psychotherapy*. London: Sage.

Rose, C. (2008) *The Personal Development Group: The Students' Guide*. London: Karnac.

Rose, S. (2006) *The 21st Century Brain: Explaining, Mending and Manipulating the Mind*. London: Jonathan Cape.

Rose, T. and Loewenthal, D. (2006) 'Heuristic research', in Loewenthal, D. and Winter, D. (eds) *What Is Psychotherapy Research?* London: Karnac. Chapter 11.

Rosenthal, R. and Fode, K. (1963) 'The effect of experimenter bias on performance of the albino rat', *Behavioral Science*, 8: 183–9.

Rosenthal, R. and Jacobson, L. (1992) *Pygmalion in the Classroom* (expanded edn). New York: Irvington.

Rosenzweig, S. (1936) 'Some implicit common factors in diverse methods of psychotherapy', *American Journal of Orthopsychiatry*, 6: 412–15.

Rothschild, B. (2000) *The Body Remembers: The Psychophysiology of Trauma and Trauma Treatment*. New York: W. W. Norton.

Rothschild, B. (2006) *Help for the Helper: Self Care Strategies for Managing Burn-out and Stress*. London: W.W. Norton.

Rowan, J. (2005) *The Transpersonal: Spirituality in Psychotherapy and Counselling* (2nd edn). London: Routledge.

Rowan, J. and Cooper, M (eds) (1999) *The Plural Self: Multiplicity in Everyday Life*. London: Sage.

Rowan, J. and Jacobs, M. (2002) *The Therapist's Use of Self*. Buckingham: Open University Press.

Ruesch, J. and Bateson, G. (1951) *Communication: The Social Matrix of Psychiatry*. Canada: W. W. Norton.

Ryde, J. (2009) *Being White in the Helping Professions: Developing Effective Intercultural Awareness*. London: Jessica Kingsley.

Ryle, A. (1990) *Cognitive-Analytic Therapy: Active Participation in Change. A New Integration in Brief Psychotherapy*. Chichester: John Wiley.

Safran, J. D. (2003) 'The relational turn, the therapeutic alliance, and psychotherapy research: Strange bedfellows or postmodern marriage?', *Contemporary Psychoanalysis*, 39: 449–75.

Safran, J. D. and Muran, J. C. (2000) *Negotiating the Therapeutic Alliance: A Relational Treatment Guide*. New York: The Guilford Press.

Safran, J. D., Muran, J. C., Samstag, L. W. and Stevens, C. (2002) 'Repairing alliance ruptures', in Norcross, J. C. (ed.) *Psychotherapy Relationships that Work: Therapist Contributions and Responsiveness to Patients*. New York: Oxford University Press, pp. 235–54.

Sampson, V. (2009) 'Staying in touch with our ecological self', Landscapes of the Mind conference, The Eden Project.

Samuels, A. (2008) 'Psychotherapy and spirituality, ethics and social responsibility'. Keynote presentation, 'Sound Foundations', Westminster Pastoral Foundation (WPF) Group Conference, London.

Sanders, D. and Wills, F. (2003) *Counselling for Anxiety Problems* (2nd edn). London: Sage.

Sanders, D. and Wills, F. (2005) *Cognitive Therapy: An Introduction*. London: Sage.

Sands, A. (2000) 'Shutting the stable door after the horse has bolted', *Self and Society*, August–September, 28 (3). http://g.o.r.i.l.l.a.postle.net/clientcorner/asandscomplete.htm (accessed 14 April 2011)

Sartre, J. P. (1990) *Being and Nothingness: Essay on Phenomenological Ontology* (new edn). London: Routledge.

Schon, D. (1983) *The Reflective Practitioner: How Professionals Think in Action*. London: Temple Smith.

Schore, A. (2001) 'Minds in the making: attachment, the self-organising brain and developmentally-oriented psychoanalytic psychotherapy', *British Journal of Psychotherapy*, 17 (3): 299–328.

Schore, A. (2003) *Affect Regulation and the Repair of the Self* (Norton Series on Interpersonal Neurobiology). New York and London: W. W. Norton.

Schore, A. (2009) 'The paradigm shift: the right brain and the relational unconscious', plenary address, Annual Convention, American Psychology Association, Toronto, Canada.

Scott, T. (2004) *Integrative Psychotherapy in Healthcare: A Humanistic Approach*. Basingstoke: Palgrave Macmillan.

Segal, Z. V., Williams, J. M. G. and Teasdale, J. D. (2002) *Mindfulness-based Cognitive Therapy for Depression: A New Approach to Preventing Relapse*. London: The Guilford Press.

Seligman, P. (2002) 'Clients' views of systemic therapy', personal communication.

Semmler, P. L. and Williams C. B. (2000) 'Narrative therapy: a storied context for multicultural counselling', *Journal of Multicultural Counselling and Development*, 28 (1): 51–62.

Siegel, D. J. (1999) *The Developing Mind: How Relationships and the Brain Interact to Shape Who We Are*. New York: The Guilford Press.

Siegel, D. J. (2010) *Mindsight: The New Science of Transformation*. New York: Bantam Books.

Sills, F. (2009) *Being and Becoming: Psychodynamics, Buddhism, and the Origins of Selfhood*. Berkeley, CA: North Atlantic Books.

Slote, M. (2007) *The Ethics of Care and Empathy*. London: Routledge.

Smith, J. and Osborn, M. (2003) 'Interpretative phenomenological analysis', in Smith, J. A. (ed.) (2004) *Qualitative Psychology: A Practical Guide to Research Methods*. London: Sage. pp. 51–80.

Soderlund, J. (2009) 'Prejudiced about prejudice: an interview with Gianfranco Cecchin', *New Therapist*. www.newtherapist.com/cecchin.html (accessed 24 April 2011).

Spencer, L. (2006) 'Tutors stories of personal development training – attempting to maximize the learning potential', *Counselling and Psychotherapy Research*, 6 (2): 108–14.

Spinelli, E. (2007) *Demystifying Therapy*. Ross-on-Wye: PCCS Books.

St Clair, M. (1996) *Object Relations and Self Psychology*. London: Brooks/Cole.

Stern, D. B. (2009) *Partners in Thought: Working with Unformulated Experience, Dissociation, and Enactment*. Hove, East Sussex: Routledge.

Stern, D. N. (1985) *The Interpersonal World of the Infant: A View from Psychoanalysis and Developmental Psychology*. New York: Basic Books.

Stern, D. N. (1995) *The Motherhood Constellation: A Unified View of Parent-Infant Psychotherapy*, New York: Basic Books.

Stern, D. N. (2004) *The Present Moment in Psychotherapy and Everyday Life*. London: W. W. Norton.

Stolorow, R. D. and Atwood, G. E. (1992) *Contexts of Being: The Intersubjective Foundations of Psychological Life*. Hillsdale, NJ: The Analytic Press.

Stolorow, R. D., Atwood, G. E. and Brandschaft, B. (eds) (1994) *The Intersubjective Perspective*. London: Jason Aronson.

Stolorow, R. D., Atwood, G. E. and Orange, D. M. (2002) *Worlds of Experience: Interweaving Philosophical and Clinical Dimensions in Psychoanalysis*. New York: Basic Books.

Stroebe, M. and Schut, H. (1999) 'The dual process model of coping with bereavement: rationale and description', *Death Studies*, 23 (3): 197–224.

Strong, T., Lysack, M. and Sutherland, O. (2008) 'Dialogic cognitive therapy', in House, R. and Loewenthal, D. (eds), *Against and For CBT: Towards a Constructive Dialogue?* Ross-on-Wye: PCCS Books.

Summers, R. F. and Barber, P. (2010) *Psychodynamic Therapy: A Guide to Evidence-Based Practice*. New York, London: The Guilford Press.

Taylor, K. (1995) *The Ethics of Caring*. Santa Cruz, CA: Hanford Mead Publishers.

Taylor, M., Redmond, J. and Loewenthal, D. (2006) 'The use of discourse analysis of psychotherapists thinking about their practice', in Loewenthal, D. and Winter, D. (eds) *What Is Psychotherapeutic Research?* London: Karnac. Chapter 8.

Teasdale, J. D. (1988) 'Cognitive vulnerability to persistent depression', *Cognition and Emotion*, 2: 247–74.

Thomas, K. (1996) 'The defensive self: a psychodynamic perspective', in Stevens, R. (ed.), *Understanding the Self*. London: Sage/The Open University.

Timulak, L. (2008) 'Significant events in psychotherapy: an update of research findings', paper presented at the ScotCon/Scottish SPR Seminars, Glasgow.

Tommel, S. E. (2010) 'Culture-oriented psychoanalysis: on taking cultural background into account in the therapy of migrants', in Schloesser, A.-M. and Gerlach, A. (eds) *Crossing Borders – Integrating Differences: Psychoanalytic Psychotherapy in Transition*. London: Karnac.

Treasure, J. and Schmidt, U. (2008) 'Motivational interviewing in the management of eating disorders', in Arkowitz, H., Westra, A. H., Miller, W. R. and Rollnick, S. (eds) *Motivational Interviewing in the Treatment of Psychological Problems*. New York: The Guilford Press.

Tudway, J. (2009) 'Relational ethics from a cognitive behavioural perspective', in Gabriel, L. and Casemore, R. (eds), *Relational Ethics in Practice: Narratives from Counselling and Psychotherapy*. Hove, East Sussex: Routledge.

Tyson, K. (1995) *New Foundations for Scientific Social and Behavioral Research: The Heuristic Paradigm*. Needham Heights, MA: Allyn and Bacon.

Vaidhyanathan, S. (2007) 'On Robert', *The Philosopher's Magazine*, 39 (3rd quarter): 31–2.

Van Deurzen, E. and Arnold-Baker, C. (eds) (2005) *Existential Perspectives on Human Issues: A Handbook for Therapeutic Practice*. Basingstoke: Palgrave Macmillan.

Van Ooijen, A. (1989) 'Untitled', in *Het Stille Weten: 1980–1992*. Unpublished manuscript, December 1989.

Van Ooijen, E. (2000) *Clinical Supervision: A Practical Guide.* Edinburgh: Churchill Livingstone/Elsevier.

Van Ooijen, E. (2003) *Clinical Supervision Made Easy.* Edinburgh: Churchill Livingstone/ Elsevier.

Von Bertalanfy, L. (1969). *General System Theory.* New York: George Braziller.

Von Glaserfeld, E. (1992) 'Knowing without metaphysics: aspects of the radical constructivist position', in Steier, J., *Research and Reflexivity.* London: Sage.

Vygotsky, L. S. (1978) *Mind in Society: The Development of Higher Psychological Processes.* Cambridge, MA: Harvard University Press.

Wachtel, L. (2007) *Relational Theory and the Practice of Psychotherapy.* New York: The Guilford Press.

Wahl, B. (2001) 'Rethinking humanistic therapy', *Self & Society*, 29 (4): 5–12.

Wampold, B. E. (2001) *The Great Psychotherapy Debate: Models, Methods and Findings.* Mahwah, NJ: Erlbaum.

Warner, M. (2000) 'Person-centred therapy at the difficult edge: a developmentally based model of fragile and dissociative process', in D. Mearns and B. Thorne, *Person-Centred Therapy Today: New Frontiers in Theory and Practice.* London: Sage. pp. 144–71.

Watson, G. (2008) *Beyond Happiness. Deepening the Dialogue between Buddhism, Psychotherapy and the Mind Sciences.* London: Karnac.

Watson, J. B. (1928). *Psychological Care of Infant and Child.* New York: W. W. Norton.

Watson, J. B. (1930) *Behaviorism* (revised edn). Chicago: University of Chicago Press.

Watzlawick, P., Bevan, J. H. and Jackson, D. D. (1967) *Pragmatics of Human Communication.* London: Faber & Faber.

Watzlawick, P., Weakland, K. and Fisch, R. (1974) *Change: Principles of Problem Formation and Problem Resolution.* New York: W. W. Norton.

Weishaar, M.E. (1993) *Aaron T. Beck.* London: Sage.

Wellings, N. and McCormick, E. (2005) *Nothing to Lose: Psychotherapy, Buddhism and Living Life.* London: Continuum.

West, W. (2001) 'Beyond grounded theory: the use of a heuristic approach to qualitative research', *Counselling and Psychotherapy Research*, 1 (2): 126–31.

Wharton, B. (2005) 'Ethical issues in the publication of clinical material', *Journal of Analytical Psychology*, 50: 83–9.

White, M. (1988) 'The externalizing of the problem and the re-authoring of lives and relationships', *Dulwich Centre Newsletter*, Summer.

White, M. (1995) *Re-authoring Lives: Interviews and Essays.* Adelaide, South Australia: Dulwich Centre Publications.

Wilber, K. (2000) *Integral Psychology.* Boston, MA: Shambhala.

Wilkinson, R. G. (2005) *The Impact of Inequality: How to Make Sick Societies Healthier.* Abingdon, Oxfordshire: Routledge.

Willig, C. (2001) *Introducing Qualitative Research in Psychology: Adventures in Theory and Method.* Buckingham: Open University Press.

Wills, F. (2008) *Skills in Cognitive Behaviour Counselling and Psychotherapy.* London: Sage.

Wills, F. and Sanders, D. (1997) *Cognitive Therapy: Transforming the Image.* London: Sage.

Winnicott, D. W. (1953). 'Transitional objects and transitional phenomena', *International Journal of Psychoanalysis*, 34: 89–97.

Winnicott, D. W. (1954) 'The depressive position and normal development', in *Collected Papers by D. W. Winnicott.* London: Tavistock.

Winnicott, D. W. (1964) 'Further thoughts on babies as persons', in *The Child, the Family, and the Outside World.* Harmondsworth: Penguin Books, pp. 85–92.

Winnicott, D. W. (1965a) 'Ego distortion in terms of true and false self', in *Maturational Process and the Facilitating Environment: Studies in the Theory of Emotional Development.* New York: International Universities Press, pp. 140–52.

Winnicott, D. W. (1965b) *The Maturational Processes and the Facilitating Environment.* London: Hogarth Press.

Winnicott, D. W. (1971) *Playing and Reality.* London: Tavistock.

Wittgenstein, L. (1953) *Philosophical Investigations.* Trans. G. E. M. Anscombe. Oxford: Basil Blackwell.

Wittstock, B., Rozental, S., Shuda, S. and Makgatho B. (1992) 'Links between rituals, ecologies of ideas, health and illness', in Mason, J., Rubenstein, J. and Schuda, S. (eds), (1992) *From Diversity to Healing.* Durban: SAIMFT.

Wood, D. (1998) *How Children Think and Learn* (2nd edn). Oxford: Blackwell Publishing.

Woodcock, J. (1997) 'Groupwork with refugees and asylum seekers', in Mistry, T. and Brown, A. (eds), *Race and Groupwork.* London: Whiting & Birch.

Woodcock, J. (2010) 'Home, emotion and deep subjectivity', *Context,* February: 11–13.

Worden, W. J. (2001) *Grief Counselling and Grief Therapy: A Handbook for the Mental Health Practitioner.* New York: Springer.

Worden, W. J. (2009) *Grief Counselling and Grief Therapy: A Handbook for the Mental Health Practitioner* (4th edn). New York: Springer.

Wundt, W. ([1874] 2002) *Principles of Physiological Psychology.* Black Mask Online Books.

Young, J. E., Klosko, J. S. and Weishaar, M. E. (2006) *Schema Therapy: A Practitioner's Guide.* New York and London: The Guilford Press.

Index